TAROT
A N D
ASTROLOGY

About the Author

Corrine Kenner specializes in bringing metaphysical subjects down to earth. She's a certified tarot master and the author of many books, including the *Wizards Tarot Guidebook*, *Tarot for Writers*, *Simple Fortunetelling with Tarot Cards*, *Tarot Journaling*, and *Tall Dark Stranger: Tarot for Love and Romance*. She's the designer of three decks: The *Wizards Tarot*, the *Epicurean Tarot*, and the *Victorian Christmas Tarot*.

Corrine has lived in Brazil and Los Angeles, where she earned a bachelor's degree in philosophy from California State University. She now lives in Minneapolis, Minnesota, with her husband and their daughters. She reads tarot professionally and offers regular classes and workshops, both in person and online. For more information, visit her website at corrinekenner.com.

To Write to the Author

If you wish to contact the author or would like more information about this book, please write to the author in care of Llewellyn Worldwide and we will forward your request. Both the author and publisher appreciate hearing from you and learning of your enjoyment of this book and how it has helped you. Llewellyn Worldwide cannot guarantee that every letter written to the author can be answered, but all will be forwarded. Please write to:

Corrine Kenner
℅ Llewellyn Worldwide
2143 Wooddale Drive
Woodbury, MN 55125-2989
Please enclose a self-addressed stamped envelope for reply,
or $1.00 to cover costs. If outside the U.S.A., enclose
an international postal reply coupon.

Many of Llewellyn's authors have websites with additional information and resources. For more information, please visit our website at http://www.llewellyn.com.

Corrine Kenner

TAROT
A·N·D
ASTROLOGY

Enhance Your Readings
with the
Wisdom of the Zodiac

Llewellyn Publications
Woodbury, Minnesota

First Edition
Eleventh Printing, 2020

Book designed by Steffani Sawyer
Edited by Lee Lewis
Cover and card art © 2011 John Blumen
Cover design by Lisa Novak
Chart wheels of public figures were produced using Solar Fire 7 software by permission of Astrolabe, Inc. (http://astrolabe.com). All charts are based on data collected from birth certificates. (Rodden Rating: AA)
Interior illustrations by the Llewellyn Art Department

Llewellyn Publications is a registered trademark of Llewellyn Worldwide Ltd.

Library of Congress Cataloging-in-Publication Data

Kenner, Corrine, 1964–
     Tarot and astrology : enhance your readings with the wisdom of the zodiac / Corrine Kenner. — 1st ed.
       p. cm.
     Includes bibliographical references.
     ISBN 978-0-7387-2964-0
     1. Tarot. 2. Astrology. I. Title.
BF1879.T2K463   2011
133.3'2424—dc23   2011036392

Llewellyn Publications
A Division of Llewellyn Worldwide Ltd.
2143 Wooddale Drive
Woodbury, MN 55125-2989
www.llewellyn.com

Printed in the United States of America

Other Books by Corrine Kenner

The Wizards Tarot

Tarot for Writers

Simple Fortunetelling with Tarot Cards

Tarot Journaling

Tall Dark Stranger: Tarot for Love and Romance

The Epicurean Tarot

Strange But True

Crystals for Beginners

Forthcoming Books by Corrine Kenner

The Tarot of Physics

Astrology for Writers

The Victorian Christmas Tarot

Acknowledgments

I am indebted to Storm Cestavani and Julie Dass for reviewing the astrological information in this book, and I'm thankful for John Blumen, who illustrated the *Wizards Tarot* cards. I also appreciate the generosity of Thraicie Hawkner and Jane Hanson, owners of the Eye of Horus Metaphysical shop in Minneapolis, where I wrote—and tested—a good portion of the material in this book.

Contents

List of Cards.. ix

Introduction... xi

Overview... xiii

Part One: Tarot Planets and Signs............................ 1

One: The Building Blocks of the Tarot 3

Two: The Planets, Astrology's Guiding Lights.................. 11

Three: Signs of the Times..................................... 39

Part Two: The Minor Arcana 75

Four: Elementary Astrology.................................... 77

Five: Tarot, Astrology, and Qabalah 85

Six: The Numbered Cards 93

Seven: The Planets in the Signs................................105

Eight: The Court Cards.......................................197

Part Three: Astrology In-Depth 223

Nine: The Houses of the Horoscope...........................225

Ten: How to Read a Horoscope Chart.........................251

Eleven: A Simplified Guide to Chart Interpretation 257

Conclusion 283
Glossary of Astrological Terms 285
Quick Reference Guide: Horoscope Keywords 294
Recommended Reading and Resources 295

List of Cards

The Fool	33	The World	30
The Magician	20	Ace of Wands	81
The High Priestess	17	Two of Wands	111
The Empress	23	Three of Wands	113
The Emperor	43	Four of Wands	115
The Hierophant	45	Five of Wands	139
The Lovers	48	Six of Wands	141
The Chariot	50	Seven of Wands	143
Strength	52	Eight of Wands	167
The Hermit	54	Nine of Wands	169
The Wheel of Fortune	27	Ten of Wands	171
Justice	57	Page of Wands	200
The Hanged Man	35	Knight of Wands	214
Death	59	Queen of Wands	204
Temperance	61	King of Wands	208
The Devil	63	Ace of Cups	84
The Tower	25	Two of Cups	132
The Star	65	Three of Cups	134
The Moon	67	Four of Cups	136
The Sun	13	Five of Cups	159
Judgment	37	Six of Cups	161

The Seven of Cups   163
Eight of Cups   188
Nine of Cups   190
Ten of Cups   192
Page of Cups   203
Knight of Cups   218
Queen of Cups   207
King of Cups   212
Ace of Swords   83
Two of Swords   152
Three of Swords   154
Four of Swords   156
Five of Swords   181
Six of Swords   183
Seven of Swords   185
Eight of Swords   125
Nine of Swords   127
Ten of Swords   129

Page of Swords   202
Knight of Swords   206
Queen of Swords   210
King of Swords   217
Ace of Pentacles   82
Two of Pentacles   174
Three of Pentacles   176
Four of Pentacles   178
Five of Pentacles   118
Six of Pentacles   120
Seven of Pentacles   122
Eight of Pentacles   146
Nine of Pentacles   148
Ten of Pentacles   150
Page of Pentacles   201
Knight of Pentacles   209
Queen of Pentacles   215
King of Pentacles   205

Introduction

For centuries, the art of tarot and the science of astrology have been closely linked. Now, with the help of *Tarot and Astrology*, you'll master the connections between astrology and tarot—not as two separate fields of study, but as a seamless, integrated whole.

If you're a tarot reader, this book will help you learn astrology. If you're an astrologer, this book will help you learn tarot. And if you already use the two arts in combination, *Tarot and Astrology* will help you master both specialties. How? If you're a tarot reader, this guide will show you how to add depth to your readings by adding astrological symbolism, interpretations, and methods. If you're a practicing astrologer, this book will show you how to bring your charts to life with the visual imagery of the cards. In short, *Tarot and Astrology* will give you the tools you need to combine the science of astrology with the art of tarot.

The History of Tarot and Astrology

If you could travel back in time 6,000 years, to a towering, multitiered ziggurat in Babylonia, you could stare, transfixed, at the planets and the stars alongside a Chaldean astrologer.

If you could travel back 600 years, to the Italian villas where tarot was first introduced, you could play cards at night—and you could hold the power of a gilded Sun and silver Moon in the palm of your hand.

Either way, you would be working with the same archetypal imagery and symbolism that people have been studying since the dawn of time.

Tarot and astrology have always been connected. The earliest tarot decks depicted the Sun, the Moon, and the Star, alongside gods with cosmic connections like Jupiter, Saturn, and Venus.

Tarot's more scholarly association with astrology, however, is much more recent. In 1785, the French occultist Jean-Baptiste Alliette devised a full-fledged set of correspondences between astrology and tarot. And as time passed, other mystics and philosophers began to notice an intriguing number of similarities between the structure of the tarot deck, the Hebrew alphabet, and the Qabalah, a form of Jewish mysticism. In each case, astrological correlations ran like a silver thread through all of their compositions.

The Dawn of Modern Tarot and Astrology

Modern tarot was born in the late 1800s, when a London group of mystics and philosophers founded the Hermetic Order of the Golden Dawn. Together, they attempted to unify several branches of metaphysics, including astrology, numerology, and Qabalah—and they consolidated their theories in a deck of tarot cards.

The group's tarot manual, MacGregor Mathers' *Book T*, described the cards' astrological, qabalistic, elemental, and spiritual attributes. The guide also included a method for associating all 78 cards with the zodiac.

In 1909, Arthur Edward Waite and Pamela Colman Smith designed their own version of the Golden Dawn tarot deck. The result, popularly known as the *Rider-Waite* tarot, is the best-selling tarot deck in the world. In 1943, Aleister Crowley and Lady Frieda Harris also created their own version, the *Thoth* tarot. They, too, used Golden Dawn attributions for most of their astrological correspondences. Today, many tarot artists and deck designers base their work on those Golden Dawn designs—which means that ancient astrology is finding its way into contemporary tarot cards, as well.

This book is illustrated with the *Wizards Tarot*, a deck by myself and artist John Blumen. It was designed with astrology in mind—and since it pictures teachers and students at a school of mystery and magic, it makes an excellent teaching guide for the marriage of astrology and tarot.

Tarot and Astrology in Action

In this guide, I'll show you how to combine tarot and astrology, starting with the basics of both subjects. We'll build, step by step, to full-fledged readings that bring out the best of both fields.

Astrology and Tarot isn't devoted only to theory. This book also includes practical spreads and techniques—all based on standard astrological and tarot practices—along with real-life examples and sample readings.

To get the most from this guidebook, you'll need a deck of tarot cards and access to horoscope charts. You can order custom charts from any astrologer or metaphysical shop. You can also create your own charts, online or with specialized software. Visit corrinekenner.com, for up-to-date suggestions and recommendations. As soon as you're ready to dive in, simply turn the page.

Overview

As we survey the starry landscape that unites tarot and astrology, we'll start with simple relationships and move toward a more comprehensive description of the two subjects.

- We'll open with the correspondence between the planets and the cards.
- After that, we'll cover the twelve signs of the zodiac and the corresponding cards from the Major Arcana.
- Next, you'll learn how astrology's reach extends into the Minor Arcana, courtesy of the four elements: earth, air, fire, and water.
- We'll explore the detailed, multilayered associations of the numbered cards of the four suits, all of which have a place on the Wheel of the Year.
- You'll meet the intriguing members of the zodiac court, who spin the Wheel of the Year.
- And you'll discover how tarot cards can help you visualize the signs and planets in the houses of the horoscope.

The All-Star Lineup

The most recognizable correspondences between tarot and astrology occur in the tarot's Major Arcana—the first twenty-two cards of the deck—which dovetail almost perfectly with the planets and signs of astrology.

Before we delve too far into the technical details of tarot and astrology, let's look at some of the most obvious connections in those cards.

The Fool, who doesn't care what society thinks, is assigned to Uranus, the planet of rebellion and revolution.

The Magician, the master of banter and fast talk, is assigned to Mercury, the planet of speed and communication. You'll often see him pointing heavenward, conveying messages from the heavens above to the Earth below.

The High Priestess, the archetypal psychic, is assigned to the Moon, the luminous orb of reflection and intuition. Most depictions of the High Priestess include lunar imagery.

The Empress, wife and mother, is assigned to Venus, the planet of love and attraction. You can find the astrological glyph for Venus in many renditions of the card.

The Emperor, master and commander, is assigned to Aries, the sign of leadership. Look for images of the Aries ram on your Emperor card.

The Hierophant, the keeper of tradition, is assigned to Taurus, the sign of stability, luxury, and pleasure. Some Hierophant cards feature Taurus glyphs and symbolism.

The Lovers, who think and speak as one, are assigned to Gemini, the sign of thought and communication. The Lovers themselves are twin souls, with their arms and hearts entwined.

The Chariot, the protected home on wheels, is assigned to Cancer, the sign of motherhood, home, and family life. Cancer's crab carries his home on his back.

Strength, the master of gentle force and control, is assigned to Leo, the sign of lionesque courage and heart.

The Hermit, the quiet leader, is assigned to Virgo, the sign of responsibility and dedicated service to others.

The Wheel of Fortune is assigned to Jupiter, the expansive planet of luck and burgeoning growth.

Justice, the model of fairness and equanimity, is assigned to Libra, the sign of equality and social grace. Libra is usually represented by a balanced set of scales.

The Hanged Man, suspended in an alternate reality, is assigned to Neptune, the planet of mysticism and illusion. The glyph, King Neptune's trident, symbolizes a watery world that exists alongside our own earthly reality.

Death, the ruler of the Underworld, is assigned to Scorpio, the sign of sex, death, transformation, and other people's money. The scorpion associated with the sign has a deadly sting.

Temperance, who straddles a divide between two worlds, is assigned to Sagittarius, the sign of long-distance travel, philosophy, and higher education. The Sagittarian archer—half horse, half man—also combines two widely different experiences, while his arrow soars across long distances on its way to new horizons.

The Devil, the embodiment of physical and material temptation, is assigned to Capricorn, the sign of business, career success, and worldly status. The mountain-climbing goat associated with the sign bears a striking resemblance to some depictions of the Devil himself.

The Tower, perpetually guarded and under attack, is assigned to Mars, the planet of energy, war, aggression, and assertiveness. The astrological glyph associated with Mars is a shield and a spear.

The Star, a glimmering light of hope and inspiration, is assigned to Aquarius, the airy sign of social groups and futuristic thinking.

The Moon, which rules the night, is assigned to Pisces, the sign of the mystical and the subconscious. The Pisces fish swim in the reflecting pond that's pictured in most versions of the card.

The Sun, the sustainer of life, naturally corresponds with the Sun, the source of energy and enlightenment.

Judgment, a last call for awareness, understanding, and acceptance, is assigned to Pluto, the planet of death, resurrection, and unavoidable change.

The World, our earthly home, is assigned to Saturn, the ringed planet of boundaries, limitations, restrictions, and structure.

◆ Astrology in Action: **The Sun Sign Spread** ◆

One of the easiest tarot and astrology readings you can try is a simple comparison between the two cards that represent your Sun sign. First, pull the Sun card itself from your tarot deck. Then pull the card that corresponds to its sign.

Which Major Arcana card corresponds to your Sun sign? How do the two cards—the Sun and its sign—complement or contradict each other? How do they describe your personality, individuality, and sense of self? What can you learn from your first tarot and astrology spread?

The Sun in Pisces

Sample Reading: Celeste's Midnight Sun

When Celeste was born on March 7, the Sun was in Pisces. That means her Sun card is paired with the Moon, the card that corresponds to the sign of Pisces.

Oddly enough, Celeste has always been a night owl. She feels most alive after dark, when the Sun sets and the Moon rises. Her emotions ebb and flow like the tide, and she cycles through life like a living lunar goddess. She even looks like a creature of the night, with pale skin and wide-set, luminous eyes.

"It's true," she exclaimed, when she saw the two cards side by side. "I am the Moon! That explains so much. I like the Sun as much as anyone, but I'd much rather live my life by moonlight."

◆　◆　◆

Part One

◆

TAROT PLANETS AND SIGNS

In this section, we'll take a closer look at the correspondences between the Major Arcana cards, the planets, and the signs of the zodiac.

One

♦

The Building Blocks of the Tarot

We'll start our study of tarot and astrology by going over the basic structure of a tarot deck.

The Infinite Universe of the Tarot

When you shuffle a deck of tarot cards and lay them on the table, you're actually putting an entire universe into motion. Every time you deal the cards, you're creating a new reality—just as the planets and signs of astrology align to represent a new reality for every child born on Earth.

A typical tarot deck has seventy-eight cards. At first glance, the sheer number of cards can seem overwhelming—and some people spend years trying to memorize them, studying the symbols and signs of each image, and attempting to decode the hidden meanings of the deck.

While that's a fascinating pursuit, you don't need to devote countless hours to a study of the cards before you can read them. You just need to understand the structure of the deck.

The tarot's seventy-eight cards are divided into two groups: the Major Arcana, which is Latin for "greater secrets," and the Minor Arcana, which means "lesser secrets."

The Major Arcana cards are the big-picture cards. They depict monumental, life-changing events and experiences, like falling in love, giving birth, starting a new job, or finding a new home. Sometimes, because the Major Arcana cards are so dramatic, the experiences they depict seem as if they're outside our control.

The Minor Arcana cards, on the other hand, are the everyday cards. They picture ordinary people doing everyday things, like dancing, drinking, eating, and sleeping. The Minor Arcana cards are divided into four suits, just like a deck of ordinary playing cards. Each suit has ten numbered cards and four Court Cards, and each suit represents a separate area of life: spiritual, emotional, intellectual, and physical. As a whole, the Minor Arcana cards are just as important as the Major Arcana cards, because they show us how we live out big events on a day-to-day basis.

Together, the major and Minor Arcana cards combine to form a cosmology—a framework for seeing the world and for categorizing the human experience.

The structure and the symbolism of the tarot deck make it easy to study the human condition—and even to grasp some of life's greatest mysteries.

The Major Arcana

The Major Arcana cards are the cards people tend to remember most after a tarot reading. That's because Major Arcana cards are forceful and dramatic. They feature figures and characters that seem larger than life, and which just happen to correspond to the planets and signs of astrology.

The figures on the Major Arcana cards are archetypes—cosmic stereotypes that transcend the limits of time and place. They are the heroes of ancient myth and legend, and they still populate the lead roles in contemporary movies, television shows, plays, and books. Artists, writers, and musicians regularly tap into the waters of the collective unconscious for inspiration and explanations of the human condition. Psychotherapist Carl Jung believed that the symbols, myths, and archetypes that regularly appear in our dreams, our myths, and our stories all spring from that same source—which explains why so many people and cultures share similar legends and make use of the same symbols, regardless of time and place.

The Major Arcana cards all depict major events that can change one's life. While we can classify them as cosmic mysteries, they're not inexplicable puzzles: each one also depicts a life lesson that makes each mystery clear.

On a symbolic level, the Major Arcana cards are also mentors, teachers, and guides: they hold the keys to the mysteries of life, and they help guide our passage through every station of the journey.

The Minor Arcana

The Minor Arcana is divided into four suits, just like a deck of ordinary playing cards. Those four suits are usually called Wands, Cups, Swords, and Pentacles. Depending on the deck you use, Wands also can be called Rods, Batons, Staffs, or Staves. Cups may be called Chalices. Swords may be called Blades, and Pentacles may be called Coins, Disks, Stones, Worlds, or Stars. Those subtle variations, however, don't make any difference in how the cards are read.

While the Major Arcana cards depict the mysteries of life, the Minor Arcana cards show how you experience those mysteries on a daily basis. They depict the way you live your life, and how you manage the various facets of your existence.

Spheres of Influence

Some people call the Minor Arcana the "pip" cards, because pips are the marks that indicate the suit or numerical value of a playing card—six hearts, for example, or seven diamonds.

In the tarot, however, pip cards take on a significance that most poker players would never dream of, because each one of the four suits corresponds to a separate area of life.

- **Wands** cards symbolize spiritual life and inspiration.
- **Cups** hold the secrets of emotional matters.
- **Swords** illustrate intellectual concepts.
- **Pentacles** represent the realities of physical and material existence.

There's also a second, equally important layer of symbolism to consider—one that's so simple, it's elementary.

The Four Elements

The four elements—fire, earth, air, and water—have played an important role in science and philosophy for thousands of years, ever since the ancient Greeks identified them as fundamental components of the physical world.

Obviously, modern science has changed our understanding of the universe. Even so, the four elements still serve as a useful psychological model. We often describe people as "fiery," "airy," or "earthy," for example. Elemental associations are essential to an understanding of astrology, and they're a fundamental component of some Eastern beliefs, too, such as feng shui.

In the tarot, each one of the four suits of the Minor Arcana is associated with one of the four elements, and each element corresponds to a separate area of life. The imagery on each card makes those associations easy to remember.

Wands, the fiery cards of spirit, are associated with passion and inspiration. In most tarot decks, Wands look like wooden branches that could be set on fire like a torch. Wands can be a source of illumination and, sometimes, they can spark an entire conflagration of ideas.

Cups, the watery cards of emotion, are associated with deeply felt affairs. Cups can hold water, of course. We also use Cups to hold other liquids with emotional significance: we toast each other in celebration. We commune with others during religious ceremonies and, sometimes, we even try to drown our sorrows.

Swords, the airy cards of the intellect, are associated with conscious awareness and communication. Swords symbolize our thoughts, ideas, and attempts to communicate. Swords, like words, move through the air. We even compare our words to the double-edged weapons when we say, "The pen is mightier than the sword."

Pentacles, the earthy cards of material existence, are associated with the physical realities of life in our four-dimensional world. In most tarot decks, Pentacles look like coins with star-shaped designs. That pattern is symbolic of the human physical form. Think of Leonardo da Vinci's Vitruvian Man: his body, with arms outstretched and legs spread wide, creates the shape of a five-pointed star. Pentacles symbolize the tangible realities of physical existence: the things you can touch and feel, and the money you need to keep body and soul together. Pentacles also symbolize spiritual and emotional treasures, including the values you hold dear, the traditions you cherish, and the people you love most.

Those people, by the way, have their own place in the structure of the tarot deck.

The Four Royal Families

Each suit in the Minor Arcana has a set of four Court Cards: a page, a knight, a queen, and a king. Depending on the deck you use, the Court Cards could have other titles. Crowley's royal families in the *Thoth* tarot, for example, consist of princesses, princes, queens, and knights. The cards themselves are roughly equivalent between decks, as long as you can keep their respective hierarchies straight in your mind.

The four members constitute an ideal family on a symbolic level: a father, a mother, a son, and a daughter. Some of the Court Cards are masculine, and some are feminine. Some are active, and some are receptive. Together, the sixteen Court Cards are well suited to reign over the four realms of the tarot—spiritual, emotional, intellectual, and physical—and to describe the unique combinations of qualities and characteristics that make up your personality.

Pages, knaves, and princesses are young and enthusiastic. They are students and messengers, children who must learn the fundamentals of the family's rule. During the Renaissance, pages were the youngest members of the royal court. It was their job to study—and to run errands, like ferrying messages from one person to another.

When pages show up in a tarot reading, they typically represent young people, students, or messages.

Knights. When pages grow to the age of knighthood, they must be tested. They're expected to embark on a quest, master a challenge, and demonstrate that they are not only strong enough and smart enough to succeed, but also that they can live up to the family's heritage. Historically, knights were rescuers and adventurers.

When knights show up in a tarot reading, they may suggest that a new quest or adventure is about to begin, or that rescue is on its way.

Queens. As adults, both men and women ascend to the throne, where they control the monarchy. Generally speaking, the tarot's queens are all mature women who tap into their feminine qualities to safeguard, nurture, and protect their realms. Queens are stereotypically female; they represent ideal women. They are compassionate, creative, receptive, empathic, and intuitive. They also are able to exert their power behind the scenes, convincing—or cajoling—others to adopt their point of view.

When queens show up in a reading, they often suggest that a similarly caring person will be working to safeguard, nurture, and protect your realm.

It's interesting to note that in Crowley's *Thoth* tarot, the transfer of power from one generation to the next takes on a complicated, soap-opera quality, as the Court Cards battle it out for power and authority. In an endless, overlapping cycle, the princes fight the knights for the throne. When a prince vanquishes the knight, he marries the princess, and she assumes the throne of her mother, the queen. And then, the cycle repeats.

Kings. The tarot's four kings are protectors, providers, and seasoned, experienced leaders. All four successfully managed to complete the mission they undertook as knights. They are skilled commanders, confident in the knowledge they acquired during their quests. They are also stereotypically masculine: they are authoritarian, assertive, and alert. They can even be aggressive. They guard their kingdoms with passion and force, and they're not afraid to make executive decisions.

When kings show up in a reading, they may suggest that someone is willing to mount an aggressive defense or even wage war on your behalf.

Your Own Royal Court

Obviously, the Court Cards are more than characters in a Renaissance drama. They sometimes represent the people in your life, such as family members, friends, employers, and coworkers. But at the same time, they also depict facets of your own personality, whether you're young and enthusiastic, or savvy and experienced. The connection is forged in a psychological principle called projection. When you like or dislike other people, it's often because they remind you of your own strengths and weaknesses.

When you find yourself dealing with people—or Court Cards—that you like, it's probably because they remind you of your strengths—your clever sense of humor, your keen intelligence, or your spirit of fun. You share similar ideas about the state of the world, and similar plans for the future.

When other people or Court Cards rub you the wrong way, it might be because they reflect aspects of your personality that you normally keep hidden—like your occasional selfishness, laziness, or bitterness. (But don't worry. Those weaknesses are between you and the cards.)

By the Numbers

In the Major Arcana, the numbered cards are often said to represent stations on the journey through life. In the Minor Arcana, the numbered cards also symbolize a progression of events: Aces represent beginnings, while tens represent conclusions. The suits, of course, indicate which events are unfolding: Wands symbolize spiritual experiences, Cups represent emotional affairs, Swords depict intellectual issues, and Pentacles relate to physical realities.

Obviously, the tarot deck is meant to be shuffled, so Minor Arcana cards rarely turn up in sequential order during a reading. You might be surprised, however, by how often you'll see the same numbers pop up in a tarot reading: it's not uncommon to find a preponderance of early, middle, or end cards in a tarot spread, or various cards relating to, say, the number seven.

All in all, if you can remember the significance of each suit, as well as the fact that each numbered card represents a separate stage in that area of life, you'll be able to interpret the cards without memorizing the individual meanings of all seventy-eight cards in the deck. The Ace of Wands, for example, often symbolizes the beginning of a spiritual quest. The

Five of Wands suggests the halfway point of a spiritual experience, and the Ten of Wands typically signifies the conclusion of a spiritual journey.

Tarot Spreads and Layouts

Most tarot readers have two or three favorite tarot spreads and layouts. Several new astrology-based spreads are illustrated in this guide.

Two

◆

The Planets, Astrology's Guiding Lights

We'll continue our study of tarot and astrology with the planets and the luminaries—the major players in the study of the stars.

The Planets

☉	**The Sun,** the source of heat and light on Earth, represents energy, enlightenment, radiance, and illumination. Because the Sun is the center of our universe, it also symbolizes the center of every individual's world—the self, or the ego. It's an active, masculine symbol, and the astrological glyph for the Sun depicts it at the center of the solar system.
☽	**The Moon,** which reflects the light of the Sun, symbolizes reflection and receptivity. It also represents the cyclical, changing nature of existence. It's a feminine symbol, and its glyph looks like the softly rounded curves of a woman's body.
☿	**Mercury,** the fastest-moving planet, symbolizes speed. Because Mercury was the messenger of the gods, it also symbolizes communication. The glyph for Mercury looks like a stick-figure sketch of the young Greek god in his winged helmet.
♀	**Venus,** the planet of love and beauty, symbolizes attraction, romance, and fertility. Venus was also the Greek goddess of love and attraction. The glyph for Venus looks like a woman's hand mirror.

♂	**Mars**, the red planet, symbolizes energy and masculine force. Because Mars was the god of war, it also symbolizes self-defense and aggression. The Mars glyph looks like a shield and spear.
♃	**Jupiter**, the largest planet, symbolizes growth, expansion, luck, and enthusiasm. Its glyph looks like the lucky number 21, as well as the number 4, which sounds like "fortune."
♄	**Saturn**, the ringed planet of boundaries and limitations, symbolizes discipline, clear-cut definitions, and tradition. The Saturn glyph looks like a church with a steeple and a cross.
♅	**Uranus**, the futuristic planet of freedom and rebellion, symbolizes independence. The Uranus glyph looks like a satellite with antennas.
♆	**Neptune**, the vaporous planet of illusion, symbolizes glamour and sensitivity. Its glyph looks like King Neptune's trident.
♇ ⯓	**Pluto**, the planet of death and regeneration, symbolizes unavoidable change. The Pluto glyph looks like someone rising from the dead; technically, it's a coin and a chalice, symbols of payment for everlasting life. An alternate version of the glyph combines the letters "P" and "L."

The Sun ☉

The God of Light

THE SUN

We relate to the Sun as we relate to God himself. The Sun is our source of light, heat, and radiant, life-giving energy. We measure our days by the rising and setting Sun. It's a metaphor for life and death, and a symbol of our hope for rebirth.

In most tarot decks, the Sun card depicts a golden child. You might recognize him as Apollo, the Greek and Roman god of music, healing, divination, truth, and light.

The Sun is an important focal point in any astrological chart; it represents the ego and the self. It symbolizes confidence and self-esteem, willpower, purpose, and drive. It suggests virility, vitality, energy, and strength. It also represents consciousness and enlightenment. It's a depiction of your inner light, and it describes the ways in which you shine.

Because the Sun is so visible, its placement in an astrological chart can highlight areas of fame, public recognition, and acclaim, and can also represent a strong male figure, like a father, a boss, or a respected teacher. The Sun's energy is masculine and direct.

The Sun rules Leo, the sign of creativity, recreation, and procreation.

The Sun is associated with the heart and the spine. Both find expression in everyday language when we describe people with courage and heart, or willpower and backbone.

The Sun card corresponds to the element of fire.

Cosmic Connection: DARK SHADOWS: SOLAR AND LUNAR ECLIPSES

Eclipses, which are part of the dance between the Sun and the Moon, cast long shadows over the Earth and force us to see familiar landscapes in a dim and mysterious light.

Solar eclipses, caused when the Moon travels between the Earth and the Sun, cut us off from the source of our creation. They obscure our conscious understanding and everyday awareness.

Lunar eclipses, triggered when the Earth moves between the Sun and the Moon, plunge the world into darkness and force us to explore the shadow side of our existence.

Solar eclipses occur during a New Moon, when the Sun and the Moon are conjunct; lunar eclipses occur during a Full Moon, when the Sun and the Moon are in opposition. The New Moon is connected to fresh starts and new beginnings, while Full Moons represent culmination and harvest.

Like the Sun and the Moon, lunar eclipses come in pairs. Total lunar eclipses are always preceded or followed by a solar eclipse, with exactly two weeks between the two.

Because eclipses cast their shadows over wide swaths of the globe, they affect nations and groups more than individuals. Ancient astrologers believed that solar eclipses signified the fall of the mighty: as the Sun's light was extinguished, people in positions of power would fall. Lunar eclipses, when the Moon looked red and covered with blood, foretold calamities like crop failures and famines.

Both solar and lunar eclipses, however, are relatively common, and today we realize they're not actually harbingers of doom.

◆ Astrology in Action: **The Eclipse Spread** ◆

If you're dealing with an issue that seems clouded or confused, this simple spread can quickly provide enlightenment.

Pull the Sun and the Moon cards from your deck to represent the Sun and the Moon, and lay them side by side. Shuffle the rest of the cards, and deal a single card between them to show you what part of your life is being eclipsed. Later, you'll pull a second card to show how you can bring light back into your life, illuminate the issue, and resolve your problems.

THE MOON   THE INITIATE   THE SUN

Sample Reading: Constantine's Creative Block

Constantine, normally a prolific writer and artist, has been feeling unusually blocked in his creative pursuits.

"I just can't seem to get any work done," he says. "I sit down at my writing desk, and I find myself surfing the Web, catching up with friends online, and reading the news. When I move to a drawing program, I stare at a blank screen and decide to check my e-mail or do errands instead. I've started to miss deadlines on some important projects, and while it's not too late to catch up, I'm starting to worry. Why can't I work?"

While the Moon and the Sun are powerful Major Arcana cards, the answer to Constantine's question comes in the form of the Fool, which is arguably the most powerful card in the entire deck. As the unnumbered first card—the leader of the pack—the Fool represents everyone who comes to the tarot reader's table for answers and advice. In fact, many tarot readers describe the rest of the cards as "the Fool's Journey." In this case, the symbol-rich Initiate card from the *Wizards Tarot* reveals several issues contributing to Constantine's creative block.

The card's association with initiation hints at one of Constantine's frustrations: his professional obligations are time-consuming, which leaves him almost no time to start new creative projects. As an artist, he enjoys the process of inspiration just as much as—or more than—the process of completion.

What's more, the Initiate's openness to new adventures suggests that Constantine has also lost his sense of fun and exploration. Despite the fact that his work is actually many people's idea of play, deadlines and commitments cast an air of drudgery over his daily routine.

The Initiate's connection to Uranus, the planet of revolution and rebellion, also indicates that Constantine is rebelling against the authority of his editors and publishers, either consciously or unconsciously. By missing deadlines and waiting until the last minute to fulfill his obligations, he might be trying to imbue his work with a sense of excitement, nonconformity, even a little danger.

So how can Constantine overcome his creative blocks and get back on task?

The Ace of Cups suggests that Constantine should start, of course, by submerging himself in the projects he's already begun. He should unplug himself from the Internet and turn his back on the distractions of the outside world.

More importantly, the Ace of Cups indicates that he will soon dive head-first into an entirely new project, one designed solely to bring him artistic pleasure and creative satisfaction, and guaranteed to get his creative juices flowing again.

◆　　◆　　◆

The Moon ☽
The High Priestess

The Moon is the ruler of the night, the keeper of secrets, and the guardian of dreams. When she takes the form of the High Priestess, the Moon becomes a close and trusted confidante, able to help us understand the cycles of life and measure our responses to the ebb and flow of time.

Tarot readers often recognize themselves in the High Priestess. She's a mystic, seated at the gateway between this world and the next. She knows the secrets of the universe, but she shares them only with the wise.

Most depictions of the High Priestess include lunar imagery. In the *Wizards Tarot*, for example, the High Priestess reads cards by the guiding light of the Full Moon. She wears a headpiece made up of the waxing, full, and crescent moons, as well as gleaming, moonlike pearls.

In fact, the High Priestess is the embodiment of the Moon, the luminous orb of reflection and intuition. If she seems to represent the Goddess in the process, that's no accident. In ancient Greece, Selene was the goddess of the Moon. She would rise from the oceans each night, freshly bathed and crowned with a crescent Moon. In ancient Rome, she was Luna, Latin for "Moon." The Moon is constantly changing form—as Moon goddesses often do—so the Greeks also knew her as Artemis, the goddess of the hunt, wild animals, wilderness, childbirth, women, and girls. The Romans knew Artemis by the name Diana.

The Moon is almost always paired with the Sun. Some cultures consider the two luminaries brother and sister, while others refer to them as husband and wife. In either case, they are a primordial couple, and their heavenly partnership symbolizes the constant give and take between light and dark, action and reaction, masculine and feminine, radiance and reflection, and the conscious and subconscious mind.

In fact, from our vantage point on Earth, the Moon and the Sun seem to be the same size. Like Selene and Helios, Luna and Sol, or Diana and Apollo, they are a cosmic pair, equal in size and engaged in a perpetual race through the heavens. Where the Sun is masculine and active, the Moon is feminine and receptive. The Moon doesn't generate light and heat of its own. Instead, it reflects the light of the Sun—changing and adapting each day as it orbits around the Earth.

Just as the Moon reflects the Sun's light, it also reflects our unconscious needs and desires. Because the Moon is shrouded in shadows and darkness, it represents secrets and mysteries that may not be understood—or even recognized.

The Moon symbolizes the rocky landscape of memory and feeling—brilliantly illuminated when the Moon is full, but dark and shadowy when her face is hidden from view.

The Moon reflects our fears and insecurities, as well as our desires for nurturing and safety. It describes our sensitivities: our inborn responses to emotional triggers, our instinctive responses to threats, and our immediate reactions to predatory behavior. It can relate to early childhood memories, the past, and longings for a better, more perfect life.

Astrologically, the Moon symbolizes the depths of personality. It has ties to memory, mood, and motherhood—along with corresponding issues of fertility, rhythms, and the need to nurture our creations.

The Moon rules Cancer, the sign of home and family. It also rules the fourth house of the zodiac, where modern astrologers look for information about childhood, motherhood, and nurturing.[1]

The Moon rules the breasts, stomach, ovaries, and womb—a reminder of the nurturing power expressed through mother's milk and comfort food.

The Moon card corresponds to the element of water.

---

1. Some astrologers believe that mothers belong in Saturn's tenth house of structure and discipline, because mothers set the standards for their children's behavior. In that case, they would put fathers in Cancer's fourth house of caregiving and parenting. Your interpretation will probably depend upon your own experience and observations.

Cosmic Connection: THE VOID-OF-COURSE MOON

As the Moon orbits the Earth, it travels through the signs of the zodiac. Along the way, it moves into geometric aspects with other planets. When the Moon runs out of aspects in a sign, however, it's said to be void-of-course.

Sometimes, the Moon is only void of course for a few seconds, and then it moves into the next sign. Occasionally, however, the Moon can be void-of-course for a day or two.

Symbolically, when the Moon is void-of-course, it's floating, unconnected to any other planets, and disconnected from the rest of the universe. It's no longer grounded in reality. You might even say it's sleepwalking.

When the Moon is void-of-course, it's a good time to focus on spiritual concerns or creative matters, but it's not a good time for important decisions or activities. Delay critical real-world matters until the void-of-course period has ended.

THE MAGICIAN

Mercury ☿
The Magician

In the tarot, Mercury comes to life in the form of the Magician—the master of space, time, and cosmic energy. He's proof that our perception of the world changes the world, and that the mind truly is more powerful than matter.

The Magician himself is a channel for transformation and change. He conducts cosmic energy through his body, and he uses that power to manifest his own reality.

In most depictions of the card, he holds one arm above his head, like a lightning rod. His stance is a reminder of the Hermetic maxim, "As above, so below." That's the same principle that is often used to explain why astrology and tarot are such effective tools. They both tap into powers greater than ourselves, and use the world of ideas to help us understand the world of matter.

In other words, the Magician shows us that the outer world of cause and effect and the inner world of personal experience aren't so far apart. We are each a microcosm of the macrocosmic universe.

In Rome, the archetypal Magician was known as Mercury. In Greece, he was called Hermes. He was depicted wearing winged boots and a winged helmet, and he was the god of speed, communication, salesmen, orators, tricksters, and thieves. Today, he still serves as an emissary between the realm of ideas and the world of physical existence.

Mercury is the closest planet to the Sun, so it has the shortest orbit: eighty-eight days. The planet's speed and agility mark it as the quick-thinking, versatile ruler of short trips, neighborhood errands, everyday commerce, and workday commutes.

In astrology, Mercury rules messages and communications. It represents logic, reason, wit, writing, and speech. It describes early schooling and primary education, as well as our childhood peers: neighbors, siblings, and cousins from whom we learn much of our communication methods and style.

Mercury is a multitasker. It rules two signs: Gemini, which is associated with the Lovers card, and Virgo, which is associated with the Hermit. Mercury also rules the third house of communication and the sixth house of work and service to others.

Mercury rules our biological message system, too. It regulates the brain, the central nervous system, and the sense organs.

The Magician, like Mercury, corresponds to the element of air.

Cosmic Connection: THE TRICKSTER PLANET: MERCURY RETROGRADE

Mercury, like the Magician, was also the trickster god—and to this day, three or four times a year, Mercury still plays a trick on our senses.

As Earth passes Mercury in its orbit around the Sun, the small messenger planet seems to travel backward through the stars. It's an optical illusion—just as a car you pass on the highway seems to go backward as you pull ahead of it.

When Mercury is retrograde, double-check details, cross your t's and dot your i's, because the trickster energy can wreak havoc with communications. Check and recheck your work. Back up important files.

Other planets go retrograde, too, but none seem to have the same upsetting effect on our daily lives. That's because Mercury rules the stuff of everyday life—messages, errands, appointments, neighborhood jaunts, and family connections.

Retrogrades and Tarot Reversals

In many ways, retrograde planets are like reversals in a tarot reading. Cards that fall upside-down don't reverse the meaning of a card. Instead, they put a new spin on a situation, call attention to details that you might otherwise overlook, and force you to change your perspective.

When a planet is in retrograde motion at one's birth, its energy is turned inward and must be developed from an inner awareness before it can be fully expressed externally.

Venus ♀
The Empress

In the Empress card, Venus takes human form, and one of the cosmos' most heavenly bodies finds an outlet for her creative nature.

The Empress is an archetypal mother who constantly generates new life. Perpetually pregnant, she's a symbol of fertility and growth.

Like Mother Nature, she's usually pictured in a lush garden setting. She sits comfortably on a cushioned throne, in keeping with her craving for stability and comfort, and she wears a crown of twelve stars—one for every month of the year, and every sign of the zodiac.

Both Venus and the Empress share a love of beauty—and love and attraction are powerful forces for creation. In ancient Rome, Venus was the goddess of beauty, love, and attraction. In Greece, she was known as Aphrodite.

The Empress, of course, is married; she's a loving partner to the Emperor.

In an astrological chart, Venus graces everything she touches with ease, comfort, affection, and enjoyment. She is generous to a fault. Like Jupiter, she's a benefactor; ancient astrologers called her the Lesser Benefic. That's usually a good thing, but not always—especially if she overindulges her children and they grow spoiled.

Venus rules pleasure and enjoyment, as well as a love of beauty and the arts. She is sensual and romantic, gracious and kind, gentle and sympathetic.

In keeping with her role as the morning and evening star, Venus rules two signs: Taurus and Libra. She also rules the corresponding second house of treasures and possessions, as well as the seventh house of marriage, partnerships, and personal relationships.

As the ruler of Taurus and the second house, Venus shows us what we love. As the ruler of Libra and the seventh house, she describes how we share that love with others. Her involvement leads to strong attachments, both to property and people.

Venus rules the throat—which puts her firmly in control of sweet talk and love songs. As the planet of pleasure and consumption, Venus is also associated with blood sugar levels and venereal disease.

The Empress card corresponds to the element of earth.

THE TOWER

Mars ♂
The Tower

Mars is the warrior planet of energy, aggression, assertiveness, and self-defense. At the same time, the Tower is a bastion—a fortification and a stronghold, built to withstand the forces of time and nature.

In this case, however, the warrior planet is in full attack mode. The Tower is under assault from all four elements: a fiery burst of lightning strikes its peak, wind and clouds roil the air, a raging sea pounds at its foundations, and the earth quakes.

Both the card and the planet symbolize quick, sudden bursts of energy and power. They represent intensity, potency, drive, and desire. They are markers of inspiration and the impetus for change. In most cases, it's impossible to resist a bolt from the blue—or a direct hit from Mars' machinery of war.

In a tarot reading, the Tower usually heralds a dramatic change. It sometimes refers to breakups or breakdowns, and the disintegration or collapse of a structure you thought was stable—like a relationship, a home, or a career. It can symbolize the destruction of false ideas and beliefs, a purge, or an intervention.

Just as frequently, however, the Tower represents enlightenment, inspiration, and release. For anyone trapped in an outgrown situation, it's a "Get Out of Jail Free" card. Ultimately, the Tower experience is one of purification, protection, and self-preservation, as an old structure is torn down so that renovation can begin.

Astrologically, Mars is associated with confidence and power. It symbolizes sexuality, stamina, and strength. It governs ambition, aggression, assertiveness, and impulse. Mars also rules sports and competitions—war games that take the place of battle during peacetime.

Mars rules Aries, the sign of leadership and action, along with the first house, where astrologers look for information about self-image and physical appearance.

In medicine, Mars presides over blood and the male sex organs. It's traditionally associated with fever, accidents, trauma, pain, and surgery.

The Tower corresponds to the element of fire.

THE WHEEL OF FORTUNE

Jupiter ♃
The Wheel of Fortune

Astrologers call Jupiter the Greater Benefic, the bringer of luck and good fortune. The expansive planet is the perfect match for the Wheel of Fortune.

As the largest planet in our solar system, Jupiter symbolizes growth—especially on a philosophical level. It represents the process of expanding your worldview through travel to distant lands, friendships with foreign people, and higher education.

Jupiter's greatest gifts are wisdom and success, long life, good health, and all the uplifting experiences the world has to offer: family, friendship, travel, philosophy. Jupiter gives you the good fortune to experience the fullness of life—along with the depth to remember what you've been, the insight to realize what you are, and the imagination to visualize what you'll be. In the *Wizards Tarot*, the imagery melds the memory of the past with a vision of the future.

Most versions of the Wheel of Fortune card depict the spinning wheel of destiny and fate. It moves through time and space, constantly cycling and recycling energy and matter. It serves as a measure of existence, and implies that there's an element of chance in everybody's life. It's a vivid reminder that what goes up must come down—and what goes around, comes around.

Both the planet and the card symbolize luck and opportunity and the twists and turns of fate, prosperity, and success.

In Roman mythology, Jupiter was the ruler of the gods and their guardian and protector. In the same way, the planet Jupiter is the king of the other planets, a giant in size with spectacular, brightly colored clouds and intense storms.

Jupiter rules Sagittarius, the sign of philosophy and adventure, and the ninth house of the zodiac, where astrologers look for information about higher education and long-distance travel. It is associated, like Sagittarius, with the hips and thighs.

The Wheel of Fortune corresponds to the element of fire.

Cosmic Connection: THE PART OF FORTUNE ⊗

In astrology, the Part of Fortune, sometimes called Fortuna, is a popular Arabic Part. Arabic Parts are sensitive points in a chart, calculated according to ancient mathematical formulas.

The Part of Fortune's location in a chart will often pinpoint the place where good fortune can be found. Its sign and house will offer valuable clues to the skills, talents, and abilities that can lead to worldly acclaim, career success, prosperity, and health.

THE WORLD

Saturn ♄
The World

While the World might seem limitless, both Saturn and the physical universe operate according to scientific law and principles of reason. Both have clearly defined parameters. Saturn, the ringed planet of structure, boundaries, limitations, and restrictions, finds perfect peace in the well-ordered physical plane of Earth.

The traditional version of the World card features a dancer, spinning endlessly in her own world. A wreath, a symbol of eternal life, forms a protective enclosure that frames her every movement. It's a symbol of simple physics: we are made of energy, and energy is never created or destroyed. It's just transformed.

While the World card usually suggests an entire universe of possibilities, Saturn's connection serves as a reminder that reasonable people also recognize their limits, and make wise choices to make the most of the time and space they're allotted.

Most people, of course, rebel at boundaries. They like to feel free and unencumbered. Saturn brings us down to earth and teaches us the practical realities of earthly existence.

Even though Saturn's rings imply a certain number of limitations and restrictions, they also delineate boundaries that can help us define our position and relate to other people without losing our own individuality. Boundaries keep outside forces out, and contain what belongs inside. In other words, Saturn's boundaries don't merely confine us: they define us.

Saturn is the rule-maker. It makes sure that we all share a common language of values, mores, and expectations, so that we're all on the same page. Saturn can also be a control freak: it likes to control the environment and the outcome.

Of course, part of the outcome is predetermined. Saturn is connected to death, and the ringed planet of limitations and restrictions sets definite boundaries for our earthly existence. When our name is written in the book of life, we all know how the story will eventually end. Like the ancient god Kronos, the god of time who ate his children, the years eventually destroy all of the earth's creations.

In Roman mythology, Saturn was the god of agriculture and conformity, and founder of civilizations and social order.

Saturn rules Capricorn, the sign of work and responsibility. It also rules the tenth house of the zodiac, where astrologers look for information about discipline, career success, public image, and social standing.

Saturn is associated with the bones and skin, which provide structure and stability to the human form.

The World corresponds to the element of earth.

Cosmic Connection: THE SATURN RETURN

The Saturn Return is one of astrology's best-known milestones. It's an astrological phenomenon that occurs every twenty-nine years or so—the time it takes Saturn to make one orbit around the Sun. When Saturn returns to the degree it occupied at the time of one's birth, we cross over a major threshold and into the next chapter of life.

The Saturn Return symbolizes three distinct stages of experience. For women, it marks the transition from maiden, to mother, to crone. For men, it denotes the process of growing from scout, to soldier, to chief.

During the first Saturn Return, a person leaves youth behind and enters adulthood. By the second return, that person has matured. And with the third return, he or she has become a wise, experienced elder, who's learned from each stage that has come before.

The first Saturn Return is usually the hardest, because it's the first test of character and strength. Saturn insists upon strong structures and foundations. If there is weakness to be found, the first Saturn Return will mark a period of upheaval and rebuilding. It's not uncommon to lose bad relationships, unfulfilling jobs, or tenuous living situations during any Saturn Return.

The result is worth it. Sometimes, a Saturn setback is just the impetus we need to move forward.

THE INITIATE

Uranus ⛢

The Fool

Uranus, the planet of freedom, revolution, rebellion, and reform, is assigned to the free-thinking Fool.

Both are idealists, masters of initiation and change, fresh starts and new beginnings. Both think in terms of extremes: they're willing to destroy the old to make room for the new.

Both are also regarded as eccentrics. They're unable—or unwilling—to meet customary norms and expectations.

Most versions of the Fool card depict a young man or woman about to take a leap of faith—a free spirit plunging ahead without regard for the past, the present, or the future. The card symbolizes hope and change, without respect for the traditions of the past or the cares of the present. It represents blind trust in the universe, and the conviction that individual action is the way to blaze a path to the future. Some even say that the Fool is a soul in search of experience, willing to trade innocence for wisdom. That's almost never an easy exchange.

Uranus is the planet of sudden and unexpected changes. It rules independence and originality. In society, it rules radical ideas and people, as well as revolutionary events that upset established structures. It displaces and overthrows any establishment that has outlived its useful life span. It's the planet of revolution and progress.

The glyph for Uranus looks like a satellite, and the planet is often associated with technological advancements and innovations. In fact, most tarot readers believe that the Fool carries the tools of tarot in his backpack, which equip him for any eventuality he'll encounter along his journey. The Fool and Uranus both symbolize the spirit of invention and innovation, as well as the freedom that can result.

In Greek mythology, Uranus was the personification of the heavens and the night sky—but from an astronomical perspective, the planet itself is unusual. It rotates on its side, so that its two poles face the Sun in turn. During its revolution, one hemisphere is bathed in light while the other lies in total darkness.

Uranus rules Aquarius, the sign of futuristic thinking, and the eleventh house of the zodiac, where astrologers look for information about social groups and idealistic causes. Like Aquarius, Uranus is associated with the lower legs, the ankles, and the circulatory system.

The Fool card corresponds to the element of air.

Neptune Ψ
The Hanged Man

THE HANGED MAN

The Hanged Man spends hours—or even days—suspended in a trancelike alternate reality. He is in perfect synch with Neptune, the planet of spiritual and psychic enlightenment.

The Hanged Man's consciousness transcends the physical, just as Neptune itself seems to escape the ordinary bounds of physics. After all, the planet is composed mostly of ethereal mist and gasses. It's a planet of dreamlike illusion, as well as an existence removed from the limitations of physical concerns.

From that vantage point, mystical experiences come easily. Both Neptune and the Hanged Man are associated with fantasy, imagination, and visionary art. They are idealistic, sensitive, and exceptionally psychic.

Neither one is very good at establishing boundaries. The real world can be a dark and dangerous place, and both the Hanged Man and the Neptunian spirit quickly learn to escape through meditation, prayer, sleep, and dreams.

Occasionally, they seek refuge in alcohol and drugs. Sometimes, those substances are a form of self-medication, in an effort to block the unsolicited psychic messages that flood the Neptunian soul.

In a tarot reading, the Hanged Man card often represents a period of willing self-sacrifice and the suspension of everyday cares and concerns. It could suggest a retreat or a change in perspective.

While most versions of the card show the Hanged Man upside down, he rarely seems to be in any pain or discomfort. Instead, he seems to be tuned in to a higher consciousness—and it's a reward, not a punishment.

In Roman mythology, Neptune was the god of the sea. He ruled the tides and the tide pools, as well as the dark, mysterious world of the ocean's depths. Seas would rise and fall at his command, and he could drown his opponents in an uncontrollable swell of unfathomably violent emotion.

Neptune rules Pisces and the twelfth house of the zodiac, where astrologers look for secrets. It also rules the places where those secrets are confined and locked away: hospitals, prisons, and mental institutions. In medicine, Neptune is associated with mysterious illnesses and neuroses.

The Hanged Man corresponds to the element of water.

Pluto ♀ ♇

Judgment

Pluto might have been written off by scientists, but astrologers and tarot readers never say die. The planet of transformation is a key player in contemporary astrology, and its role in tarot is equally established.

Pluto is the planet of death and destruction—ominous-sounding words that are softened by their presentation in the Judgment card. Most versions of the card depict people who are in the act of being judged; in the *Wizards Tarot*, the card features a group of students taking their final exams.

Because tarot readers read ahead, we know that, in the end, the students will pass the test. They'll be left standing, and freed to go on to the next chapter of their lives.

Pluto and the Judgment card both teach that endings are merely part of the cycle of resurrection and rebirth, and inevitably lead to a second chance at a new life.

In astrology, Pluto symbolizes death, resurrection, forgiveness, and release. It can indicate areas of testing and challenge, power struggles, and resistance. It's a planet of evolution and unavoidable change.

In a tarot reading, the Judgment card is often a call for discernment and decision-making. It compels us to release anything that's no longer living up to our needs or expectations, so we can recycle and reuse that energy in better ways.

In ancient myth, Pluto was the god of the Underworld. He ruled Hades, where souls would travel after their physical death.

Pluto rules Scorpio, the sign of mystery. It also rules the eighth house, where astrologers look for information about sex, death, and inheritance.

The Judgment card corresponds to the element of fire.

Cosmic Connection: KARMIC LESSONS AND THE POINT OF NODE RETURN

Many astrologers include the Moon's nodes in their calculations. The nodes are mathematical points that show where the Moon's orbit and the Sun's path happen to intersect.

☋ **The South Node** highlights a point of natural ability—a talent or skill that's innate, inborn, already mastered. It could be a karmic lesson that was learned in a past life, so you feel no urge or obligation to repeat it in this one. It's a marker of inherited skill and ease.

☊ **The North Node** indicates a karmic lesson you were born to learn. It's related to possibilities, growth, challenges, and opportunities for improvement.

If your south node is in Cancer in the fourth house, for example, you might not feel the need to have children. Instead, your focus will be on career—because your north node, on the other side of your chart, is in Capricorn in the tenth house; that's the sign of ambition in the house of status.

The north node and the south node are always exactly opposite each other in the chart, so some charts will only show one of the two nodes.

Three

◆

Signs of the Times

Thousands of years ago, when astrologers were first developing the principles of their art, they saw the Sun rise and set against the backdrop of a different constellation each month. Eventually, 12 constellations became the 12 signs of today's tropical zodiac: Aries, Taurus, Gemini, Cancer, Leo, Virgo, Libra, Scorpio, Sagittarius, Capricorn, Aquarius, and Pisces.

♈ **Aries,** the ram. The glyph for Aries looks like the horns of a ram.

♉ **Taurus,** the bull. The glyph for Taurus looks like the head of a bull.

♊ **Gemini,** the twins. The glyph for Gemini looks like two people.

♋ **Cancer,** the crab. The glyph for Cancer looks like the claws of a crab.

♌ **Leo,** the lion. The glyph for Leo looks like a lion's mane or tail.

♍ **Virgo,** the virgin. The glyph for Virgo looks like the wings of an angel or a V and an M, the initials of the Virgin Mary.

♎ **Libra,** the scales. The glyph for Libra looks like a pair of perfectly balanced scales.

♏ **Scorpio,** the scorpion. The glyph for Scorpio looks like a scorpion with a stinger.

♐ **Sagittarius,** the archer. The glyph for Sagittarius looks like an arrow.

♑ **Capricorn,** the goat. The glyph for Capricorn looks like a goat's head.

♒ **Aquarius,** the water bearer. The glyph for Aquarius looks like waves of water.

♓ **Pisces,** the fish. The glyph for Pisces looks like two fish tails.

Cosmic Connection: PRECESSION OF THE EQUINOXES

Every now and then, you'll hear media reports that the zodiac has shifted, and your Sun sign isn't really your sign.

Don't panic. It's simply an attention-getting way to describe an astronomical phenomenon known as the Precession of the Equinoxes.

The Earth rotates on an axis that's tilted. Our equator isn't quite aligned with the Sun and the Moon. As a result, both the Sun and the Moon exert a gravitational pull on the equator, which makes the Earth wobble a bit.

Over time, that wobble realigns our view of space. The position of the fixed stars gradually changes, and the Sun seems to rise and set against a slowly shifting backdrop of constellations.

The Greek astronomer Hipparchus first noted the phenomenon in 134 BC. Since then, the background constellations have continued to drift, and now they're about a month out of synch with our traditional frame of reference—which is known as the tropical zodiac.

In tropical astrology, we start each celestial year on the vernal equinox, or the first day of spring. We refer to that date as the start of Aries, no matter where the Sun actually rises or sets among the stars. It's mostly as a matter of convenience, because the tropical zodiac aligns so well with the mythology and symbolism of western civilization. Once we have Aries marked in the heavens, we simply measure out the remaining signs in twelve segments of 30 degrees each.

There is one branch of astrology that has kept up with the times. Vedic astrologers, who generally practice in India, use a sidereal zodiac, which accurately reflects the current position of the stars as seen from Earth.

Neither system is right or wrong. In fact, both systems are equally effective, because both tropical and sidereal astrologers rely on most of the same astrological principals.

The animal imagery of the signs is important. The word zodiac means "circle of animals," and the characteristics of each creature can be valuable clues to personality.

Sign Language

The symbolism of the signs involves multiple layers of meaning. Before we dive into the cards that correspond to each sign, let's look at the characteristics that all of the signs have in common.

Modes, Qualities, and Quadruplicities

Astrology is a calendar-based study, and the twelve signs, just like the twelve months of the year, can be grouped into four seasons: spring, summer, fall, and winter. Each season is three months long, and each season has a beginning, middle, and end.

The signs fall into three corresponding modes: cardinal, fixed, and mutable. Loosely put, those modes conform to the beginning, middle, and end of each season, so they—and their corresponding cards—are evenly spaced around the Wheel of the Year. The modes are sometimes called quadruplicities, because there are four signs for each mode.

Cardinal signs start each season with a bang. Each one marks a definite starting point on the Wheel of the Year, so they correspond to new beginnings. The first day of Aries marks the first day of spring. The first day of Cancer is the first day of summer. The first day of Libra is the first day of fall, and the first day of Capricorn is the first day of winter.

Cardinal signs are unstoppable forces of nature. They're leaders with a take-charge, can-do attitude. They're courageous, self-motivated, quick to take the initiative, and energetic. They're fast. They think on their feet, and take immediate action. They initiate change with sudden bursts of inspiration. All told, the cardinal signs convey a sense of inspiration and fresh starts.

Fixed signs mark the high point of each season. Just as you know that summer days are hot and winter nights are cold, the fixed signs—Taurus, Leo, Scorpio, and Aquarius—are clearly defined. They are thorough, unstoppable, and enduring. The fixed signs dig in and are able to hold steady in their goals to achieve something solid. It's hard for them to change, which gives them a reputation for being stubborn—but they're also very dependable. They are respected for their reliability and sense of purpose. They have the strength and endurance to see things through and to uphold the status quo. They need stable homes, careers, and partnerships, and prefer the known to uncertainty.

Mutable signs—Gemini, Virgo, Sagittarius, and Pisces—are flexible, adaptable, and changeable, because they typically usher in the change of seasons. They pave the way for change, and offer a sense of closure. They're transitional; they represent the breakdown of the old season before the new season begins, so there's a touch of chaos to their nature. They're versatile, but they can also be scattered, fickle, inconstant, and restless. They can see life from many perspectives, making them great communicators, and they can steer projects through periods of transition to bring them to a successful conclusion.

The Triplicities of the Four Elements

The twelve signs can also be grouped according to element. The elements are sometimes called triplicities, because there are three signs in each.

Fire signs—Aries, Leo, and Sagittarius—are as mesmerizing as fire itself. They give off heat and light that's impossible to ignore and difficult to contain. They're energetic, enthusiastic, spontaneous, impulsive, and optimistic.

Earth signs—Taurus, Virgo, and Capricorn—are as stable as the ground beneath your feet. They're solid, supportive, reliable, practical, physical, sensible, and capable. They're also cautious, slow-moving, thorough, and unhurried.

Air signs—Gemini, Libra, and Aquarius—are quick-witted and as fleeting as the wind, filled with ideas and imagination. They're light and airy; they can shoot the breeze with anyone. They're conversational and communicative. Sometimes, they can also be elusive.

Water signs—Cancer, Scorpio, and Pisces—are emotional and intuitive. Their moods can rise and fall like the tides. They can be turbulent and swirling, or deep and calm. Still waters run deep, and most water signs are placid—but they're also susceptible to passing storms of anger.

Dualities

In a world where opposites attract, all of the signs have characteristics that make them either masculine or feminine—or, in other words, active or receptive, extroverted or introverted, energetic or magnetic, linear or circular, or yin or yang.

Masculine Fire and air signs are masculine. They're outspoken, confident, assertive, courageous, and bold. They don't wait for results: they make things happen.

Feminine Earth and water signs are feminine. They're quiet, responsive, intuitive, and understanding. They're patient and strong, and they have the wherewithal to see events through to their conclusions.

Now let's take a look at the Major Arcana cards that correspond to each sign.

Aries ♈
The Emperor

Aries comes to life in the form of the Emperor. Whether you think of him as an astrological sign or a tarot card, he's the leader of the pack.

The Emperor typifies the Aries personality: fearless, confident, courageous, and completely in control. He's a master and commander, a visionary ruler, and lord of all he surveys. He creates order out of chaos and transforms his conquests into an empire and a civilization of his own design.

The Emperor is ready to protect and defend his realm at a moment's notice—like Aries, the Greek god of war for whom the sign was named. The Romans called him Mars, and the planet named in Mars' honor is assigned to the Tower card. Even today, the warlike god is remembered in terms like "martial arts" and "martial law."

As the embodiment of the first sign, the Emperor symbolizes leadership and initiation. He's adventurous, pioneering, and decisive. He is forceful, blunt, and direct. And just as Aries leads all the other signs, the Emperor leads a vast collection of kingdoms, lands, and territories.

You'll discover clues to the Emperor's Aries nature in most versions of the Emperor card. The Aries glyph looks like the horns of a ram—and, in fact, images of rams and rams' horns are incorporated in many artists' renditions of the Emperor card. In the *Wizards Tarot*, the Aries influence is prominently featured in the warrior's helmet with the horns of a ram.

Aries rules the head. True to form, the Emperor leads with the head, not the heart. He is willful, stubborn, and strong—and he rules through logic and reason. He can be rigid and inflexible: his word is law.

The connection isn't limited to health and physical issues: think broadly and symbolically. The Emperor is the head of state. Aries, the first sign of the zodiac, occupies the first house of the natural horoscope, so it's the head of the zodiac household, too. The first house is where astrologers look for information about first impressions and physical appearance.

Aries is a fire sign. In both astrology and tarot, the element of fire symbolizes spiritual energy. As a result, the Emperor can be hot-headed. All that fire makes him passionate about the causes he believes in. He's bold, brash, and self-confident. He doesn't doubt himself for a moment, or question the rightness of his cause.

People with a strong Aries influence in their charts can seem like rams—and Emperors. They're not afraid to butt heads, or to use their heads as battering rams. In an argument, the heady Emperor can outsmart, outmaneuver, and browbeat almost any opponent. He holds a battery of facts at his disposal. He's hard-headed, too; it's not easy to get him to change his mind. Occasionally, the Emperor is even called upon to give up his life for his people or his cause. After all, rams were sacrificial animals in the ancient world.

Aries' ruler, Mars, is the red planet, traditionally associated with the unbridled energy and passion of war, as well as aggression, self-defense, and action. The mythic cross-connections don't stop there. In mythology, Mars and Venus were lovers, and in tarot, Venus is assigned to the Empress card. While the Empress holds court in a lush and fertile garden, the Emperor rules from a far more Spartan landscape. He's all business.

In tarot, Mars corresponds to the Tower card.

The Sun travels through Aries between March 21 and April 20. The sign marks the first month of spring and the first day in the astrological year. That makes it a cardinal sign: it's an initiator and a self-starter. The Emperor doesn't wait to take action, or look around for someone else to take the lead. While Aries introduces new beginnings, other signs will step in to provide the follow-through that an Emperor requires from his followers.

Aries rules the first house of self, where astrologers look for information about physical appearance and first impressions.

Taurus ♉
The Hierophant

THE HIEROPHANT

Taurus plays for keeps, especially when it comes to matters of spiritual value. That's what makes the sign such a perfect match for the Hierophant, the card of time-honored values and beliefs.

Taurus is the sign of stability and convention, while the Hierophant is a traditionalist who values faithfulness, monogamy, and procreation. Both Taurus and the Hierophant are committed to structure and propriety, along with creature comforts and objects of beauty that represent spiritual treasures.

In ancient Greece, the hierophants were priests who guided their followers through the sacred rites of the Eleusinian Mysteries—a mythic scenario of death and rebirth—by enacting the story of Persephone. She was the maiden goddess who was kidnapped by Hades, the god of the Underworld. Her disappearance plunged the world into a long winter of bitter cold and deprivation—but it was fertile ground for ruminations about life after death. Today, the role of the hierophant lives on in every spiritual teacher and guide who leads followers through seasons of hope and experience.

The word "hierophant" shares the same origin as the word "hierarchy," which means an organization with varying levels of authority; a hierophant is the final authority on matters of faith. He has the power to speak on behalf of God, to explain the teachings of divine wisdom, and to serve as a bridge between this world and the next.

The glyph for Taurus looks like the head of a bull, or the ring in a bull's nose. Most Hierophant cards feature Taurus glyphs carved into pillars of the church, or heavy, earthy animals like bulls or elephants.

Like bulls in a meadow, Taurus and the Hierophant are committed to creature comforts—as well as the comfort and stability of long-standing ritual and practice. Both can be bull-headed: stubborn, immovable, and almost impossible to placate. Both can be bullish when it comes to the practice of their beliefs. But both can also be a rock of solidarity and comfort in difficult times. They are determined and loyal, dedicated, and enduring. In a sense, the Hierophant is a spiritual beast of burden.

Taurus is the second sign. It rules the second house of the zodiac, where astrologers look for information about money and possessions, as well as the spiritual values they represent.

Taurus, in turn, is ruled by Venus, the planet of love, beauty, and attraction. In the tarot, Venus is assigned to the Empress card; she offers a physical form of nurturing that complements the Hierophant's spiritual training.

The Sun is in Taurus between April 21 and May 21. Taurus marks the second month of spring. That makes it a fixed sign: when Taurus is in play, the season of spring is in full flower.

Taurus is also an earth sign. In both astrology and tarot, the element of earth symbolizes physical energy. It's practical and reliable, patient and persevering. It's feminine and receptive: it provides fertile soil for growth and development.

Taurus rules the neck and throat—which means that Taurus can be remarkably expressive through spoken language and song. Similarly, hierophants have always relied on speeches, sermons, and hymns to lead and uplift their followers.

Cosmic Connection: CHIRON, THE WOUNDED HEALER ⚷

In the *Wizards Tarot* deck, the Hierophant is Chiron, the wounded healer of myth and legend. A centaur—half human, half horse—he represents a magical blend of man and beast, body and spirit, and intelligence in animal form.

Chiron was an immortal creature who served as a teacher to the ancient Greeks and Romans. He even tutored the legendary hero Hercules. When Hercules accidentally shot him with a poisoned arrow, however, Chiron's immortal essence condemned him to suffering without end. As Chiron sought relief for his crippling injuries, he accumulated a vast store of medical knowledge. He shared that wisdom with others, which led to his legendary reputation as a wounded healer. Eventually, the gods took pity on Chiron's suffering. They relieved him of his mortal form and gave him a heavenly home in the stars.

In astrology, Chiron is a comet with a unique and erratic orbit. Modern astrologers look to Chiron for information about the wounded healer that resides in every person's birth chart, along with corresponding efforts toward healing and recovery.

The glyph for Chiron looks like the Hierophant's key to the kingdom of heaven.

Gemini ♊
The Lovers

It is often said that people born under the sign of Gemini are the great communicators of the zodiac. They are insatiably curious, talkative, flirtatious, and playful.

One could say the same thing about the Lovers, the tarot card associated with Gemini.

The Lovers are twin souls, with a wide range of thoughts, interests, and experiences to share and compare. They're quick thinking and smart—and they're versatile, lighthearted, adventurous, and inquisitive, too.

While the card can have romantic connotations, it's more important to note that the Lovers are kindred spirits, who speak the same language and exchange thoughts and ideas freely and openly. Their love and affection for each other could just as easily be Platonic as romantic.

Most people put a romantic spin on the Lovers card, but its astrological significance applies to siblings, too. You might even think of a sibling relationship as a profound soul mate connection. In fact, most people have a longer-lasting relationship with their brothers and sisters than they do with their husbands, wives, or romantic partners.

The Gemini glyph depicts Castor and Pollux, twins who hatched from the egg of their mother Leda, following her seduction by Zeus. They were great warriors, noted for their devotion to each other. Zeus created the constellation Gemini in their honor.

The glyph for Gemini looks like two people standing side by side, with their arms around each other, perhaps smiling for the artist who first etched their image on a cuneiform tablet.

The sign represents the duality of two separate individuals working in tandem—one that makes the most of two identities, two ideals, and the intersection of two points of view. Both the Gemini twins and the two Lovers in the tarot card represent a diversity of thoughts and experiences, and the versatility and expanded point of view that a partnership can bring to any situation.

The sign also describes the intersection of those viewpoints, primarily through communication, which it rules. People send and receive information in a variety of ways; Gemini covers the spoken word, written word, and body language.

Together, the combination of Gemini and the Lovers demonstrates that two heads are better than one—and that two points of view can coexist harmoniously.

Gemini rules communication. It controls the free and open expression of ideas, and it lends a sense of magic to written and verbal messages. Gemini rules sibling relationships, because we so often learn how to communicate with others based on our exchanges with brothers, sisters, and related peer groups. Gemini also rules short errands and neighborhood trips—the kind we embark upon when we're first learning to navigate the world as children.

Gemini is the third sign. It rules the third house of the zodiac, where astrologers look for information about communication, sibling relationships, and elementary education. Gemini, in turn, is ruled by Mercury, the planet of speed and communication. In tarot, Mercury corresponds to the Magician card.

Gemini is also an air sign. In astrology, just as in tarot, the element of air symbolizes intellectual energy.

Gemini is ambidextrous: it's associated with the dual embrace of arms and hands. It also rules the twin chambers of the lungs, which control the air we breathe and use to communicate.

The Sun is in Gemini between May 22 and June 21. The sign marks the third and final month of spring. That makes it a mutable sign: it's flexible, spontaneous, and adaptable, to ease the transition from one season to the next.

THE CHARIOT

Cancer ♋
The Chariot

The Chariot card corresponds to Cancer, the sign of motherhood, home, and family life.

At first glance, the sign doesn't seem to have much in common with the adventurous spirit of the Chariot card. Look again, though, and you'll soon discover that the high-flying charioteer never leaves her home and family for long.

The typical Cancer individual is far more like the Charioteer than you might expect. After all, the first charioteers traveled in an early version of the mobile home. Both Cancer and the Charioteer are also remarkably resourceful, intuitive, and protective—all valuable resources for the traveler on the go.

In almost every version of the card, the Charioteers are adventurers—but their quests have a practical purpose. Some are warriors, determined to protect and defend their communities. Some travel for the sake of business and trade, in order to make a better life for their families. Some journey in pursuit of knowledge and experience, and to make new connections with people in other parts of the world.

No matter where they travel, however, the Cancerian charioteers bring a little piece of home along for the ride. In most versions of the card, the Chariot is itself a home away from home. In the *Wizards Tarot*, the Chariot is a broom—a staple tool of hearth and home, and a must for proper homemaking.

The glyph for Cancer looks like a crab's claw—and both Cancer and the Charioteer can be defensive. The crab's hard shell offers a tough, nearly impenetrable barrier between the dangers of the outside world and the vulnerable creature inside.

Crabs scuttle sideways when they move; they rarely move in a direct course. They even put out feelers to sense the direction they should travel. When they sense danger, they lash out with sharp, pinching claws that can maim those who threaten or torment them.

And because they're water creatures, Cancerians are sensitive and intuitive. They're moody: just as the Moon changes from day to day and the tides rise and fall in response, they can be wildly responsive to fluctuations in the environment around them.

They can be possessive and overly protective. Overall, however, Cancers are sensitive, kind, gentle, imaginative, affectionate, and nurturing.

Cancer is the fourth sign. It rules the fourth house of the zodiac, where astrologers look for clues about home and family life, as well as nurturing influences. Cancer, in turn, is ruled by the Moon, the planet of reflection, intuition, and inspiration. The Moon is assigned to the High Priestess card—which is a good fit, as she represents those same qualities.

The Sun is in Cancer between June 22 and July 23. The start of the sign, on the summer solstice, is also the first day of summer. That makes it a cardinal sign of leadership and new beginnings. Both the sign and the Chariot card represent leaders who aren't afraid to dive into new experiences and adventures.

Cancer is also a water sign. In astrology, just as in tarot, the element of water symbolizes emotional energy.

Cancer rules the breasts and stomach, which clearly indicates a mother's lifelong role as a nurturing presence in her children's lives. For most mothers, feeding their children is a primary part of their job—first, by nursing their children as infants, and later by filling their stomachs with home-cooked meals.

STRENGTH

Leo ♌

Strength

Strength is the card of courage and self-discipline. It symbolizes bravery and determination, even in the face of overwhelming obstacles. It also suggests the confidence and calm that come from overcoming fear.

The young woman in the card might seem fearless, but that's not necessarily the case. She'd be the first to tell you that she both fears and respects the power of every wild creature. She's learned, however, to maintain her composure, even in the face of danger.

She's also learned that some animals feed on fear, so she refuses to display any hint of vulnerability. Instead, she snatches victory from the jaws of defeat.

In older tarot decks, Strength was called Fortitude—a cardinal virtue, aligned with Temperance, Justice, and Prudence. In a similar vein, Leo is also a sign of valor, daring, and willpower.

Both Leo and Strength are generous, warm, dramatic, flamboyant, magnetic, strong-minded, optimistic, honorable, loyal, frank, energetic, and regal.

Most Leos, the strong, self-confident showmen of the zodiac, would have no qualms about stepping into the center ring of the circus if it meant that they could demonstrate their courage and ability to a crowd of admirers. Like the brave young lion-tamer in the Strength card, they take a certain pride in their ability to shine in the spotlight.

In fact, the ferocious beast in most versions of the Strength card is simply a reminder of Leo's signature animal, the lion. Leo people are usually as strong, brave, inspiring, and showy as the Strength card would suggest. They can also be vain, proud, and self-important—but, having tamed lion after lion, they probably have earned the right to show off a bit.

Lions hunt and dispatche their prey without bitterness, recrimination, or regret. The lion is also an alchemical symbol for the Sun—Leo's ruling planet—along with gold and sulphur.

The glyph for Leo looks like a lion's tale or a lion's mane. Most versions of the card feature both the glyph and a lion—or a similarly formidable creature of the wild, like a tiger or a dragon. In the *Wizards Tarot*, the Strength card depicts a wyvern—a dangerous, dragon-like creature, with wings, two legs, and a serpent's tail. While the wyvern isn't likely to bite the hand that feeds him, any close interaction with the creature entails an element of risk.

Leo rules the fifth house of the zodiac, where astrologers look for information about creativity—creation, procreation, and recreation.

Leo, in turn, is ruled by the Sun, the radiant center of our solar system. Leo personalities typically like to be in the spotlight of center stage. In astrology, the Sun symbolizes the ego and individuality of the self.

The Sun is in Leo between July 21 and August 23. Leo rules the hottest month of summer, when the Earth is closest to the Sun, the days are long and scorching, and the season is at its peak. That makes it a fixed sign: established, clearly defined, and unmistakably fiery.

Leo is also a fire sign. In both astrology and tarot, fire represents spiritual energy, passions, and drive. Leo is one of the most flamboyant signs, determined to shine and stand out from the rest of the celestial crowd.

Leo rules the heart and spine. It's no accident that we use the terms heart and backbone to describe the bravery and determination of heroes.

The Hermit

Virgo ♍

The Hermit

Any hermit can tell you that it's lonely at the top—especially when others are expecting you to shine a light of wisdom and experience to guide them, too.

The Hermit isn't part of ordinary civilization, but he does keep watch over the world from his hermit's cave, where he maintains a collection of universal wisdom and learning. He's reclusive, but he's not exclusive; his followers know where to find him. He even holds a lamp of wisdom to serve as a beacon and a guide.

In astrology, Virgo is the sign of duty, work, and service to others, and the Hermit typifies the Virgo personality: self-disciplined, conscientious, reliable, and exacting—a troubleshooter who can spot flaws and fix them.

The Hermit card usually represents wisdom, prudence, and illumination, as well as philosophy, introspection, and meditation. The card illustrates the concepts of solitude, silence, and leadership by example.

Virgo is represented by the virgin—more spiritual than physical, almost holy, and pure. In fact, the glyph for Virgo looks like a pair of angel wings, or a "V" and an "M"—the initials of the Virgin Mary.

That doesn't mean that the Hermit is destined for a life of celibacy. In Latin, "Virgo" means "unmarried" or "self-possessed." Virgos give of themselves by choice, not out of a sense of duty. They have integrity, and they always stay true to themselves. Historically, unmarried temple virgins served their communities by living exemplary lives of public service and personal responsibility. Hermits are solitary and self-possessed, too, but they carry the light of wisdom for others to follow, and they tend to attract fellow seekers and believers.

At their core, Virgos are somewhat isolated. It's their rational, practical, and analytical nature at work. In order to live up to their own high standards, Virgos often have to separate themselves from those who aren't as hard-working, resourceful, and well organized. They're detail-oriented, and they can be critical—although usually they are most critical of themselves. They are also extremely helpful. Once you seek them out, they are more than willing to share the wisdom they have accumulated on their own journeys.

Virgo is the sixth sign and rules the sixth house of the zodiac, where astrologers look for information about work and service to others.

Virgo, in turn, is ruled by Mercury, the planet of communication. In tarot, Mercury corresponds to the Magician card. The combination of the wise old Hermit and the brash young Magician relates directly to Virgo's desire to teach and help other people.

The Sun is in Virgo between August 24 and September 23. The sign marks the third and final month of summer. That makes it a mutable sign: it's changeable and varied, to ease the transition from one season to the next.

Virgo is also an earth sign. In both astrology and tarot, the element of earth symbolizes stability and practicality.

Virgo is associated with the nervous and digestive systems. Most Virgos are very conscious of their health, and pay keen attention to diet and clean living.

Cosmic Connection: SATURN'S CLOAK

If you're coming to tarot from an astrology background, you might think the Hermit is associated with Saturn or Kronos, the ancient gods of time and harvest. You wouldn't be completely off-base: there is plenty of room for overlap in the archetypes of the tarot. Some early versions of the card did depict him as a robed and bearded man, holding a Saturnine hourglass. The *Rider-Waite's* designer, however, described the Hermit as a variant of Prudence, which aligns the card with Virgo, too.

Libra ♎

Justice

The goddess of Justice has assumed many forms, from her earliest incarnations in ancient Egypt to her prominent position in modern-day courtrooms. She comes to life in the Justice card, where she balances an archetypal set of scales and serves as a compelling witness to the importance of honesty and truth.

You might recognize her as Ma'at, the Egyptian goddess of truth who weighed the hearts of the dead before they could pass into the Afterlife. On her scales, a pure heart would weigh no more than a feather. Ma'at, like Libra, was the embodiment of cosmic order: she was responsible for ensuring that the universe followed a consistent, predictable set of rules.

You might also know her as Themis, the ancient Greek goddess of justice. She helped keep the infant Zeus safe from his father Kronos, the god of time who destroyed all of his creations. She was also a gifted prophet who served for a time as the Oracle of Delphi, where she offered visions of truth and light to spiritual seekers.

Today, the goddess of Justice is almost always depicted with the scales of balance—the emblem of the sign of Libra. The iconographic imagery links the card to Libran concepts of balance, equanimity, and grace, both personal and political.

Libra is skilled at solving problems, compromising, and arranging diplomatic solutions for any conflict. Occasionally, Libra's need to see both sides of any issue can make it seem indecisive. Its charm, however, makes up for it.

Librans have an innate need to balance themselves through relationships with others. They are typically friendly, gregarious, and charming. They are exceptionally social creatures, with visionary social and humanitarian ideals. They tend to express themselves through artistic pursuits and have a keen appreciation for the beauty and harmony of art.

Libra is the seventh sign. It rules the seventh house of the zodiac, where astrologers look for information about marriage, partnerships, and intimate relationships.

Libra, in turn, is ruled by Venus, the planet of love, attraction, and an appreciation for beauty and harmony. For that reason, Libra rules all of the arts, from theaters, to concert halls, to art galleries.

In tarot, Venus corresponds to the Empress card. The combination lends a caring, nurturing quality to Libra's role as an emissary of balance and equanimity.

The Sun is in Libra between September 23 and October 22. Its start marks the first day of fall. That makes it a cardinal sign: it takes a leadership position, and initiates change and forward movement. Like Aries and Cancer before it, Libra is an agent of change and decisive action.

Libra is also an air sign. In astrology, just as in tarot, the element of air symbolizes intellectual energy. Libra is extroverted, communicative, and conversational. It's interested in others—and it's able to express that interest in an utterly charming fashion.

Libra rules the seat of power in the human body: the buttocks, along with the lower back and the balanced pair of purifying kidneys.

Scorpio ♏

Death

Believe it or not, the Death card isn't a bad omen. It's not a portent of doom or imminent destruction. Instead, it's a card of transition. It almost never refers to an actual, physical death. In practical terms, it's more likely to suggest a release, a change of form, a transformation, or the "little deaths" of sex and sleep.

While most people fear death, those who are born under Scorpio's influence are unafraid of darkness. In fact, they're fascinated by the interconnected mysteries of death and sex.

Scorpios understand, perhaps better than any other sign, that death does not always have the sting associated with its signature emblem, the scorpion.

Occasionally, Scorpio is also represented by an eagle, a bird of prey, or a phoenix, the mythical bird that dies and is reborn from its own ashes.[2] The bird is a symbol of destruction and purification by fire and subsequent rebirth from the ashes. It's a metaphor for transformation and change, metamorphosis and rebirth. It doesn't represent the loss of energy; instead, it symbolizes a conversion.

Like the reborn phoenix, the Death card heralds the completion of one chapter of life and the exciting new start of another.

When the Death card rears its ugly head in a tarot reading, it could also refer to a death that's already transpired—especially if that passing has gone unnoticed or unacknowledged.

---

2. The eagle is one of four zodiac creatures that make a joint appearance in other cards, too. Many versions of the Wheel of Fortune and the World feature the fiery lion of Leo, the earthy bull of Taurus, the airy human form of Aquarius, and the eagle of watery Scorpio.

It may call for the release of old habits, old patterns, and old relationships that have served their purpose and now should be relegated to the pages of history.

Scorpio is the eighth sign. It rules the eighth house of the zodiac, where astrologers look for information about sex, death, joint resources, and other people's money.

Scorpio, in turn, is ruled by Pluto, the planet of death, regeneration, and unavoidable change. In classical astrology, Mars was Scorpio's ruler—but contemporary astrologers assign the sign to Pluto, and the tarot does, too.

In tarot, Pluto corresponds to the Judgment card. The combination of the Death and Judgment cards reaffirms Scorpio's grasp of the deep mysteries of life, as well as its appreciation for the life to come. The sign is inextricably linked to the transformative powers of sex, death, and inheritance.

Scorpio is a water sign. In astrology, just as in tarot, the element of water symbolizes deep emotional energy.

The Sun is in Scorpio between October 23 and November 22. That's the second month of autumn, when the days and nights are in perfect balance and the season is at its peak. It's a fixed sign: established, clearly defined, and undeniably forceful in its autumnal energy.

Scorpio is associated with the reproductive organs, which guarantees that the ongoing cycle of birth and death will never end.

Sagittarius ♐
Temperance

THE ALCHEMIST

In most tarot decks, the Temperance card depicts the alchemical process of blending and mixing disparate elements. Wet and dry, hot and cold, male and female … there is no end to the various combinations and permutations we can explore, and in most cases, the adventure of discovery is more fulfilling than any final result.

For Sagittarius, the sign of long-distance travel, higher education, and philosophy, the journey is also more important than the destination. Sagittarius is always chasing the adventure and excitement that awaits just over the horizon—whether that borderline is literal or figurative.

The archer of Sagittarius is a wily creature, a restless adventurer and offbeat philosopher. Half man, half horse, he's a seamless blend of man and beast. He's a happy-go-lucky explorer who travels the world in search of honest and visionary companions. He is enthusiastic, independent, footloose, and fancy-free.

The glyph for Sagittarius looks like an arrow. With a single movement, the archer can unleash his weapon and send it soaring to a new horizon. Just as an arrow flies through time and space, physical and intellectual journeys broaden the mind and expand our horizons.

Sagittarius is the ninth sign. It rules the ninth house of the zodiac, where astrologers look for information about higher education, philosophy, and long-distance travel.

In turn, Sagittarius is ruled by Jupiter, the planet of luck and expansion. In the tarot, Jupiter is assigned to the Wheel of Fortune card. The combination of Temperance and the Wheel of Fortune depicts Sagittarius' balanced, optimistic nature.

Temperance was one of the five cardinal virtues in ancient Greece, and it's one of the four cardinal virtues of the Catholic Church. While the current interpretation of the word implies a total abstinence from alcohol, it also refers to a mechanical process: just as steel is tempered by fire and ice, people are tempered—made harder and more durable—by time and experience.

The Sun is in Sagittarius between November 21 and December 20. The sign marks the third and final month of fall. That makes it a mutable sign: it's changeable and varied, to ease the transition from one season to the next.

Sagittarius is a fire sign. In astrology, just as in tarot, the element of fire symbolizes spiritual energy.

Sagittarius is associated with the hips and thighs—the "horsey" part of the body that can bear weight and carry a rider across long distances of time and space.

THE DARK LORD

Capricorn ♑
The Devil

The Devil knows how to make the most of first impressions—and he knows how to intimidate his opposition.

But if anyone could beat the Devil at a game of cards, it would be a Capricorn. That's because the stereotypical Capricorn businessman and the Devil share an important trait: both understand all too well the trials and temptations of the material world.

Capricorn is the sign of business, career, worldly success, and social standing. It's the sign of tangible property, material resources, and physical existence. People who are born when the Sun is in Capricorn are usually hard workers, high achievers, and responsible partners, both at work and at home.

The dark lord of the Devil card, however, offers a secret glimpse at every person's dark side. He's obviously connected to sin and temptation, as well as the pitfalls of human existence like lust, gluttony, greed, sloth, wrath, envy, and pride. He knows that wealth and material success can liberate us—or enslave us.

Most Capricorns are keenly aware of their social status. Like their symbol, the sure-footed mountain goat, they are constantly climbing, and constantly seeking greener pastures. They are ambitious, driven, disciplined, and industrious. They are prudent, patient, stable, and enduring and they're willing to give the Devil his due.

Capricorn is ruled by Saturn, the planet of boundaries and limitations. In tarot, Saturn is assigned to the World card. The combination is effective: the Devil is an earthly creature, firmly rooted in the material world, and closely associated with both the pleasures and pain of physical existence.

People with a strong Capricorn influence usually feel driven to prove themselves in business and society. In this case, however, the Devil demonstrates that an obsession with outward appearances can imprison the spirit in the material world.

The Devil is a Christian invention—but many of his characteristics happen to be derived from Pan, the mythical god of music, nature, sheep, and shepherds. Pan's head and torso looked human, but from the waist down, he was a goat, with fur-covered legs and animal hooves.

Pan was a god of physical pleasures, including sexuality, food, and drink. He was a close associate of Dionysus, the god of wine. As a result, the Devil card occasionally symbolizes alcohol and drug abuse. Pan was wild: he could even inspire panic. Because of his association with Pan, the Devil has come to symbolize erotic pleasure, wild behavior, and unbridled desire.

Some astrologers depict Capricorn as a hybrid creature, half goat and half fish. The imagery dates back to myths about Pan, who jumped into the Nile to escape the monster Typhon. Submerged from the waist down, his legs turned into a fish tail, while his upper body maintained its goat-like form. The Capricorn glyph looks like the profile of a goat-fish.

The Devil card can also be connected to Cernunnus, the horned nature and fertility god of the Celts, and Baphomet, the imaginary creature that's sometimes depicted as a goat's head superimposed on an inverted pyramid. Occasionally, the Devil card relates to Pluto or Hades, the lord of the Underworld and the king of the dead.

Capricorn is the tenth sign of the zodiac. It rules the tenth house of career and social status—both of which often come at great expense. No one understands that cost better than a Capricorn, who will pay almost any price for the privilege that power can bring.

Capricorn is ruled, in turn, by Saturn, the ringed planet of boundaries and limitations. In tarot, Saturn corresponds to the World card.

Not surprisingly, Capricorn is an earth sign. In both astrology and tarot, the element of earth symbolizes stability and practicality. It's the sign of tangible property, material resources, and physical existence.

The Sun is in Capricorn between December 21 and January 20. The sign marks the beginning of winter. It's a cardinal sign of leadership and initiation, which introduces a season of change and new beginnings.

Capricorn is associated with the knees, shins, and ankles—three components that are critical to anyone who wants to climb mountains and reach the pinnacle of career and social success.

Aquarius ♒
The Star

THE STAR

What could be more astrological than the stars? The constellations and the signs of the zodiac have helped shape our very understanding of the human psyche.

In tarot, the glimmering Star card is associated with Aquarius, the sign of social consciousness and futuristic thinking. The stars of Aquarius are the altruistic visionaries, revolutionaries, and pioneers who dream of a brighter tomorrow.

Aquarius can be an unpredictable sign. Aquarians are usually unconventional free thinkers, and they can sometimes be eccentric. Despite their love of humanity, they occasionally spurn intimate, one-on-one relationships. They can even be aloof. Don't take it personally. Most Aquarians are just a little farsighted, being focused on the future as they are.

The Star card illustrates the power of myth. Since the dawn of time, storytellers have gathered around campfires and used the stars as an aid to describe our most secret hopes and dreams. Every constellation in the night sky is associated with a corresponding myth or legend.

Aquarius, is sometimes linked to Ganymede, the handsome young cupbearer of the Greek gods. He kept their cups filled with ambrosia—the water of life, the nectar of the gods, and the drink of immortality.

The goddess depicted in the *Wizards Tarot* Star card might be Nut, the Egyptian goddess of the night sky. Her name itself means night: she arched protectively over the Earth, covered in stars, and she served as a barrier between chaos and the orderly workings of the cosmos. Each night she would swallow the Sun so that she could give birth to the morning.

The Egyptians identified with Nut: they used to say that every woman was a *nutrit*, a little goddess.

The Star is also associated with Phospheros and Hesperos—two names for the rising and setting morning and evening star. The Star might also be Sirius, the Dog Star, the Star of Bethlehem, the Star of the Magi, or the North Star that guides sailors through the night. According to some traditions, each star is an unborn or departed soul.

For thousands of years, people have looked to the night sky for guidance—and the Star still symbolizes direction. Sailors navigate by the North Star. Small children make wishes on the evening star. Young lovers watch for shooting stars, so they can make wishes for their happiness. And astrologers look to the stars when they chart the course of their clients' lives.

Aquarius is the eleventh sign of the zodiac. It rules the eleventh house, where astrologers look for information about social groups, social causes, utopian visions, and technology.

Aquarius is ruled, in turn, by Uranus, the planet of freedom, rebellion, and reform. In tarot, Uranus corresponds to the Fool. The combination of the Star and the Fool is a clear depiction of the dreamer who is not afraid to follow his heart.

The Sun is in Aquarius between January 21 and February 20. The sign marks the middle month of winter. That makes it a fixed sign: like a fixed star, it's unmoving and clearly placed.

Aquarius is an air sign. In astrology, just as in tarot, the element of air symbolizes intellectual energy. And while Aquarius is an air sign, its symbol is a water bearer—so the glyph represents waves of both air and water.

Aquarius rules the shins, calves and ankles—the parts of our body that are immersed when we wade into the rivers of time.

Pisces ✳
The Moon

Pisces is often said to be the most mystical sign of the zodiac. While most people live entirely on the dry land of observable reality, the Pisces fish are equally comfortable swimming through the deep waters of intuition and spiritual transformation.

On land, Pisces can be restless, changeable, and self-destructive. In water, its energy flows in more appropriate channels. It becomes adventurous, imaginative, creative, and artistic.

Those otherworldly qualities are reflected in the Pisces card, the Moon—and they're fully expressed in the goddess on the card.

Like the Moon, Pisces is changeable. It is sensitive, compassionate, selfless, and intuitive. It can also be restless, self-destructive, self-pitying, and secretive.

Throughout myth and history, the Moon has usually been a feminine symbol; since it reflects the light of the Sun, it's often perceived as a mate or companion to the Sun. The Moon is also the Earth's companion, a partner in time and space. She reveals herself in bits and pieces, and she hides the dark side of her nature.

In tarot, the Moon card is associated with the Greek goddess Artemis, the goddess of the hunt. (The Romans knew her as Diana.) Her hounds accompanied her as she chased playfully through the skies with her twin brother Apollo, god of the Sun.

In her role as hunter, Artemis could take life, cleanly and without reservation. She wasn't a goddess of death, however. In fact, she was the goddess of childbirth, and she was dedicated to shepherding new life into the world. Immediately after she was born, she helped deliver her own twin brother. In ancient Greece, women in labor would cry out to Artemis for relief; they believed that she could either kill their pain, or kill them to end their suffering.

The Moon also represents the changing nature of existence and the cycles of our lives. It moves through all of the signs every month, and it's actually full in each sign once a year. Because the lunar and solar calendars aren't perfectly synchronized, the Moon makes a complete orbit around the Earth every 28 days, and catches up with the Sun every 30 days.

The Moon symbolizes fertility and creativity, because its 28-day cycles are typical of most women's monthly cycles. It is also linked to pregnancy and childbirth, because its phases so clearly match the pregnant female form: slim, then round and full, then slim again.

The goddess on the *Wizards Tarot* Moon card embodies all three forms of the triple goddess: maiden, mother, and crone. Her figure is slim, like a young woman's. However, her stomach is curvy and her breasts are full. She has either given birth recently, or she's in the early stages of pregnancy. At the same time, her hair is silver, which suggests the wisdom and experience of the crone.

Pisces is a water sign. In astrology, just as in tarot, the element of water symbolizes emotional energy. The Moon moves those waters, as it rules the ebb and flow of the tides.

Pisces is the twelfth sign. It rules the twelfth house of the zodiac, where astrologers look for information about our deepest, darkest secrets and desires—all submerged in the waters of memories, dreams, and reflections.

Pisces, in turn, is ruled by Neptune, the planet of mystery and illusion. In tarot, Neptune corresponds to the Hanged Man, the visionary whose body exists in suspended animation, freeing his spirit to travel through an alternate reality.

The Sun is in Pisces between February 19 and March 20. The sign marks the third and final month of winter. That makes it a mutable sign: it's changeable and varied, to ease the transition from one season to the next.

The Pisces glyph looks like two fish tails. In Greek mythology, the two fish were Aphrodite and her son, Eros. They turned into fish to escape the monster Typhon, and they tied their tails together to make sure they didn't lose each other.

Pisces rules the feet—the one part of the human form that's most in contact with the grounding qualities of the earth, but always ready to wade into the watery realm of emotion.

◆ Astrology in Action: **The Phases of the Moon Spread** ◆

This spread, based on the phases of the Moon, is especially good for project planning. It can help you set goals and manage the creative growth and development of any undertaking.

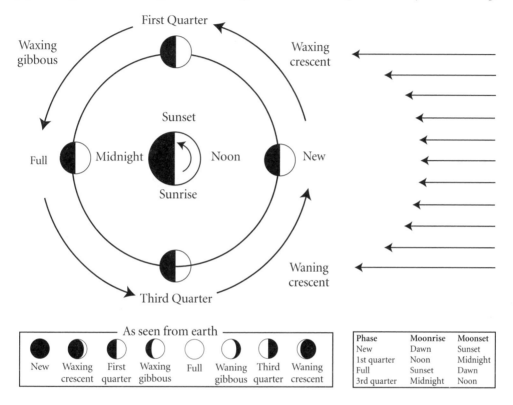

As seen from earth

Phase	Moonrise	Moonset
New	Dawn	Sunset
1st quarter	Noon	Midnight
Full	Sunset	Dawn
3rd quarter	Midnight	Noon

To start, choose a significator, a card that represents the subject of your reading. A significator card will help you focus your thoughts, clarify your question, and visualize the starting point of your reading.

You can shuffle the deck and choose the significator at random, or you can pick a card that represents the matter at hand. If you'd like to tune into the lunar energy of the moment, you can also refer to an astrological calendar and choose a card that corresponds to the Moon's current sign. If you look ahead to the next Full Moon, you'll even see what type of work you should be trying to manage.

Shuffle the rest of the deck and lay four cards around the significator. Start with a card in the New Moon position, and continue counter-clockwise. If you're working in a tight space, you can also lay the cards in a straight row under the significator; you can use the four key cards, or go all out and lay additional cards for the waxing and waning crescent and gibbous Moons. Those extra cards will clarify and enhance the information in the four key cards.

● **The New Moon** represents a starting point. It's the darkest phase of the Moon, but it also marks the beginning of the two-week period when the Moon moves away from the Sun and increases in light. It's a good time to plant seeds, both literally and metaphorically.

◐ **The Waxing (First Quarter) Moon** grows larger, day by day. The card that lands here will help you determine the healthiest avenue for your project's growth and development.

○ **The Full Moon** depicts the peak intensity of the project, when it reaches its fullest potential. The card that lands in this position will describe the best results you can hope to achieve.

◑ **The Waning (Third Quarter) Moon** symbolizes the steps you'll need to take to finish the project, and it could even suggest possibilities for a follow-up project.

To measure your progress in real life, look at the Moon—and picture the Moon goddess' canine companions. Over the course of a month, the Moon's curvy side will spell the word "dog." D is the Waxing Moon, O is the Full Moon, and G is the Waning Moon.

Sample Reading: Magic Moonbeams

Jane owns a busy metaphysical shop in Minneapolis. She'd like to produce a podcast to expand the store's outreach, but she doesn't know where to begin or how to proceed. What light can the Moon shed on her plans?

First Quarter:
The Wheel of Fortune

Full Moon:
The Empress

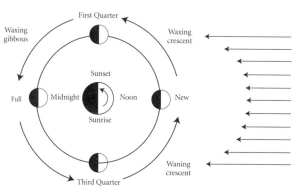

The New Moon:
The Six of Swords

Third Quarter:
The Lovers

● **The New Moon:** The Six of Swords depicts Mercury, the messenger of the gods, in his adjunct role as a psychopomp—a conductor of souls. As Jane embarks on her journey into broadcasting, it might be a good idea for her to recruit a guide, someone who has already garnered some experience as the host or producer of a successful radio program.

◑ **First Quarter:** The Wheel of Fortune, associated with Jupiter, is the card of growth and expansion. It suggests that Jane should take advantage of any opportunities she can to reach as many people as possible, even in the show's beginning phases. She should make her recordings available through multiple outlets, not just her store's website.

○ **Full Moon:** The Empress card corresponds to Venus, the planet of love, attraction, and pleasure. While radio broadcasts are designed to be heard, Jane might also want to design programming—and packaging—that will appeal to several senses. She can develop attractive visuals to accompany the downloads. She can augment recorded interviews with a theme song, bumper music during transitions, and live studio performances by singers and musicians. And she can devise program ideas that focus on her store's fragrant oils and candles.

◐ **Third Quarter:** The Lovers, a Gemini-themed card of partnership and communication, seems to indicate that as her show grows more successful, Jane will need to add a co-host. In this case, two heads are better than one: adding a second regular voice to the program will boost its interest, appeal, and versatility.

◆　◆　◆

Summary: Major Arcana Correspondences

Glyph	Planet or Sign	Significance	Tarot Card*
☉	Sun	Illumination, the self, the ego; the glyph looks like the Sun at the center of the solar system. A masculine symbol, the Sun can represent a husband, father, or authority figure.	The Sun
☽	Moon	Cycles, reflection; the glyph looks like a crescent Moon. A feminine symbol, the Moon can represent mothers or motherhood.	The High Priestess
☿	Mercury	Speed, communication; the glyph looks like Mercury, messenger of the gods, in his winged helmet.	The Magician
♀	Venus	Love, attraction, spiritual treasure, fertility; the glyph looks like a woman's hand mirror.	The Empress
♂	Mars	Energy, aggression, self-defense, action; the glyph looks like a shield and spear.	The Tower
♃	Jupiter	Luck, growth, expansion, enthusiasm; the glyph looks like the lucky number 21 or the number 4, which sounds like "fortune."	The Wheel of Fortune
♄	Saturn	Discipline, limits, boundaries, tradition; the glyph looks like a church and steeple.	The World
♅	Uranus	Independence, rebellion, freedom, technology; the glyph looks like a satellite and antenna.	The Fool (The Initiate)
♆	Neptune	Glamour, illusions, sensitivity; the glyph looks like Neptune's trident.	The Hanged Man
♀ ♇	Pluto	Death, regeneration, unavoidable change; one glyph looks like a chalice and coin, symbols of resurrection and rebirth. The alternate glyph looks like the first two letters of the word Pluto.	Judgment
♈	Aries, the ram	(March 21–April 20) The initiator; ruled by Mars; the glyph looks like the horns of a ram.	The Emperor
♉	Taurus, the bull	(April 21–May 20) The maintainer; ruled by Venus; the glyph looks like a bull's head.	The Hierophant
♊	Gemini, the twins	(May 21–June 20) The questioner; ruled by Mercury; the glyph looks like two people side by side.	The Lovers
♋	Cancer, the crab	(June 21–July 20) The nurturer; ruled by the Moon; the glyph looks like the claws of a crab or a woman's breasts.	The Chariot

♌	Leo, the lion	(July 21–August 20) The loyalist; ruled by the Sun; the glyph looks like a lion's mane or tail.	Strength
♍	Virgo, the virgin	(August 21–September 20) The modifier; ruled by Mercury; the glyph looks like an angel's wings or a V and an M, the initials of the Virgin Mary.	The Hermit
♎	Libra, the scales	(September 21–October 20) The judge; ruled by Venus; the glyph looks like a balanced set of scales.	Justice
♏	Scorpio, the scorpion	(October 21–November 20) The catalyst; ruled by Pluto; the glyph looks like the stinger of a scorpion's tail.	Death (Transfiguration)
♐	Sagittarius, the archer	(November 21–December 20) The adventurer; ruled by Jupiter; the glyph looks like an arrow.	Temperance (The Alchemist)
♑	Capricorn, the goat	(December 21–January 20) The pragmatist; ruled by Saturn; the glyph looks like the head and body of a goat.	The Devil (The Dark Lord)
♒	Aquarius, the water bearer	(January 21–February 20) The reformer; ruled by Uranus; the glyph looks like rolling waves of water or air.	The Star
♓	Pisces, the fish	(February 21–March 20) The visionary; ruled by Neptune; the glyph looks like two fish kissing or bound together by the tails.	The Moon

*Card titles often vary from deck to deck. This chart lists each card's standard *Rider-Waite* title, along with the corresponding *Wizards Tarot* title in parentheses.

Part Two

◆

THE MINOR ARCANA

*In this section, you'll discover just how seamlessly
astrology's reach extends into the Minor Arcana.*

- *The Aces correspond to the four elements: fire, earth, air, and water.*
- *The numbered cards correspond to the decans,
  the 10-degree subdivisions of each sign.*
- *And the Court Cards spin the Wheel of the Year.*

Four

◆

Elementary Astrology

Every card of the tarot deck corresponds to one of the four elements: fire, earth, air, and water. In the Major Arcana, the elemental correspondences are based on zodiac signs. In the Minor Arcana, the elemental correspondences are based on the nature of the four suites.

The fire signs of Aries, Leo, and Sagittarius correspond to Wands, the cards of spirit. The Wands cards typically include fiery colors and a bright, sunny landscape. Wands cards depict spiritual life, energy, and drive. In most tarot decks, Wands look like freshly cut branches from leafy trees. That is your cue that Wands can be set on fire and burned. You might want to picture each wand as a flaming torch that can be used for light and heat—or, in other words, enlightenment and inspiration. Our spiritual lives can catch fire. Our spiritual development can be ignited by our ideals and fueled by our passions, hopes, fears, and desires.

The earth signs of Taurus, Virgo, and Capricorn correspond to Pentacles, the cards of physical and material existence. In most tarot decks, Pentacles look like coins with star-shaped designs. Pentacles symbolize the tangible realities of physical life—the things we can touch and feel. They can represent money or property, and also spiritual and emotional treasures—the values we hold dear, the memories that are close to our hearts, and the people and things we love most and carry with us always.

The air signs of Gemini, Libra, and Aquarius correspond to Swords, the cards of the intellectual realm and communication. Swords cards describe the way we think and communicate our ideas to others. The cards, like real-life Swords, can often be pointed; they frequently cut right to the point. They can even draw blood—at least on a symbolic level. The cards in the suit of Swords usually feature symbols of air, such as windswept landscapes, clouds, and flying birds.

The water signs of Cancer, Scorpio, and Pisces correspond to Cups, the cards of relationships and emotional affairs. Cups can hold water—the essence of life—or, for that matter, any liquid that holds sentimental significance, such as wine or champagne. The connection to emotion is clear: we use cups to toast each other in celebration, to commune with others during religious ceremonies, and sometimes we use cups to drown our sorrows. Cups cards serve as a reminder that the well of human emotion runs deep. Just as the human body is 75 percent water, the human psyche is driven by an overwhelmingly emotional combination of wants, needs, drives, and desires.

Elemental Dignities

For centuries, philosophers believed that the entire universe consisted of four elements: fire, water, air, and earth. They agreed that each element had primary and secondary characteristics that determined how well the elements would mix and match.

According to their system:

- Fire is hot and dry.
- Water is cold and wet.
- Air is wet and hot.
- Earth is dry and cool.

Symbolically, the elements sustain and complement each other. Air feeds fire, and water nourishes earth, for example. They can also be enemies; water extinguishes fire, and air blows earth away. They can work at cross-purposes: water extinguishes fire, and air evaporates water. Even complementary elements can have a destructive effect if they're unbalanced: earth and air can also extinguish fire, fire can evaporate water, and water can turn earth into mud. An idealized universe—like an idealized horoscope chart—includes a balance of all four elements.

Some tarot readers use the elements to enhance their readings, by referring to the elemental dignities in a spread.

The Elemental Dignities Spread[3]

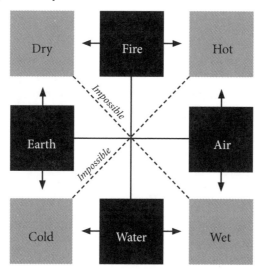

This introductory spread will help you see how the four elements work in combination. Don't think about any elements pictured on the cards themselves. For this practice reading, simply work with the positions in the spread.

1. Start by laying the four central cards. Lay one card for each element: fire, air, water, and earth.

2. Lay four more cards in the corners, to represent the characteristics of the elements: dry, hot, cold, and wet.

3. Use the diagram to determine how well the cards relate to each other on an elemental level.

    -   The three cards along any one side, like fire, hot and dry, will work well together; the two cards on either side will reinforce the card in the middle.

    -   Any two element cards that share a corner card—fire and air, air and water, water and earth, or earth and fire—can also work together.

    -   The cards in the Fire and Water positions—as well as the cards in earth and air—will be diametrically opposed to each other, but they can meet in the middle.

---

3. This spread originally appeared in the *Wizards Tarot Handbook* (Llewellyn, 2011) by Corrine Kenner.

- The cards in opposite corners—dry and wet, or hot and cold—will be impossible to reconcile.

The Elemental Aces

The elemental associations are clearly illustrated in the ace cards.

In theory, the aces represent pure potential. They're the seeds from which the rest of the Minor Arcana cards will sprout—and they're filled with promise and possibility.

Ace of Wands △
The Power of Fire

In ancient mythology, when Prometheus stole fire from the gods, he also appropriated much of the gods' power for mankind. On our behalf, he took control of the power to create and destroy, to illuminate the night, to vanquish darkness, and to promote civilization. Fire separated men from beasts, and made it possible for people to manufacture tools and technology and forge ahead in their development.

Today, we use fire as a metaphor for energy, drive, desire, and enlightenment. In both astrology and tarot, fire symbolizes our burning passions, our primal drives, and our most fervent desires. Like any tool, it can be used for constructive purposes, to heat and illuminate—or it can be misused, to wreak havoc, to burn, damage, and destroy.

Wands themselves symbolize the careful use, consideration, and application of will and intention—often as summoned and channeled through the power of a magic wand.

Wands are active, and they make an excellent counterpart to the watery receptivity of the Cups.

The Ace of Wands symbolizes all the powers of fire—as well as the fire signs of Aries, Leo, and Sagittarius. Fire, like the Sun, is a focal point for attention, as well as a source of enlightenment and understanding. It's hot, quick, active, uncontainable, spontaneous, impulsive, and immediate. You'll find those qualities, to some degree or another, in all of the Wands cards. Most Wand cards feature fiery red and orange colors and imagery.

The glyph for the element of fire is an upward-pointing triangle. Its shape looks like a campfire.

The Ace of Wands corresponds to the season of summer.

Ace of Pentacles ▽
The Power of Earth

We are children of the earth. We spend most of our lives held fast to its surface, tethered to our mother planet by the sheer force of gravity, and we rely on the earth to support our weight. Earth is solid, practical, supportive, reliable, physical, tangible, and material.

Earth, however, is more than just our foundation. It's the very substance of our physical makeup. We rise from ashes and return to ashes, and transition from dust to dust.

The earth is also our vantage point for our vision of the stars; it's our ride through outer space.

The Ace of Pentacles symbolizes all the powers of earth—as well as the earth signs of Taurus, Virgo, and Capricorn.

They correspond to the coin-shaped Pentacles. Like money, Pentacles represent treasure—both material and spiritual. Pentacles serve as a reminder that the tangible objects we prize have significance and meaning far beyond their monetary value. In addition to the prominent coins on each card, the images in the suit often include rich, green, gardenlike scenes that serve as a reminder of earth's bounty.

Pentacles are receptive, and they make an excellent counterpart to the airy energy of the Swords.

The glyph for the element of earth is a downward-facing triangle. It features a horizontal line that operates like the force of gravity, forcing the element down to earth.

The Ace of Pentacles corresponds to the season of winter.

Ace of Swords △
The Power of Air

From our first breath to our last, air is the invisible force that keeps our spirits linked to our physical form. Air is the invisible whisper of spirit that maintains the pulse of life.

Air is the realm of thought and communication. Our thoughts and ideas travel through the air, both literally and symbolically. We transmit our outbound broadcasts, and we receive inbound messages and bulletins.

The airwaves used to be a purely philosophical construct. Today, in the era of mass media beamed from space, wireless communication is a fact of life.

Symbolically speaking, however, air is still an intellectual concept. The element of air is mental, light, elusive, uncontainable, conversational, and social.

The Ace of Swords symbolizes all the powers of air—as well as the air signs of Gemini, Libra, and Aquarius. Swords move through the air, like words and unspoken thoughts.

Swords are active, and they make an excellent counterpart to the earthy energy of the shield-like Pentacles.

The Sword cards often incorporate the color yellow, which represents the element of air. They also feature symbols of air, such as windswept landscapes, clouds, and flying birds.

The glyph for the element of air is an upright triangle, like the tip of a sword. It features a horizontal line, like air rising up from the surface of the earth.

The Ace of Swords corresponds to the season of spring.

ACE OF CUPS

Ace of Cups ▽
The Power of Water

Still waters run deep, and the Ace of Cups is a bottomless font of feelings, emotions, desires, joys and sorrows. It's a significant card that reflects the importance of emotional life and relationships.

People are creatures of sentiment and feeling: we spend the majority of our time assessing our feelings, gauging our reactions, and wondering how other people feel about us. The ratio can be likened to the physical properties of water in the human body—60 to 75 percent. Similarly, the oceans cover about 75 percent of the Earth's surface.

The card symbolizes the healing power of love, as well as the grace of compassion and forgiveness. It also serves as a reminder of the power of intuition, which we achieve by tapping into the undercurrents of human emotion. What's more, its womblike shape represents creativity and fertility.

Cups are receptive, and they make an excellent counterpart to the fiery energy of the Wands.

In the watery world of emotions, Cancer, Scorpio, and Pisces are all water signs. They correspond to the suit of Cups.

The Cup cards usually include a lot of watery greens and blues, and they feature lakes, rivers, streams, and oceans.

The glyph for the element of water is a downward-pointing triangle that looks like drop of water.

The Ace of Cups corresponds to the season of autumn.

Five

◆

Tarot, Astrology, and Qabalah

The Golden Dawn's tarot designers based many of their astrological associations on Qabalah, a mystical philosophy first developed by the ancient Jews.

In essence, Qabalah is a belief system that describes the creation of the universe, as well as man's place in the world. It serves as a framework and a filing system for almost every metaphysical subject you can imagine.

In fact, the Golden Dawn mystics who developed the astrological correspondences in this book actually used tarot as a way to unify several branches of metaphysical thought on the qabalistic Tree of Life.

Some basic principles of qabalistic thought appear throughout most standard tarot decks. For example:

- According to qabalistic belief, the universe was created in a single, lightning-like flash—a cosmic "Big Bang." You'll see that lightning flash on most versions of the Tower card.

- At that moment of creation, the energy of pure thought was instantaneously transformed into physical matter.

- Although the creative process was practically instantaneous, there were ten separate stages in the creation of the universe. The energy followed a zigzag course—first right, then left, then right again.[4] The energy of the tree flowed back and forth, from side to side, keeping it in harmony until it finally came to rest in perfect balance in the physical world.

- Along the way, there were ten stages of creation—one at each turning point.
- A diagram called the Tree of Life depicts those ten stages in the creation of the universe. On the Tree of Life, each stage is depicted as a *sepheroth*, or sphere, which dangles like fruit on the branches of the tree. The ten spheres correspond to the ten numbered cards of each suit in the tarot.
- The numbered position of each sephira has symbolic meaning. The first sphere is pure energy and potential, like the ace cards. With each subsequent stopping point, that energy becomes less refined and more weighed down by the realities of physical existence.
- Human beings live in the tenth sphere, the world of matter. In one sense, the physical world is the least spiritual sphere of existence; in another sense, however, the physical world represents the culmination of God's creative efforts.
- According to qabalistic thought, the Tree of Life is actually four trees in one, linked together from top to bottom. The four worlds of the four trees correspond to the four suits of the Minor Arcana:
  1. **Atziluth**, the world of archetypes, ideas, and the urge to create, corresponds to the fiery suit of Wands, which symbolizes passion and inspiration.
  2. **Briah**, the archangelic world of fertility and creation, corresponds to the watery suit of Cups, in which ideas can gestate and take shape.
  3. **Yetzirah**, the astral plane of thought and form, corresponds to the airy suit of Swords, in which specific patterns and designs can be drawn up.
  4. **Assiah**, the material plane, corresponds to the physical world of pentacles, in which inspiration, gestation, and design can coalesce into physical existence.
- The ten spheres on the Tree of Life are linked by twenty-two paths, which also correspond to the twenty-two letters of the Hebrew alphabet and the twenty-two cards of the Major Arcana. The twenty-two Major Arcana cards serve as guardians and guides on the paths that connect the spheres.

---

4. Because the Tree of Life was a Jewish construct, it reads from right to left, like Hebrew.

- While the energy of creation flows from the top down, Kabbalistic philosophers believe that humans can use the paths to climb back up the Tree of Life and rejoin their creator.

- According to Jewish tradition, God's name is composed of four Hebrew letters: *Yod Heh Vau Heh*. In English, these letters are usually pronounced "Jehovah." Also referred to as the Tetragrammaton, the letters correspond to the four elements and suits of the tarot—*Yod* with fire, *Heh* with water, *Vau* with air, and *Heh* with earth.

- The forty pip cards of the Minor Arcana—those that are left when the Court Cards are removed—also correspond to the four letters in the name of God.

- Those four letters are also reflected in the Minor Arcana's Court Cards, which consist of four families of four members each.

The Numbered Cards and the Tree of Life

As we move through the regular numbered cards of the Minor Arcana, the significance of the Qabalistic Tree of Life will come into play—because the numbers on each card are all designed to remind us of the numbered spheres on the Tree of Life.

Spheres (Sepheroth)	Cards	Astrological Associations	Description
1. Kether, the Crown	The four Aces	Aether, the realm of spirit	The aces—the first card in every suit—represent a singularity. They symbolize unity, a single purpose, and a sole point of origin. The aces are the source of all creation, and in the four worlds of the Qabalah, they each represent a separate element: fire, water, air, and earth. However, the elements aren't manifested in material form. They're still in a state of pure potential. Like seeds, they contain the promise and possibility of all the numbered cards that follow.
2. Chokmah, the sphere of Wisdom	The Kings and the Twos	Purely elemental	The twos represent duality. They mark a split, a division, a point and a counterpoint. They make it possible to compare and contrast any concept—which is also the starting point for wisdom and understanding. Twos also symbolize reflection, which leads to self-awareness. In tarot, the twos represent partnership and attraction, and the corresponding concepts of love, pleasure, and harmony.
3. Binah, the sphere of Understanding	The Threes and the Queens	Saturn, the planet of structure	The third sphere, like a womb, is a vessel for creation. Saturn's energy provides shape and form. In tarot, the threes symbolize creation, just as a child is born from the union of a mother and father.
4. Chesed, the sphere of Mercy	The Fours and the Pages	Jupiter, the planet of expansion	In the fourth sphere, creations materialize and become solid. Jupiter, the expansive planet of growth, pushes for continued development. That's one reason the universe is constantly expanding. In tarot, the fours symbolize growth and stability, along with the four dimensions of space: length, width, height, and time.
5. Geburah, the sphere of Strength and Power	The Fives	Mars, the planet of war	The fifth sphere is the halfway point in the ten stages of existence. In most case, nature's creations have to fight for their right to survive—but they're made stronger in the process. It's all part of the cycle of life: while Jupiter expands, Mars contracts, and the red planet's aggressive energy reigns in the otherwise uncontrolled chaos of unbridled creativity. In tarot, the fives are cards of crisis and conflict. They depict tests of skill and talent, and challenges of spirit and will.

Spheres (Sepheroth)	Cards	Astrological Associations	Description
6. Tipareth, the sphere of Beauty	The Sixes and the Knights	The Sun, the light of recognition	The sixth sphere is the realm of the gods, perpetually dying and being resurrected, just like the Sun rising and setting every day. Those who were tested in the fifth sphere of Mars can reawaken in the sixth. It's the realm of union and reunion, where opposing forces meet and meld. The sixth sphere reestablishes balance and harmony. In tarot, the sixes symbolize accomplishment.
7. Netzach, the sphere of Victory	The Sevens	Venus, the planet of love and attraction	The seventh sphere helps us appreciate the beauty and pleasure of life. It embodies delight and passion, and moves us to interact with others. Unfortunately, the seven cards in tarot can be weak and unbalanced, because we occasionally fall prey to Venus' glamour, and the unrealistic emotions and illusions she inspires.
8. Hod, the sphere of Splendor and Glory	The Eights	Mercury, the planet of thought and communication	The eighth sphere is ruled by Mercury, an airy, fleeting planet that doesn't always have a firm hold on material reality. While Mercury can offer mental clarity, it only introduces the beginnings of reason and thoughtful understanding. It's the place where we begin to assimilate our emotions and experience.
9. Yesod, the sphere of Foundation	The Nines	The Moon, the orb of reflection	The ninth sphere is ruled by the light of the Moon, which makes it hard to distinguish reality from shadowy illusion. The Moon is part of our world—but at the same time, it's not our world. It's a place of imagination and dreams.
10. Malkuth, the Kingdom	The Tens and the Pages	The Earth, our worldly home	In the tenth sphere—and the final cards of each suit—the elements exhaust the energy of development and come to rest in the fixed reality of physical existence. In tarot, the tens represent completion, as well as preparation for the next round of life and worldly experience.

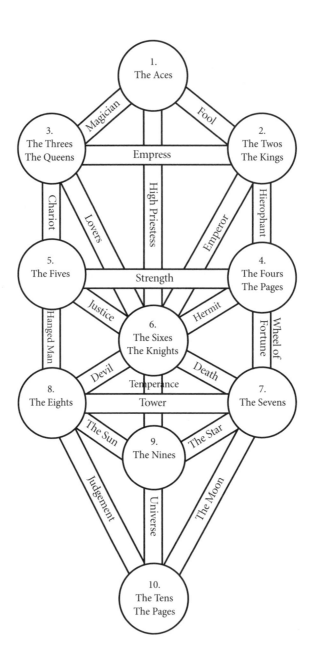

The Twenty-Two Paths

Twenty-two paths connect the spheres on the Qabalistic Tree of Life. They correspond to the twenty-two Major Arcana cards.

- Aleph—The Fool
- Beth—The Magus
- Gimel—The Priestess
- Daleth—The Empress
- Hé—The Emperor (Crowley switched the Emperor and the Star)
- Vau—The Hierophant
- Zain—The Lovers
- Cheth—The Chariot
- Teth—Adjustment
- Yod—The Hermit
- Kaph—Fortune
- Lamed—Lust
- Mem—The Hanged Man
- Nun—Death
- Samekh—Art
- Ayin—The Devil
- Pé—The Tower
- Tzaddi—The Star
- Qoph—The Moon
- Resh—The Sun
- Shin—The Aeon
- Tau—The Universe

Six

◆

The Numbered Cards

Astrologically, the numbered pip cards of the Minor Arcana are just as rich and complex as the Major Arcana cards. Each one is packed with symbolic associations to zodiac signs, planets, and rulerships—all arranged systematically around the Wheel of the Year.

To devise those associations, early deck designers simply dealt the cards around the horoscope wheel.

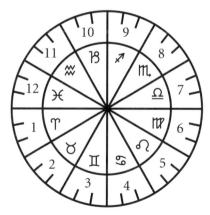

THE DECANS AND THE NUMBERED CARDS

Study this chart for a minute, and you'll see how the Minor Arcana cards are distributed by element, number, and mode.

	2, 3, 4 (Cardinal)	5, 6, 7 (Fixed)	8, 9, 10 (Mutable)
Wands (Fire)	Aries	Leo	Sagittarius
Pentacles (Earth)	Capricorn	Taurus	Virgo
Swords (Air)	Libra	Aquarius	Gemini
Cups (Water)	Cancer	Scorpio	Pisces

The Zodiac Wheel

Understanding the Wheel of the Year is the key to understanding the astrological associations of the Minor Arcana.

The zodiac wheel is divided into twelve signs. In a typical wheel, each sign occupies a pie-shaped 30-degree slice, and each slice is further subdivided into three separate 10-degree segments, called decans.

The study of the decans dates back to ancient Egypt, where early astrologers tracked thirty-six constellations that moved across the sky. The constellations rose and fell like clockwork: a new constellation would appear every ten days. The ancient stargazers referred to them like a calendar, to measure the passing of the year.

Later, the Greeks assigned the decans to zodiac signs. Since the Sun takes about thirty days to travel through each sign, it spends about ten days in each decan.

Because there are 360 degrees in the wheel, there are 36 decans of ten degrees each. The thirty-six numbered pip cards of the Minor Arcana—the twos through the tens—are assigned to those decans.

Dealing the Cards

At first glance, the distribution of the Minor Arcana cards might seem arbitrary and random—but there is a method to the madness. The cards are allotted according to the element of their suits, their numeric position in the deck, and the mode—cardinal, fixed, or mutable—of each sign.

Let's discuss the details.

Elemental Associations

We'll start with the elemental associations between the cards and the signs, because they're easy to remember. In fact, the associations are pictured right on the cards.

The fire signs of Aries, Leo, and Sagittarius are assigned to the fiery suit of Wands. The cards in this suit usually feature wooden clubs or branches that can be set ablaze and burned for light, heat, and inspiration.

The water signs of Cancer, Scorpio, and Pisces belong to the watery suit of Cups. Cups hold water, the essence of life. We toast our joys and drown our sorrows.

The air signs of Gemini, Libra, and Aquarius correspond to the airy suit of Swords, which move quickly and decisively through the element of air, like words and thoughts.

The earth signs of Taurus, Virgo, and Capricorn fit the earthy suit of Pentacles. Pentacles look like money—the coin of the earthly realm, and symbols of tangible property, material possessions, and physical existence.

Modes and Seasons

Once the elemental associations are in place, we use seasonal associations to connect individual cards to the signs. It's an easy way to plug the cards into place on the zodiac's Wheel of the Year.

Cardinal Signs: In astrology, the first day of spring begins when the Sun moves into Aries. The first day of Cancer is the first day of summer. The first day of Libra is the first day of fall, and the first day of Capricorn is the first day of winter. Accordingly, the cardinal signs represent "firsts"—so they're assigned to the first three numbered cards in each suit: 2, 3, and 4.

Fixed Signs: Taurus, Leo, Scorpio, and Aquarius, the middle months of each season, get the middle cards: 5, 6, and 7.

Mutable Signs: Gemini, Virgo, Sagittarius, and Pisces are the final months of each season. They get the last three cards in each suit: 8, 9, and 10.

The aces don't enter into this equation, because we've already seen that they're assigned to entire seasons.

Planetary Rulers and Subrulers

As the Minor Arcana cards are distributed around the wheel, they each fall into a house and a sign. The three cards that land in the first house, for example, find themselves in Aries' domain. That gives them a planetary ruler, too: Aries is ruled by Mars. We covered all of the planetary rulers in the section on the Major Arcana cards.

Now, in the Minor Arcana, the signs don't just have rulers anymore—they also have subrulers. In fact, each decan—each 10-degree subdivision of a sign—has a subruler.

It's a hierarchical system: a planetary subruler works under the auspices of the planetary ruler, just as a vice-principal works under the supervision of a principal. You might think of the planetary subrulers as astrology's middle managers.

As with any hierarchy, however, the organizational flow chart can be confusing—and there's one technical detail you should know before we go any further. We don't use the same formula to determine planetary subrulers that we used for planetary rulers. Back in the Major Arcana, the planetary rulers were allocated according to contemporary astrology.

Now that we're working with the Minor Arcana, however, the decans—and their planetary subrulers—are all derived from classical astrology.

I'll say that again, because it's an important distinction. We use modern planetary rulerships for our Major Arcana correspondences—but when it comes to Minor Arcana associations, we revert back to classical astrology.

It's actually an elegant system. The ancient astrologers worked with the seven lights and planets that are visible to the naked eye: the Sun, the Moon, Mercury, Venus, Mars, Jupiter, and Saturn. They assigned planetary rulerships in a parallel arrangement that started at the bottom of the wheel and moved up both sides simultaneously. Look at this chart of classical rulerships and you'll see the pattern they developed.

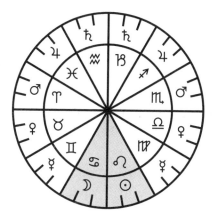

The ancients gave the rulership of Cancer to the Moon, and Leo to the Sun—the luminaries that provide most of the light and heat on Earth, both night and day. It's no coincidence that Cancer and Leo mark the longest, hottest days of the year.

The rest of the assignments were based on the other planets' proximity to the Sun. Mercury has the smallest orbit, so it's always within one sign of the Sun: it was assigned to Virgo and Gemini. Venus, which also has a relatively small orbit, is always within two signs of the Sun—so it has rulership over Libra and Taurus. Mars was assigned to Scorpio and Aries, Jupiter was given Sagittarius and Pisces, and Saturn, the coldest, most distant planet, was awarded Aquarius and Capricorn—the two signs opposite Leo and Cancer.

In modern astrology, however, we also work with Uranus, Neptune, and Pluto—three planets that were discovered with the aid of telescopes. In the twentieth century, the ancient system of rulerships was revised to incorporate those outer planets, so in contemporary astrology, Pluto rules Mars, Uranus rules Aquarius, and Neptune rules Pisces.

The next chart illustrates the difference between classical and modern rulerships. The modern planetary rulers are all shown inside the wheel. The classical rulers—which were displaced by the modern ones—are pictured outside the wheel.

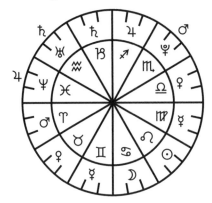

Planetary Subrulers

The Golden Dawn's deck designers traveled back to astrology's earliest days to choose planetary subrulers for the Minor Arcana cards. They traveled so far back, in fact, that they chose the Chaldean order of the planets.

In ancient Babylon, the Chaldeans were some of the world's first astrologers. They categorized the planets based on their speed; they put the Sun at the center of a continuum, with the outer planets on one side and the inner planets—those between the Sun and the Earth—on the other.[5]

♄	♃	♂	☉	♀	☿	☽
Saturn	Jupiter	Mars	Sun	Venus	Mercury	Moon

As it happens, the Chaldean system transferred seamlessly to the cards.

The deck's designers began their assignments with the first decan of Aries. They chose Mars, the planet of energy and action, to jump-start the wheel, and then they followed the Chaldean order of the planets to assign planetary subrulers to the rest of the decans.

To see how the whole system plays out, turn to the chart on page 100.

---

5. If you practice contemporary astrology, which assigns rulers for each decan based on the element of each sign, the tarot correspondences might seem incorrect to you. Don't get confused. Just remember that when it comes to tarot, Minor Arcana rulerships are based on classical astrology and the Chaldean order of the planets.

Cosmic Connection: ANCIENT INSPIRATION

Deck designers have been borrowing from and building upon each other's work for centuries. Most of today's tarot readers, however, don't realize that the Minor Arcana cards they know and love aren't just variations of classical themes and motifs. In fact, many are based on ancient astrological imagery associated with the decans.

In *Mystical Origins of the Tarot*, author Paul Huson describes the historical foundations of modern deck designs. He includes excerpts from primary sources, like the *Picatrix*, a book of astrological magic translated from Arabic into Latin around the fourteenth century. Huson's book is well worth reading if you, too, would like to dive deeply into the wellspring of tarot and astrology.

Arthur Edward Waite and Pamela Colman Smith borrowed from classical descriptions of the decans for their work on the *Rider-Waite* tarot; later, so did Aleister Crowley and Frieda Harris, who developed the *Thoth* tarot. In fact, both Waite and Crowley specifically designed their Minor Arcana cards to serve as a pictorial key to the astrological meanings of the cards.

Minor Arcana Card Assignments

Decans	Approx. Dates	Minor Arcana Cards	Planetary Subrulers
1st 0°–10° ♈	Mar 21–30	Two of Wands (fire)	Mars
2nd 10°–20° ♈	Mar 31–Apr 10	Three of Wands (fire)	Sun
3rd 20°–30° ♈	Apr 11–20	Four of Wands (fire)	Venus
1st 0°–10° ♉	Apr 21–30	Five of Pentacles (earth)	Mercury
2nd 10°–20° ♉	May 1–10	Six of Pentacles (earth)	Moon
3rd 20°–30° ♉	May 11–20	Seven of Pentacles (earth)	Saturn
1st 0°–10° ♊	May 21–31	Eight of Swords (air)	Jupiter
2nd 10°–20° ♊	Jun 1–10	Nine of Swords (air)	Mars
3rd 20°–30° ♊	Jun 11–20	Ten of Swords (air)	Sun
1st 0°–10° ♋	Jun 21–Jul 1	Two of Cups (water)	Venus
2nd 10°–20° ♋	Jul 2–11	Three of Cups (water)	Mercury
3rd 20°–30° ♋	Jul 12–21	Four of Cups (water)	Moon
1st 0°–10° ♌	Jul 22–Aug 1	Five of Wands (fire)	Saturn
2nd 10°–20° ♌	Aug 2–11	Six of Wands (fire)	Jupiter
3rd 20°–30° ♌	Aug12–22	Seven of Wands (fire)	Mars
1st 0°–10° ♍	Aug 23–Sep 1	Eight of Pentacles (earth)	Sun
2nd 10°–20° ♍	Sep 2–11	Nine of Pentacles (earth)	Venus
3rd 20°–30° ♍	Sep 12–22	Ten of Pentacles (earth)	Mercury

Decans	Approx. Dates	Minor Arcana Cards	Planetary Subrulers
1st 0°–10° ♎	Sep 23–Oct 2	Two of Swords (air)	Moon
2nd 10°–20° ♎	Oct 3–12	Three of Swords (air)	Saturn
3rd 20°–30° ♎	Oct13–22	Four of Swords (air)	Jupiter
1st 0°–10° ♏	Oct 23–Nov 2	Five of Cups (water)	Mars
2nd 10°–20° ♏	Nov 3–12	Six of Cups (water)	Sun
3rd 20°–30° ♏	Nov 13–22	Seven of Cups (water)	Venus
1st 0°–10° ♐	Nov 23–Dec 2	Eight of Wands (fire)	Mercury
2nd 10°–20° ♐	Dec 3–12	Nine of Wands (fire)	Moon
3rd 20°–30° ♐	Dec 13–21	Ten of Wands (fire)	Saturn
1st 0°–10° ♑	Dec 22–30	Two of Pentacles (earth)	Jupiter
2nd 10°–20° ♑	Dec 31–Jan 9	Three of Pentacles (earth)	Mars
3rd 20°–30° ♑	Jan 10–19	Four of Pentacles (earth)	Sun
1st 0°–10° ♒	Jan 20–29	Five of Swords (air)	Venus
2nd 10°–20° ♒	Jan 30–Feb 8	Six of Swords (air)	Mercury
3rd 20°–30° ♒	Feb 9–18	Seven of Swords (air)	Moon
1st 0°–10° ♓	Feb 19–28	Eight of Cups (water)	Saturn
2nd 10°–20° ♓	Mar 1–10	Nine of Cups (water)	Jupiter
3rd 20°–30° ♓	Mar 11–20	Ten of Cups (water)	Mars

Cosmic Connection: GUARDIANS OF HEAVEN

The designers of modern Golden Dawn tarot decks put a tremendous emphasis on the four aces. Not only do the aces represent the starting point of each suit, they are also like seeds—they contain the undeveloped nucleus of every other card in the suit.

Rather than assigning the aces to a position on the Wheel of the Year, the designers stationed the four aces along the north pole of the ecliptic. To visualize their position, picture the earth as the center of the universe, surrounded by a circular sphere of heaven—like a circle within a circle, or a ball within a ball. The north pole of the ecliptic marks the top of that celestial sphere—and from that position, the four aces guard the heavens.

The aces are grounded by the four pages, which don't have a place in the zodiac either. Instead, the four pages symbolize the four elements of fire, earth, air, and water, and they serve as the "thrones" of the aces.

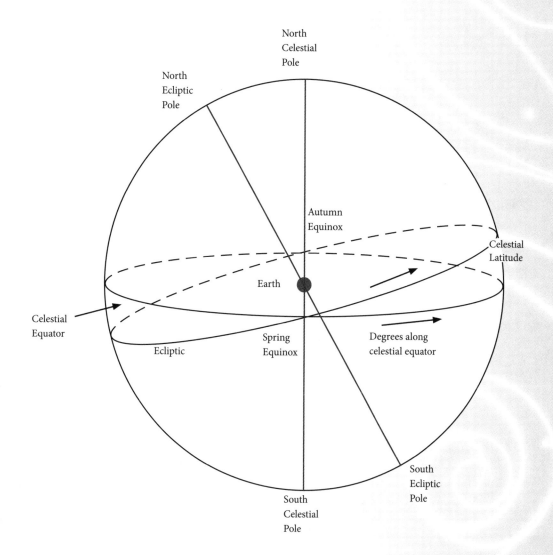

Seven

◆

The Planets in the Signs

The mechanics of the Minor Arcana might seem technical and dry, but the assignments make it possible for all the correspondences to come to life in the imagery of the cards.

Picturing the Planets

You've already met the planets and signs, back in the section on the Major Arcana cards. Now, as you move through the Minor Arcana cards, you'll meet them again.

Here the planets and signs take human form, just as they did in the Major Arcana. We first met Venus, for example, in the guise of the Empress—the goddess of love, beauty, and attraction. Normally, she's focused on the attributes of her own sign, Libra, which measures social grace and balance. But when the Empresslike Venus finds herself as the planetary sub-ruler of another sign, as she does in the fiery third decan of Aries, she also tries to work her magic there.

Naturally, some planets are more comfortable with some signs than others. Venus loves being in Libra, the sign that she rules. But send her to Aries, 180 degrees from her usual home, and she feels like a stranger in a strange land. She's forced to work with elements, energies, and an environment that are completely different from her own—which means she's at a distinct disadvantage.

Astrologers use a system of essential dignities to clarify how the planets will feel—and function—in the various signs of the zodiac. You might want to keep it in mind or refer to this chart as you try to picture the cards moving around the Wheel, visiting foreign lands and houses that aren't their own.[6]

Dignities and Debilities

Planet	Dignity (Domicile)	Exaltation	Detriment	Fall
Sun	Leo	Aries	Aquarius	Libra
Moon	Cancer	Taurus	Capricorn	Scorpio
Mercury	Gemini/Virgo	Virgo	Sagittarius	Pisces
Venus	Taurus/Libra	Pisces	Aries	Virgo
Mars	Aries/Scorpio	Capricorn	Libra	Cancer
Jupiter	Sagittarius/Pisces	Cancer	Gemini	Capricorn
Saturn	Capricorn/Aquarius	Libra	Cancer	Aries

Dignity (Domicile) Planets feel at home in their domiciles, the signs they rule. The Sun is at home in Leo, for example, while the Moon is at home in Cancer. A planet in its own home is said to be in its highest form of dignity.

Detriment Planets that find themselves 180 degrees from their usual placement are as far from home as they can go. They're forced to function in a land of opposites. They're weak; the placement is a detriment.

Exaltation Each of the seven traditional planets has its exaltation in one zodiac sign, where their energy is compatible. Planets in exaltation are honored guests in another planet's home. According to some astrologers, the exaltations were the original domiciles of the planets, before Adam and Eve's fall from grace in the Garden of Eden.

Fall On the other hand, planets in fall are in a sign 180 degrees from their exaltation. Rather than being honored guests, they're unwelcome visitors—humbled, dejected, and at their absolute weakest.

Planetary Powers

No matter what sign they land in, you'll notice some common, recurring themes among the planets as they travel through the signs of the zodiac.

---

6. Essential dignities are based on classical astrology, which refers only to the seven planets that are visible to the naked eye. The modern planets—Uranus, Neptune, and Pluto—aren't included in the system. Luckily, that's not a problem for us, because the Minor Arcana assignments are based on ancient astrology, too.

- **The Sun**, the central focus of cosmic energy and identity, highlights and personalizes everything it touches.

- **The Moon**, the orb of reflection and intuition, adds emotional depth and compassion.

- **Mercury**, the planet of speed and communication, adds a note of reason, logic, and intellectual understanding to all of its placements.

- **Venus**, the planet of love, attraction, and beauty, graces everything she touches with affection and benefic gifts.

- **Mars**, the warrior planet of aggression and assertion, powers its contact points with intensity, energy, and drive.

- **Jupiter**, the largest planet in the solar system, brings expansion and good fortune to everything in its path.

- **Saturn**, the ringed planet of limitations, boundaries, and restrictions, constricts everything it touches. While ancient astrologers thought of Saturn as a malefic planet, its influence isn't always a negative. Saturn also offers structure and discipline to those he meets along his path.

Cosmic Connection:
MINOR ARCANA CORRESPONDENCES AND YOU

As you survey the Minor Arcana cards, you might notice that some of them describe the placement of planets in your birth chart. You might have Venus in Aries, for example. Does that mean you're destined for a life of ballroom dancing, like the couple pictured on the Four of Wands?

Probably not. The Minor Arcana correspondences relate to the natural zodiac. They don't really correspond to individual birth charts. In fact, any similarities they share with other planets and signs in a real-life chart are merely coincidental.

What's more, the decans only address 36 possible combinations, so the odds are that none of the planets and signs described in the Minor Arcana cards will share the same placement as any of the planets and signs in your actual birth chart.

One of the Minor Arcana cards will correspond to your birth chart, though—based on your Sun sign. One of them will describe a significant facet of your personality or depict a theme in your life story.

To find the card that has the most significance for you, look at your birth chart and check the Sun's position. The degree and minute should be clearly labeled. If your Sun is positioned between 0° and 10° of a sign, you were born during the first decan of the sign. If the Sun is positioned between 10° and 20° of a sign, you were born during the second decan. And if the Sun is positioned between 20° and 30° of a sign, you were born during the third decan. The card that corresponds to your decan should have some personal significance for you.

The Three Decans of Aries

CARDINAL FIRE: THE TWO, THREE, AND FOUR OF WANDS

♦ ♦ ♦

We'll start our tour of the Minor Arcana with the cards that correspond to the three decanate divisions of Aries: the Two, Three, and Four of Wands.

Because Aries is a fire sign, the cards come from the fiery suit of Wands. And since it's a cardinal sign, symbolic of new beginnings, the cards are the first three numbered cards of the suit.

As we study the cards, and the characters in the cards, remember that they'll all share the same attributes of the sign.

- **Sign:** Aries, the first in the zodiac, is the sign of leadership, authority, and beginnings. All three cards in Aries depict leaders and authority figures.
- **Mode/Quality:** Aries is also a cardinal sign. Just as cardinal signs usher in a change of seasons, the characters in the cards that belong to Aries initiate change. They're decisive, quick, and energetic.
- **Element:** Aries is a fire sign, assigned to the suit of Wands. Both the element and the suit are impulsive, driven, courageous, direct, energetic, enthusiastic, and spontaneous.
- **Duality:** Fire signs are masculine: active, assertive, confident, direct, and energetic. They move in a linear fashion, from point A to point B.
- **Corresponding Majors:** Aries corresponds to the Emperor, and its ruling planet, Mars, corresponds to the Tower.

With that in mind, let's look at the first decan of the first sign, and the first numbered card of the Minor Arcana.

Cosmic Connection: HONORARY TITLES

The Golden Dawn designers of the Minor Arcana cards gave honorary titles to the planets, to describe their powers as the subrulers of each sign.

While those archaic titles can be charming, they can also seem confusing and arcane. Just remember that the titles are meant to personalize the planets, so we can remember the roles they play.

The Six of Wands, for example, depicts Jupiter in Leo. No matter where it travels, Jupiter is a benefic planet—but when Jupiter moves through Leo, the sign of courage and strength, it rewards the bravery and daring that Leo can inspire. As a result, the Golden Dawn deck designers called Jupiter in Leo the "Lord of Victory," because it dispenses victory as a reward for valor.

Two of Wands: Mars in Aries

Lord of Dominion

We first met Mars and Aries in the Tower and the Emperor cards. Now the planet and the sign make a repeat appearance in the Two of Wands, where we see Mars as the master of his own domain.

The character in the card is a younger version of the Emperor, the Major Arcana card that corresponds to Aries. He's bold, fierce, resolute, and shameless.

He's seated comfortably on a battlement, a low wall of the Tower. In tarot, the Tower card corresponds to Mars, Aries' ruling planet.

Like the Emperor, he holds a scale model of the universe in his hands—but in this case, the symbol of his power and control is a fireball, true to his fiery Aries nature, that he controls with the power of his mind.

The first decan of Aries depicts that energy in its initial, formative stages. The young man in the card has taken a spark from the Ace of Wands, and he's shaped and molded it into a ball of fire.

Mars, the red planet, is the natural ruler of Aries. When Mars is in his own sign, he's the king of the castle and the master of his realm. After all, he's in his own element, in his own sign, in his own house. He's the lord of all he surveys. In fact, the Golden Dawn designers of this card called it "Lord of Dominion" because it depicts Mars in its dignity—and dominion means governing authority and control of a territory.

In the Two of Wands, however, Mars isn't just the ruler of sign; it's the ruler of the first decan, too. That gives the Two of Wands an extra dose of powerful Mars energy. In fact, that's the reason Mars rules the first decan: its fiery drive jump-starts the zodiac and pushes the Wheel of the Year into motion.[7]

Mars is the planet of energy, action, aggression, and defense. It symbolizes protection and self-preservation, along with self-assertion, courage, daring, fearlessness, spontaneity, passion, adventure, and violence. It rules competition and combat.

Qabalistically, the Two of Wands depicts the second sphere of wisdom, Chokmah. It's positioned in Atziluth, the fiery world of inspiration. The young Emperor is actively engaged in conscious creation, reflection, and comparison.

In a tarot reading, the Two of Wands often symbolizes the establishment of a new business or enterprise.

The first decan of Aries usually falls between March 21 and 30, when the Sun is between 0 and 10 degrees Aries.

---

7. In *Book T*, one of the Golden Dawn's deck designers wrote, "There being thirty-six Decans and seven Planets, it follows that one of the latter must rule over one more Decan than the others. This is the Planet Mars, to which are allotted the last Decan of Pisces, and the first of Aries, because the long cold of the winter requires a great energy to overcome it, and initiate spring."

Three of Wands: Sun in Aries
Lord of Established Strength

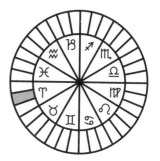

Who is that radiant young woman shining at the top of a hill? She's a fiery ruler—another young version of the Aries Emperor—and with the Sun shining on her and her realm, she's imbued with an endless supply of confidence, courage, and optimism. She also embodies her fair share of pride, nobility, and rulership.

The Sun is the source of heat and light, the center of our solar system, and the giver of life. In tarot, it symbolizes energy, enthusiasm, and enlightenment. From an astrological perspective, the Sun represents the ego, will, and self.

The Sun is exalted in Aries, where it serves as the subruler of the sign. It's a visiting dignitary and an honored guest. Here, more than anywhere else in the zodiac, the Sun is recognized as a potent source of strength, wisdom, and enlightenment.

Aries, of course, is the first sign of the zodiac. It signifies leadership and initiation—and the Sun's energy feeds Aries' need to direct and control events.

The Golden Dawn designers of this card referred to the Sun in Aries as the "Lord of Established Strength." The title describes the sheer power and force of the Sun—especially when its light shines on those in positions of power. In history and myth, the world's most influential leaders were said to be crowned with the glory and radiance of the Sun; that's one reason so many monarchs have worn gold headdresses as a sign of their divine right to rule.

As the picture of the Sun in Aries, the young woman in the Three of Wands has every reason to believe that she's in a position of power, and that she is the master of her own destiny. She stands at the crest of a hill, high above the rest of the world.

The "Three" cards symbolize creativity, and in this case, the young woman's creative powers have reached a certain height, just as Aries' strength reaches a peak here at the height of its power in the second decan of the sign.

While the pinnacle of the hill does represent a high level of command and control, the Three of Wands is a still Minor Arcana card—so we can assume that she's not particularly experienced, and that her strength hasn't been fully tested. Even so, while she waits for her ship to come in, she knows that she's made good decisions, and she seems confident that her hopes are about to be realized.

Qabalistically, the Three of Wands depicts Binah, the third sphere of understanding. It's positioned in Atziluth, the fiery world of inspiration. The third sphere corresponds to Saturn, the planet of structure and form. The young woman in the card is coming to understand her place in that world.

In a tarot reading, the Three of Wands often symbolizes the creative drive that underlies the growth of a business or enterprise.

The second decan of Aries usually falls between March 31 and April 10, when the Sun is between 10 and 20 degrees Aries.

Four of Wands: Venus in Aries
Lord of Perfected Work

FOUR OF WANDS

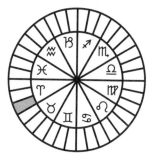

Venus, the planet of love and affection, has to travel a long way to her assignment in the third decan of Aries. In fact, Venus is in her detriment here: she's 180 degrees away from her own home on the other side of the zodiac, and Aries' fiery energy is completely different than her airy Libra élan. To picture it in tarot terms, just imagine the Venusian Empress leaving her lush and fertile arboretum to visit the Emperor in his desert-like, Aries-influenced office.

Happily, Venus is always a beneficial planet, and her grace and charm bless every sign she touches. The Golden Dawn designers of this card called Venus in Aries the "Lord of Perfected Work," because it illustrates the subtle beauty, style, and refinement that Venus brings to brash Aries.

The Four of Wands is the card of the dance. It's a metaphor for collaboration and cooperation. In a tarot reading, the Four of Wands often symbolizes a marriage or a partnership.

That's something that the young man from the Two of Wands and the young woman from the Three of Wands can take to heart, as they practice their dance steps and learn to work in concert with each other. As emperors in training, they'll need to learn how to synchronize their movements.

Venus is the planet of pleasure, music, dance, creativity, and the arts. It's the planet of beauty and attraction, and the resulting friendships and romances that result. Venus—which also rules the fixed earth sign of Taurus—also enjoys the comfort and stability that love and partnership can bring.

Let's not forget, either, that Venus corresponds to the Empress card. She's a natural match for the Emperor, the Major Arcana card that corresponds to this sign. Here in the Four of Wands, Venus aligns herself with the purpose-driven energy of Aries, and she teaches it to dance. So even though Venus is in its detriment in Aries, forced to join forces and work with a warrior mentality, the planet still manages to cast a romantic glow over an otherwise single-minded sign.

The Four of Wands could also reflect a young emperor's determination and desire to find an empress who can help him rule his empire.

Qabalistically, the Four of Wands depicts Chesed, the fourth sphere of mercy. It's positioned in Atziluth, the fiery world of inspiration. The fourth sphere corresponds to Jupiter, the planet of expansion. The young couple is solidifying their relationship and learning to reach out and grow with one another.

The third decan of Aries usually falls between April 11 and 20, when the Sun is between 20 and 30 degrees Aries.

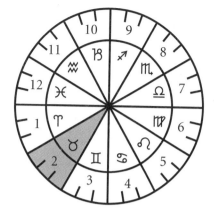

The Three Decans of Taurus

FIXED EARTH: THE FIVE, SIX, AND SEVEN OF PENTACLES

◆ ◆ ◆

We'll continue our tour of the Minor Arcana with the three cards that correspond to the three decans of Taurus: the Five, Six, and Seven of Pentacles.

Because Taurus is an earth sign, the cards come from the earthy suit of pentacles. And since it's a fixed sign, well-established and firmly set in place, the cards come from the middle of the suit.

As we study the cards, and the characters in the cards, remember that they'll all share the same attributes of the sign.

- **Sign:** Taurus, the second sign of the zodiac, is the sign of possessions, wealth, and spiritual treasures. All three cards in Taurus depict people dealing with issues that relate to money and values.

- **Mode/Quality:** Taurus is a fixed sign, stationed securely in the middle month of spring. The corresponding cards from the middle of the suit embody a stable, persistent energy.

- **Element:** Taurus is an earth sign, so it corresponds with the suit of pentacles. Both the element and the suit are solid, reliable, responsible, practical, physical, and enduring.

- **Duality:** Earth signs are feminine. They are receptive, reactive, magnetic, responsive, and patient, and their energy flows in a circular pattern.

- **Corresponding Majors:** The Hierophant corresponds to the sign of Taurus, while the Empress corresponds to Taurus' ruling planet, Venus.

Five of Pentacles: Mercury in Taurus
Lord of Material Trouble

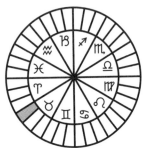

When Mercury, the Magician, finds himself in Taurus, his focus shifts. Normally, he's busy on the intellectual plane—a role that corresponds to his rulership over Gemini, the sign of communication, and Virgo, the sign of work and service to others. Here in the Five of Pentacles, however, mental Mercury is suddenly thrust into a cold, cruel world where he has to fight for physical survival.

The Golden Dawn designers of this card called Mercury in Taurus the "Lord of Material Trouble," because high-flying Mercury is weighed down here by the limits of physical existence. In earthy Taurus, Mercury is earthbound. He's trapped in human form, weighed down by the limits of physical existence—but he can transcend the physical world by turning to the spiritual realm of spiritual teaching and tradition.

Like all the cards in Taurus, the Five of Pentacles is connected to the Hierophant—and here, the pontiff is close at hand, just inside the cathedral. The light shining through the windows symbolizes the illuminated wisdom that the teacher of tradition has to offer.

Much of that wisdom focuses on the earthly realities of life on this planet, where we find our spiritual selves embodied in human form. If we're not careful, we can forget that our physical forms don't define our existence.

Like all the cards in the suit of pentacles, Taurus is associated with structure and stability, material security, and spiritual values. While Aries, the preceding sign, was focused on consciousness and self-awareness, Taurus is concerned with material and physical well-being.

It's a natural progression. Anyone who can comprehend his own existence will also recognize his mortality—and when safety and security aren't assured, most people don't have time for high-minded philosophy and spiritual ruminations. Survival is every living creature's first order of business.

That's one reason Taurus puts such emphasis on material possessions. Tangible goods represent physical security, along with a conditional guarantee that one's earthly existence will continue.

Qabalistically, the Five of Pentacles depicts Geburah, the fifth sphere of power, strength, and severity. It corresponds to Mars, the planet of war. The outcasts are wandering through Assiah, the material world, and they're facing the challenges of physical existence.

In a tarot reading, the Five of Pentacles often symbolizes a spiritual refuge and a haven from physical discomfort.

The first decan of Taurus usually falls between April 21 and 30, when the Sun is between 0 and 10 degrees Taurus.

Six of Pentacles: Moon in Taurus

Lord of Material Success

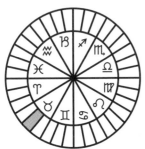

The Moon, like her counterpart the High Priestess, is exalted in Taurus. When she visits the sign, she's an honored guest—and she brings housewarming gifts.

Her presence explains the charitable giving shown in the card.

The Golden Dawn designers of this card called the Moon in Taurus the "Lord of Material Success," because it depicts the blessings of comfort and security that the silvery Moon bestows in Taurus, the sign of material and spiritual treasure.

It's not often that we associate wealth with the silvery orb of reflection—but money, like the Moon, often comes and goes in cycles. Income and expenses can ebb and flow like the tides. A silver coin in your hand can catch and reflect light like the Moon—and money, even in theory, can be just as mesmerizing as the silent guardian of the night. Both money and the Moon can symbolize the cyclical nature of life, passages, and transitions, and nurturing feminine energy.

In the Six of Pentacles, the benefactor with coins to share is a younger version of the Hierophant, showering his acolytes with blessings. The coins represent wisdom, charity, or karmic reward. The scales of Libra make an appearance in this card, too, since Taurus and Libra are both ruled by Venus.

Qabalistically, the Six of Pentacles depicts Tiphareth, the sixth sphere of beauty. It corresponds to the Sun, a symbol of radiance and enlightenment. It's positioned in Assiah, the material world, and the three people in the card are discovering the pleasure of sharing their wealth.

In a tarot reading, the Six of Pentacles often represents prosperity, power, and influence, and the charitable giving that can stem from business success. The card can represent either the giver or the receiver.

The second decan of Taurus usually falls between May 1 and 10, when the Sun is between 10 and 20 degrees Taurus.

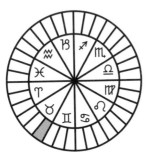

Seven of Pentacles: Saturn in Taurus
Lord of Success Unfulfilled

Saturn, the ringed planet of limitations and restrictions, imposes structure and discipline on everything it touches. When Saturn lands in Taurus, a sign of growth and fertility, it enforces a waiting period before harvest and reward.

When we first met Saturn in the World card, crowned with the laurel wreath of victory, completion and success seemed like a sure thing. Saturn's presence in the Seven of Pentacles, however, reminds us that real victory demands a long-term investment of physical endurance and spiritual strength. In this case, Saturn serves as a patient taskmaster, teaching the value of determination and perseverance.

The Golden Dawn designers of this card called Saturn in Taurus the "Lord of Success Unfulfilled," because he delays gratification and reward until they've been earned.

Like Kronos, the god of time, Saturn forces us to learn self-discipline, to manage our time wisely, and to allow nature—and life—to run its natural course. Saturn reminds us that the world is bigger than any one individual, and that others will eventually impose their will on us if we can't control ourselves.

Like all the Minor Arcana cards of Taurus, the Seven of Pentacles is connected to the Hierophant and the Empress. The Hierophant—the embodiment of Taurus—knows that our possessions reflect our values. The Hierophant's ruler, the Venusian Empress, can take that message a step further: we value things more when we wait for them. Every woman who has ever given birth—like the Empress, who is perpetually pregnant—can tell you that the last few months of pregnancy seem to stretch on far beyond their actual measure. She can also tell you that anticipation makes the final reward sweeter.

Qabalistically, the Seven of Pentacles depicts Netzach, the seventh sphere of beauty. It corresponds to Venus, the planet of love and attraction. It's positioned in Assiah, the material world, and the young gardener is contemplating the beauty of physical growth and development.

In a tarot reading, the Seven of Pentacles often symbolizes patience and reward, obstacles and delays, and worries about expected outcomes.

The third decan of Taurus usually falls between May 11 and 20, when the Sun is between 20 and 30 degrees Taurus.

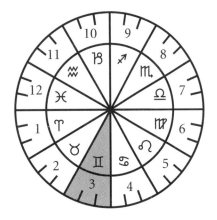

The Three Decans of Gemini
MUTABLE AIR: THE EIGHT, NINE, AND TEN OF SWORDS

◆ ◆ ◆

We'll continue our tour of the Minor Arcana with the three cards that correspond to the three decans of Gemini: the Eight, Nine, and Ten of Swords.

Because Gemini is an air sign, the cards come from the airy suit of Swords. And since it's a mutable sign, symbolic of endings and transitions, the cards are the last three numbered cards of the suit.

As we study the cards, and the characters in the cards, remember that they'll all share the same attributes of the sign.

- **Sign:** Gemini, the third sign of the zodiac, is the sign of intellect and communication. All three cards in Gemini depict intellectual concerns.
- **Mode/Quality:** Gemini is a mutable sign, transitioning from the last month of spring to the first month of summer. The corresponding cards from the end of the suit depict a versatile, flexible energy.
- **Element:** Gemini is an air sign, so it corresponds with the suit of Swords. Both the element and the suit are intellectual, communicative, social, changeable, curious, and versatile.
- **Duality:** Air signs are masculine. They are active, assertive, confident, direct, and energetic. They move in a linear fashion, from point A to point B.
- **Corresponding Majors:** Gemini is connected to the Lovers, and to the Magician, which corresponds to its ruling planet, Mercury.

Eight of Swords: Jupiter in Gemini
Lord of Shortened Force

The first decan of Gemini is ruled by Jupiter, the planet of growth and expansion. Normally, you'd probably think that would be a good thing. In theory, Jupiter could give airy, intellectual Gemini all the room it needs to let its mind roam free.

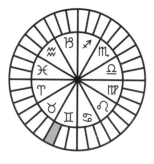

Gemini, however, doesn't need any help coming up with new ideas. In fact, Gemini already has more interests than he could ever fully explore—and multiplying those options won't make life any easier.

If you've ever seen a Gemini surrounded by a half-dozen half-done projects, unable to focus long enough to finish one before moving on to the next, you'll understand. An endless array of openings and opportunities isn't necessarily liberating.

The Eight of Swords illustrates the problem. The woman in the card is paralyzed by possibility. She's surrounded by a multitude of options, but she can't see the forest for the trees. She's trapped in a mental prison of her own making; she is stuck in the middle of Jupiter's Wheel of Fortune. She's alone, too. She's separated from her companion on the Lovers card, and she doesn't have her Gemini soulmate along to keep her company.

As it turns out, Jupiter is in its detriment in Gemini. The planet is 180 degrees from its natural home in the zodiac, so it's forced to work with energies that are radically different from its own.

The Golden Dawn designers of this card called Jupiter in Gemini the "Lord of Shortened Force," because it illustrates the crippling effect of too much of a good thing.

Qabalistically, the Eight of Swords depicts the eighth sphere of splendor, Hod. It corresponds to Mercury, the planet of thought and communication. It's positioned in Yetzirah, the airy realm of thought. The Swords that surround the young woman in the card exist solely in her mind, and her bondage will be short-lived.

In a tarot reading, the Eight of Swords often represents entrapment. It can also symbolize the process of initiation, and the recognition and reawakening that occur when you're forced to assess your situation and focus on your goals.

The first decan of Gemini usually falls between May 21 and 31, when the Sun is between 0 and 10 degrees Gemini.

Nine of Swords: Mars in Gemini
Lord of Despair and Cruelty

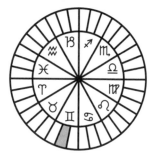

NINE OF SWORDS

Mars, the planet of energy and aggression, doesn't tone down his warlike nature when he travels through the signs. In fact, when he steps in as the ruler of Gemini's second decan, he finds a whole arsenal of mental weaponry at his disposal. In Gemini, Mars doesn't play war games—he plays mind games.

Fully armed with verbal and intellectual ammunition, Mars bombards his adversaries with a full battle array. He imprisons them in a tower of despair. He launches insults and criticism, harsh words and wicked thoughts. He plants seeds of doubt in a trusting mind, and unleashes stealth attacks in the form of nightmares and unconscious fears. He'll try every tactic in turn, in an unrelenting assault on the opponent of his choosing.

In the Nine of Swords, Mars' hapless target happens to be a young woman. She sits upright in bed and tries to clear her mind, but she can't sleep while her thoughts race through enemy territory.

There's a fine line between love and hate, and this card's link to the Gemini Lovers reminds us that former friends and confidants make the cruelest opponents. They know our weaknesses, and they're willing to exploit them. The Nine of Swords' connection to the Magician card also reminds us of Mercury's shadow side, in which the trickster god took a perverse pleasure in undermining those who trusted him.

The Golden Dawn designers of this card called Mars in Gemini the "Lord of Despair and Cruelty," because it illustrates the brutal effect of a mental assault under the cover of darkness.

Qabalistically, the Nine of Swords depicts Yesod, the ninth sphere of foundation. It corresponds to the Moon, the orb of reflection. It's positioned in Yetzirah, the airy realm of thought. The young woman's worries are merely shadows in the night; her concerns have no basis in reality.

In a tarot reading, the Nine of Swords often represents restless nights, anxious dreams, insomnia, and panic attacks.

The second decan of Gemini usually falls between June 1 and 10, when the Sun is between 10 and 20 degrees Gemini.

Ten of Swords: Sun in Gemini

Lord of Ruin

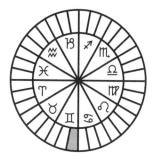

The third and last decan of Gemini is ruled by the Sun, the fiery orb of consciousness and enlightenment.

The Sun usually seems like a benevolent force: always shining, always beaming, always radiating light and life. Too much Sun, however, can burn—especially when it reveals the truth.

Gemini is a talkative sign. Unfortunately, talk often leads to backstabbing, gossip, slander, libel, and vicious personal attacks. Even when Gemini's intellectual energy is self-contained, it can pierce our confidence with pains of self-doubt.

When the Sun passes by, however, it clears away clouds and illuminates shadows, exposing the truth in the bright light of day.

Sadly, sometimes the truth hurts—especially when the Sun reveals the politics of personal destruction.

If the Nine of Swords showed the woman from the Lovers, the Ten of Swords shows the man. Both have been wounded by the trickster aspect of their ruling planet, and the young man's wounds aren't the kind that heal well.

The Golden Dawn designers of this card called the Sun in Gemini the "Lord of Ruin," because it reveals the unavoidable truth of an untenable situation.

While the illustration looks cruel, it also represents full consciousness and release. Nothing is hidden anymore. The Sun in Gemini delivers a *coup de grâce*—a final, freeing blow. The suffering ends. The soul is liberated by complete and total enlightenment. The mind is free to roam, unburdened by physical form and unhindered by gravity. At last, a higher consciousness is possible, and ruin can be followed by rebuilding.

Qabalistically, the Ten of Swords depicts Malkuth, the tenth sphere of earthly reality. It's positioned in Yetzirah, the airy plane of thought. The young man is pinned to the ground by verbal and intellectual attacks that are every bit as debilitating as physical assaults.

In a tarot reading, the Ten of Swords often represents overkill, death and rebirth, and the cycle of endings and beginnings.

The third decan of Gemini usually falls between June 11 and 20, when the Sun is between 20 and 30 degrees Gemini.

The Three Decans of Cancer
CARDINAL WATER: THE TWO, THREE, AND FOUR OF CUPS

◆ ◆ ◆

We'll leave the spring months of Aries, Taurus, and Gemini behind and continue our tour of the decans with Cancer—the first sign of summer.

Because Cancer is a water sign, the cards come from the watery suit of Cups. And since it's a cardinal sign, symbolic of new beginnings, the cards are the first three numbered cards of the suit.

As we study the cards, and the characters in the cards, remember that they'll all share the same attributes of the sign.

- **Sign:** Cancer, the fourth sign of the zodiac, is the sign of home and family life. All three cards in Cancer depict people dealing with emotional or relationship issues.
- **Mode/Quality:** Cancer is also a cardinal sign. Just as cardinal signs usher in a change of seasons, the characters in the cards that belong to Cancer initiate change. They are decisive, quick, and energetic.
- **Element:** Cancer is a water sign, so it corresponds to the watery suit of Cups. Both the element and the suit are emotional, changeable, subtle, intuitive, and flowing.
- **Duality:** Water signs are feminine. They are receptive, reactive, magnetic, responsive, and patient, and their energy flows in a circular pattern.
- **Corresponding Majors:** Cancer is associated with the Chariot, and its ruling planet, the Moon, with the High Priestess.

Two of Cups: Venus in Cancer

Lord of Love

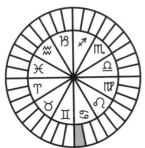

If the young lovers in the Two of Cups seem a little starstruck, it's no accident: powerful forces have drawn them together. Venus, the planet of love and romance, has made her way into the nurturing sign of Cancer—and she's been playing matchmaker. The young couple in the card could very well be an adolescent version of a Charioteer in training and the girl who will someday assume the Empress' throne.

Venus is the planet of pleasure and attraction. Her counterpart in the tarot is the Empress, a loving mother who's naturally attuned to the energy of Cancer, as well as the fourth house of home and family life.

Venus rules the fixed earth sign of Taurus, so she enjoys the comfort and stability that true love and partnership can bring. When she steps in as the ruler of Cancer's first decan, she simply lights a few candles, plays love songs in the background, and lets nature take its course.

The young lovers in the Two of Cups are depicted in the first blush of romance. Here in the first decan of what is arguably the most sentimental sign, their affection for each other seems especially wholesome and pure, innocent and uncorrupted by time or experience. They are opposites, but opposites attract. They meet in the middle.

The Golden Dawn designers of this card called Venus in Cancer the "Lord of Love," because it illustrates the sweetness and purity of true love.

This Minor Arcana cards of Cancer corresponds to the Chariot and its ruling planet, the lunar High Priestess. That connection tells us that, for now, the young couple is protected by a mother's love—but that safeguard won't last forever. Over time, they'll gain wisdom and experience as their affection for each other is tested, and both people grow and mature. Most of us learn along the way that experience comes at a cost, and early relationships often leave us sadder, but wiser.

Qabalistically, the Two of Cups depicts Chokmah, the second sphere of wisdom. It's positioned in Briah, the watery world of fertility and creation. The young couple in the card is starting to create a life together, and they'll learn from their shared experiences.

In a tarot reading, the Two of Cups often represents love—especially between childhood sweethearts, kindred spirits, and soul mates. It symbolizes equal partnership and the attraction of opposites.

The first decan of Cancer usually falls between June 21 and July 1, when the Sun is between 0 and 10 degrees Cancer.

THREE OF CUPS

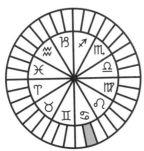

Three of Cups: Mercury in Cancer
Lord of Abundance

It's been a good year, and after a mild spring and a temperate summer, three women have gathered to celebrate a bountiful harvest. After a glass or two of wine, they'll also divide the yield—all in the spirit of Mercury, the god of commerce and exchange.

Here in the second decan of Cancer, Mercury reveals a side of himself that's been largely overlooked. While Mercury is the god of speed and communication, he's also the god of marketing and trade. He's used to the exchange of ideas—but he's also an expert in the exchange of goods.

The Golden Dawn designers of this card called Mercury in Cancer the "Lord of Abundance," because the planetary energy is focused on material exchanges and stockpiles.

Mercury is the natural ruler of Gemini and Virgo, which benefit from his expertise in business communication. Cancer welcomes that expertise, too. Cancer is the sign of home and family life, and the maternal figures that rule the sign—the Cancerian Charioteer and her ruling planet, the Moon—recognize the importance of maintaining a healthy store of provisions for the long, cold months of winter.

The Moon's influence is subtly reinforced in the imagery of the card. Most versions of the Three of Cups feature three women. The trio is easy to identify as the three faces of the goddess—maiden, mother, and crone—who are reflected in the ever-changing face of the

Moon. Every month, the Moon itself embodies the three stages of womanhood as it cycles from waxing, to full, to waning.

Some tarot readers compare the three women in the card to the three fates, the mystic sisters who know every man and woman's destiny from the moment of their birth. Mercury does rule sibling relationships, and he could certainly have a hand in the three sisters' celebration.

There's also a side of Mercury that loves to party, and the celebration here takes on an almost Dionysian quality. That could be related to Cancer's watery influence: those who submerge themselves in the world of emotion might occasionally find themselves submerged in a few drinks, too. Mercury, the great communicator and the playful trickster, celebrating good fortune and toasting success. Cancer, the sign of homemaking and nurturing, happy to be secure in a harvest bounty sure to last through the coming winter months.

Qabalistically, the Three of Cups depicts Binah, the third sphere of understanding. It corresponds to Saturn, the planet of structure. It's positioned in Briah, the watery world of fertility and creation. The three young women in the card are kindred spirits, with a deep emotional connection to one another, and a shared investment in their physical well-being.

In a tarot reading, the Three of Cups often represents a successful harvest, a celebration, a reward for effort and hard work, and prosperity to last through the winter months.

The second decan of Cancer usually falls between July 2 and 11, when the Sun is between 10 and 20 degrees Cancer.

Four of Cups: Moon in Cancer
Lord of Blended Pleasure

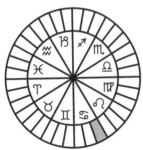

The Moon is the natural ruler of Cancer, so the High Priestess is in her dignity here. You might want to give her some space, though: as both the ruler and the subruler of the sign, the Four of Cups gets a double dose of lunar energy.

At least once a month, the Moon needs to go into hiding, to decompress and shake off the emotions she's picked up in her travels around the zodiac. As the High Priestess, a natural psychic and empath, she spends most of her time reflecting—and absorbing—energy and emotions from everyone around her. In Cancer, the sign of sensitivity and self-protection, the Moon can rebuild her strength, recharge her battery, tend to any cracks in her crab shell, and re-attune herself to the rhythms and cycles of the natural world. She can resume her circuitous route as a guiding light for the traveling Charioteer.

The Golden Dawn designers of this card called the Moon in Cancer the "Lord of Blended Pleasure," because it illustrates the quickly changing moods of the Moon in her own sign. Give Cancer some time, and she'll eventually put on a happy face.

Qabalistically, the Four of Cups depicts Chesed, the fourth sphere of mercy. It corresponds to Jupiter, the planet of expansion. It's positioned in Briah, the watery world of fertility and creation. The young man in the card is experiencing an outpouring of emotion—but in the process, he's being offered a generous gift of awareness and strength.

In a tarot reading, the Four of Cups often represents disappointment, disillusionment, and disenchantment—often despite an abundance of resources. Sometimes, that abundance is the very cause of the sadness: possessions, in and of themselves, are rarely a source of pleasure. In other words, money can't buy happiness.

The third decan of Cancer usually falls between July 12 and 21, when the Sun is between 20 and 30 degrees Cancer.

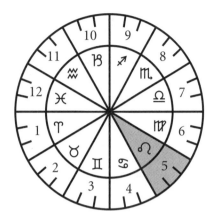

The Three Decans of Leo

FIXED FIRE: THE FIVE, SIX, AND SEVEN OF WANDS

◆　　◆　　◆

We'll continue our tour of the Minor Arcana with the three cards that correspond to the three decans of Leo: the Five, Six, and Seven of Wands.

Because it's a fire sign, the cards come from the fiery suit of Wands. And since it's a fixed sign, illustrating established principles, the cards come from the middle of the suit.

As we study the cards, and the characters in the cards, remember that they'll all share the same attributes of the sign.

- **Sign:** Leo, the fifth sign of the zodiac, is the sign of creativity, recreation, and procreation. All three cards in Leo depict people dealing with creativity issues.
- **Mode/Quality:** Leo is a fixed sign that reigns over the middle month of summer. The corresponding cards from the middle of the suit embody a stable, persistent energy.
- **Element:** Leo is a fire sign, so it corresponds to the suit of Wands. Both the element and the suit are impulsive, driven, courageous, direct, energetic, enthusiastic, and spontaneous.
- **Duality:** Fire signs are masculine. They are active, assertive, confident, direct, and energetic. They move in a linear fashion, from point A to point B.
- **Corresponding Majors:** The Strength card corresponds to Leo and the Sun card corresponds to Leo's ruling planet, the Sun.

Five of Wands: Saturn in Leo

Lord of Strife

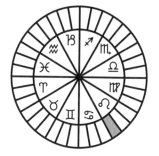

The first decan of Leo is ruled by Saturn, the ringed planet of boundaries, limitations, and restrictions. You might think that sounds oppressive, but take another look at the card. Here, five solitary practitioners are trying to join forces—and a few guidelines are definitely in order.

Leo can be self-centered, which is what got the five free and independent spirits in the card each going her own way. Normally, Leo is the star of the show. It's also a sign of courage and fortitude, as seen on the corresponding Strength card. The sign is ruled by the Sun—the center of the universe—so Leo is used to being the center of attention. In the worst-case scenario, the astrological influence can even lead to boldness, cruelty, lust, and violence.

If the young magicians want to accomplish anything as part of a group, they'll need the discipline and structure that Saturn, the planet of framework, can bring.

Of course, rivalries could ensue—but in this case, Saturn will direct their energy through regulated channels. The resulting competition will help their skills improve faster and more efficiently than even the most dutiful, self-motivated student could master on her own. In the end, they'll be masters of both the physical and spiritual world—as seen on the World card itself.

The Golden Dawn designers of this card called Saturn in Leo the "Lord of Strife." While unfriendly competition is our modern understanding of the word, strife used to refer to a strenuous or earnest effort, too. It's related to the concept of striving for improvement.

Qabalistically, the Five of Wands depicts Geburah, the fifth sphere of power and severity. It corresponds to Mars, the planet of war. It's positioned in Atziluth, the fiery world of inspiration. The group of young practitioners in the card must come to terms with each other before they can make magic together.

In a tarot reading, the Five of Wands often represents a mock battle, adolescent conflict, effort, and opposition.

The first decan of Leo usually falls between July 22 and August 1, when the Sun is between 0 and 10 degrees Leo.

Six of Wands: Jupiter in Leo

Lord of Victory

SIX OF WANDS

If you're looking for a guarantee of honor and acclaim, you've found it in the Six of Wands. Here, in the second decan of Leo, Jupiter puts Leo in the spotlight, and hands the sign all the praise and adulation it craves.

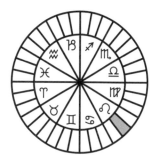

This is where Leo is at its best, shining at the height of its thirty-day reign on the Wheel of the Year. Leo is being heralded as a conquering hero, the star of the show, the center of attention, and the man of the hour—which is why the Golden Dawn designers of this card called Jupiter in Leo the "Lord of Victory."

Like a lion, Leo's signature creature, the hero of the Six of Wands can overcome quarreling, ignorance, and pretenders—and step into the spotlight as a confident, optimistic, and inspiring leader. Jupiter, the great Benefic that spins the Wheel of Fortune, gives the young hero of the Strength card a forum for leadership and acclaim.

Qabalistically, the Six of Wands depicts Tiphareth, the sixth sphere of beauty and harmony. It corresponds to the Sun, a symbol of enlightenment and recognition. It's positioned in Atziluth, the fiery world of inspiration. The young hero who sets herself apart from the crowd is learning how to harmonize her vision of the future with a group of enthusiastic believers and followers.

In a tarot reading, the Six of Wands often symbolizes success, admiration, and a position at the head of the crowd. Many renditions of the card feature a triumphal parade, born of a courageous conquest and victory in battle.

The card also serves as a reminder, though, that leaders are more than just a face in the crowd. Leadership also comes with responsibility and a certain *noblesse oblige*.

The second decan of Leo usually falls between August 2 and 11, when the Sun is between 10 and 20 degrees Leo.

Seven of Wands: Mars in Leo

Lord of Valor

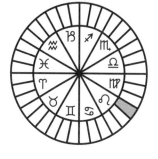

Whatever Mars touches, he imbues with a warrior's spirit. In the last decan of Leo, Mars gives a final boost to the natural courage and drive of the sign. He turns an ordinary mortal into a being of superhuman strength and ability.

Leo—which rules the heart—is all heart, and Mars gives Leo the will and determination it needs to fight for his heart's desire.

War is just as often fought defensively as offensively, and always in support of one's principles and beliefs. In this case, Mars inspires Leo to stand his ground, to face his opponents with bravery and skill.

The encroaching Wands aren't necessarily those of antagonistic forces: you could read the card as an illustration of leadership and courage, too. The young man at the top of the hill could be rallying his troops, and leading his followers into battle or forward into new adventures and experiences. The Martian warrior could be leading an assault, and storming an enemy's Tower or fortress.

In either case, he's the king of the hill. He holds the higher moral ground. The Golden Dawn designers of this card called Mars in Leo the "Lord of Valor." Valor, of course, is another word for courage.

Qabalistically, the Seven of Wands depicts Netzach, the seventh sphere of victory. It corresponds to Venus, the planet of love and attraction. It's positioned in Atziluth, the fiery world of inspiration. The young man in the card has the drive and desire to defend his dreams.

In a tarot reading, the Seven of Wands often symbolizes the courage to take a stand in the face of obstacles, opposition, and overwhelming odds. It's the picture of assertiveness, self-defense, and determination.

The third decan of Leo usually falls between August 12 and 22, when the Sun is between 20 and 30 degrees Leo.

The Three Decans of Virgo
MUTABLE EARTH: THE EIGHT, NINE, AND TEN OF PENTACLES

◆ ◆ ◆

We'll continue our tour of the Minor Arcana with the three cards that correspond to the three decans of Virgo, the Eight, Nine, and Ten of Pentacles.

Because it's an earth sign, the cards come from the earthy suit of Pentacles. And since it's a mutable sign, illustrating conclusions and the corresponding transition to new beginnings, the cards come from the end of the suit.

As we study the cards, and the characters in the cards, remember that they'll all share the same attributes of the sign.

- **Sign:** Virgo, the sixth sign of the zodiac, is the sign of work, duty, and responsibility to others. All three cards in Virgo depict people dealing with service issues; they'll either be in service to others, or on the receiving end of services from others.

- **Mode/Quality:** Virgo is a mutable sign, transitioning from the last month of summer to the first month of fall. The corresponding cards from the end of the suit depict a versatile, flexible energy.

- **Element:** Virgo is an earth sign, so it corresponds with the suit of pentacles. Both the element and the suit are solid, reliable, responsible, practical, physical, and enduring.

- **Duality:** Earth signs are feminine. They are receptive, reactive, magnetic, responsive, and patient, and their energy flows in a circular pattern.

- **Corresponding Majors:** The Hermit corresponds to Virgo and the Magician corresponds to Virgo's ruling planet, Mercury.

Eight of Pentacles: Sun in Virgo

Lord of Prudence

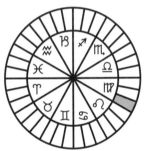

The Sun enlightens everything it shines upon, including the Virgo stonemason at his workbench. Like the Hermit, its Major Arcana counterpart, Virgo is diligent and persevering, devoted to his craft, dedicated to perfection, and true to his word.

The Sun enhances all of those qualities. It makes the apprentice even more conscientious, detail-minded, and meticulous. In short, the Sun's appearance provides a cosmic boost and influx of energy, opportunity, enlightenment, and optimism.

The Golden Dawn designers of this card called the Sun in Virgo the "Lord of Prudence," because it depicts the virtue of dedication, sound judgment, and appropriate behavior.

Prudence is the one cardinal virtue missing from the tarot's Major Arcana. Temperance, Justice, and Fortitude all have their place in the deck—even if Fortitude does go by the name of Strength. Cardinal virtues are developed through practice. Symbolically speaking, the young man in the Eight of Pentacles isn't just developing a trade or a skill. By working diligently at his craft, he's also refining his character.

Qabalistically, the Eight of Pentacles depicts Hod, the eighth sphere of splendor and glory. It corresponds to Mercury, the planet of thought and communication. It's positioned in Assiah, the material world of earthly existence. It's a card of success and achievement in the physical world—especially when accomplishments are based on creative plans and ideas.

In a tarot reading, the Eight of Pentacles often represents a high-level apprenticeship, the ability to sell one's services, and an opportunity grow and develop through work and service. The young man in the card is literally making money.

The first decan of Virgo usually falls between August 23 and September 1, when the Sun is between 0 and 10 degrees Virgo.

NINE OF PENTACLES

Nine of Pentacles: Venus in Virgo

Lord of Material Gain

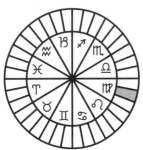

Here we see Venus, the Empress, given rulership over part of the Hermit's realm. Even in isolation, she surrounds herself with objects of beauty and comfort, symmetry, and balance.

When Venus visits the second decan of Virgo, she's in her fall—180 degrees from her exaltation in Pisces. Normally, planets in fall are like unwelcome visitors—humbled, dejected, and at their absolute weakest.

Venus, however, is always a benefic planet, so even when she seems to have fallen from grace, she manages to transform her environment into a place of pleasure and contentment. She has tamed the plants that grow there, just as she has tamed the falcon on her gloved hand. She is calm and placid, and knows that even in the slumber and solitude of winter, she can commune with the beauty of nature.

The Golden Dawn designers of this card called Venus in Virgo the "Lord of Material Gain," because Venus comes bearing gifts of prosperity and possessions. In fact, the card occasionally symbolizes money from an inheritance or a bequest.

Qabalistically, the Nine of Pentacles depicts Yesod, the ninth sphere of foundation. It corresponds to the Moon, the orb of reflection. It's positioned in Assiah, the material world of earthly existence. The young woman in the Nine of Pentacles is reflecting on her physical surroundings.

In a tarot reading, the Nine of Pentacles often represents time spent in peaceful solitude. It suggests a measure of comfort and security, as well as protection from the harsh realities of the outside world.

The second decan of Virgo usually falls between September 2 and 11, when the Sun is between 10 and 20 degrees Virgo.

Ten of Pentacles: Mercury in Virgo
Lord of Wealth

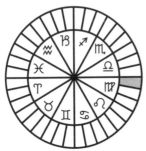

Mercury is exalted in Virgo, which means the messenger planet is an honored guest in the Hermit's home. He comes bearing messages from the outside world. He unites brothers, sisters, and extended family members: aunts, uncles, and cousins. He has an affectionate pat for the dog; the care and feeding of pets is a sixth-house Virgo concern. Most importantly, Mercury maintains his role as god of prosperity.

Wealth isn't just monetary. True wealth refers to several forms of currency: happy family relationships, healthy boundaries, a comfortable, organized, and efficient home, and money for both needs and wants. Each generation has its own space, delineated by clearly defined boundaries in the card. The walls and arched doorways symbolize a certain recognition of each person's need for privacy and respect. It's interesting to note that two dogs play a prominent role in the illustration. The sixth house is the house of pets, because caring for pets is a duty and responsibility that must be managed on a daily basis.

The Golden Dawn designers of this card called Mercury in Virgo the "Lord of Wealth," because it illustrates the fullness and richness of a life well lived. Qabalistically, the Ten of Pentacles depicts Malkuth, the tenth sphere of our earthly reality. It's positioned in Assiah, the material world of earthly existence. The three generations in the card are enjoying the fruits of physical existence.

In a tarot reading, the Ten of Pentacles often represents wealth, business success, inheritance, and multigenerational family relationships. The people in the card enjoy each other's company—in part because they recognize and respect each other's differences. They are prosperous, not just in material terms, but also spiritually and emotionally. The third decan of Virgo usually falls between September 12 and 22, when the Sun is between 20 and 30 degrees Virgo.

The Three Decans of Libra

CARDINAL AIR: THE TWO, THREE, AND FOUR OF SWORDS

◆ ◆ ◆

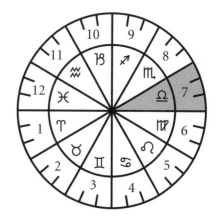

We'll continue our tour of the Minor Arcana with the three cards that correspond to the three decans of Libra: the Two, Three, and Four of Swords.

Because Libra is an air sign, the cards come from the airy suit of Swords. And since it's a cardinal sign, illustrating initiation and new beginnings, the cards come from the beginning of the suit.

As we study the cards, and the characters in the cards, remember that they'll all share the same attributes of the sign.

- **Sign:** Libra, the seventh sign of the zodiac, is the sign of relationships and intimate partnerships. All three cards in Libra depict people dealing with relationship issues.
- **Mode/Quality:** Libra is also a cardinal sign. Just as cardinal signs usher in a change of seasons, the characters in the cards that belong to Libra initiate change. They're decisive, quick, and energetic.
- **Element:** Libra is an air sign, so it corresponds with the suit of Swords. Both are intellectual, communicative, social, changeable, curious, and versatile.
- **Duality:** Air signs are masculine. They are active, assertive, confident, direct, and energetic. They move in a linear fashion, from point A to point B.
- **Corresponding Majors:** Justice is associated with the sign of Libra, and the Empress is assigned to Libra's ruling planet, Venus.

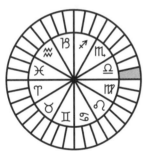

Two of Swords: Moon in Libra
Lord of Peace Restored

Two lunar goddesses merge in the Two of Swords, a card of deep reflection, contemplation, and intuition.

We first met the Moon in the guise of the High Priestess—a lunar goddess and a guide to hidden mysteries. When she steps in to serve as subruler of Libra, she merges with Justice, the archetypal goddess assigned to the sign of balance and equanimity.

Most renditions of this card feature a young woman seated alone on a shoreline, contemplating a difficult choice between two extremes. During the first ten days of the month, Libra is ruled by the Moon—the heavenly orb of intuition, not reason. So while the woman in the card is focused on a rational and balanced discernment, she's blindfolded and forced to rely on her intuition in order to come to a decision.

Visually speaking, the illustration is an echo of the Justice card. In this case, the woman in the card resembles a younger version of the goddess of Justice—but she herself is the scale, weighing both sides of an issue.

Libra is an air sign; without the influence of the Moon, she might seem detached from the watery, emotional side of the issue. The Moon, however, connects her to the emotional realm.

The Golden Dawn designers of this card called the Moon in Libra the "Lord of Peace Restored," because the Moon graces Libra with the gift of reflection, acceptance, and understanding.

The card itself is balanced at the halfway point of the wheel of the year. Libra is a cardinal sign, and when the Sun enters the sign each September, the season of fall begins.

She might be torn between two lovers. Libra rules the seventh house of relationships, which suggests that the young woman's concerns originate in the realm of partnerships and attractions. Because the Two of Swords is a Minor Arcana card—and because it's positioned in the early, first decan of Libra—it's not unrealistic to imagine that the woman in the card is young and inexperienced in affairs of the heart.

It's also possible that she's discovering a foundational truth in the book of love: we have to know and accept ourselves before we can be truly intimate with others. The symbolism of the blindfold does suggest a search for inner peace and understanding.

It might also hint at an initiation; some secret societies blindfold their newest members during their swearing-in.

Libra is ruled by Venus, the planet of love and affection. In tarot, Venus corresponds to the Empress card. Like any loving mother, the young woman in the card doesn't see external appearances. Instead, she's attuned to inner beauty—even if the object of her affection has a face only a mother could love.

Qabalistically, the Two of Swords depicts Chokmah, the second sphere of wisdom. It's positioned in Yetzirah, the airy plane of thought. That makes it a card of carefully considered decision-making and discrimination.

In a tarot reading, the Two of Swords often symbolizes a difficult decision or a choice between two paths.

The first decan of Libra usually falls between September 23 and October 2, when the Sun is between 0 and 10 degrees Libra.

THREE OF SWORDS

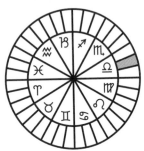

Three of Swords: Saturn in Libra

Lord of Sorrow

Most versions of the Three of Swords feature blood-filled, beating heart, pinned to a backdrop of rain and clouds by three silver swords.

The second decan of Libra is ruled by Saturn—the ringed planet of boundaries and limitations—and at this point, Libra is forced to recognize its restrictions all too well.

That explains the grief and sorrow associated with the Three of Swords. Despite the fact that Libra is at the height of its power and potential, it's not free to float among the clouds as its airy, intellectual nature would like. Instead, Libra is weighed down by the wordly restrictions that Saturn imposes.

Some of those impediments are simply the result of being human. On earth, our time is limited, and our physical, spiritual, and emotional energy is closely tied to our bodies and our surroundings. In Roman mythology, Saturn was the Titan god who consumed his own children. The Greeks knew Saturn as Kronos, the god of time. Those ancient myths illustrate the fact that no one lives forever, and that time will eventually take us and all our creations, too.

Libra's emphasis on relationships also generates its own fair share of sorrow. While we tend to idealize seventh-house issues of love, romance, marriage, and partnerships, it's a sad fact of life that affairs of the heart almost never come without a price. Even the best relationships demand to be constantly weighed, balanced, and adjusted.

That's where the iconography of the Justice card comes into play. Justice is the card that's assigned to the entire month of Libra, and the imagery of the Three of Swords is vaguely reminiscent of the scales of Justice. The Swords might be gruesome, but the illustration itself is perfectly balanced, with two Swords on either side of a central pivot point—like two scales, on either side of a fulcrum. In that sense, the card illustrates mental anguish, as Libra struggles to come to terms with two seemingly irreconcilable differences or points of view. Both extremes are piercing, but the sword in the middle demonstrates that a painful compromise is usually possible.

The Major Arcana connections don't end there, either. Libra is ruled by Venus, the planet of love and devotion. In tarot, Venus is assigned to the Empress card. The Christian mystics who designed tarot decks often had the Virgin Mary in mind when they depicted the Empress—and the Virgin Mary is commonly depicted with her heart exposed and pierced with Swords.

The Golden Dawn designers of this card called Saturn in Libra the "Lord of Sorrow," because Saturn dispenses a fair measure of misery in its travels through the sign.

Saturn is exalted in Libra: it loves the finely honed sense of balance and precision it can find in the sign.

Qabalistically, the Three of Swords depicts Binah, the third sphere of wisdom. It corresponds to Saturn, the planet of structure. It's positioned in in Yetzirah, the airy plane of thought. The wisdom and understanding that are born from painful experience might seem like mortal wounds—but whatever doesn't kill us makes us stronger.

In a tarot reading, the Three of Swords often symbolizes hearts that have been broken by infidelity, divorce, or miscarriage.

The second decan of Libra usually falls between October 3 and October 12, when the Sun is between 10 and 20 degrees Libra.

Four of Swords: Jupiter in Libra

Lord of Rest from Strife

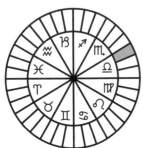

The third and last decan of Libra is ruled by Jupiter, the Greater Benefic. That gives our young friend depicted in the Four of Swords a chance to catch up on some much-needed sleep.

Libra is an air sign, and its intellectual focus is clearly symbolized by the four swords in the card. Three swords are suspended in midair, and one is carved into the young man's bench, like an additional framework or support.

Clearly, he's been thinking and studying, analyzing and judging, and obsessing about intellectual issues. But like a kindly uncle, Jupiter has come into the card, and he has slowed the Wheel of Fortune enough to give Libra a break from its usual worries and concerns.

The Golden Dawn designers of this card called Jupiter in Libra the "Lord of Rest from Strife," because it depicts a much-needed period of rest and recuperation—a gift from the Great Benefic in an otherwise troubled time of anxiety and turmoil.

Even so, the imagery of Libra's Major Arcana counterpart, the Justice card, is still in play. Justice is assigned to the entire month of Libra, and the three Swords above the young man look like a pair of scales in the process of balancing.

Other versions of this card often depict the young man as a knight in effigy, like a sculpture on a tomb. Effigies are usually carved and displayed in a place of honor, like churches and mausoleums. In that sense, the imagery serves as a reminder that all soldiers in the battle of life are waiting for their ultimate reward. It suggests that resurrection and new life await everyone who fights the good fight.

Qabalistically, the Four of Swords depicts Chesed, the fourth sphere of mercy. It corresponds to Jupiter, the planet of expansion. It's positioned in Yetzirah, the airy plane of thought. The gentle giant Jupiter truly does take mercy on those who need rest and recuperation from the trials of the mind.

In a tarot reading, the Four of Swords often represents a temporary reprieve from problems, a stay of execution, a retreat, or a recovery period.

The third decan of Libra usually falls between October 13 and 22, when the Sun is between 20 and 30 degrees Libra.

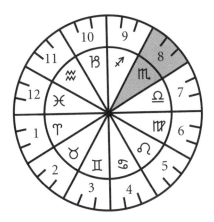

The Three Decans of Scorpio

FIXED WATER: THE FIVE, SIX, AND SEVEN OF CUPS

◆ ◆ ◆

We'll continue our tour of the Minor Arcana with the three cards that correspond to the three decans of Scorpio: the Five, Six, and Seven of Cups.

Because it's a water sign, the cards come from the watery suit of Cups. And since it's a fixed sign, illustrating established principles, the cards come from the middle of the suit.

As we study the cards, and the characters in the cards, remember that they'll all share the same attributes of the sign.

- **Sign:** Scorpio, the eighth sign of the zodiac, is the sign of sex, death, transformation, and other people's money. All three cards in Scorpio depict people dealing with intense issues.
- **Mode/Quality:** Scorpio is also a fixed sign, stationed securely in the middle month of fall. The corresponding cards from the middle of the suit embody a stable, persistent energy.
- **Element:** Scorpio is water sign, so it corresponds to the watery suit of Cups. Both the element and the suit are emotional, changeable, subtle, intuitive, and flowing.
- **Duality:** Water signs are feminine. They are receptive, reactive, magnetic, responsive, and patient, and their energy flows in a circular pattern.
- **Corresponding Majors:** The Death card is assigned to Scorpio, and Judgment is assigned to Scorpio's ruling planet, Pluto.

158 • The Planets in the Signs

Five of Cups: Mars in Scorpio
Lord of Loss of Pleasure

It's no coincidence that Halloween falls during the first decan of Scorpio. On Halloween, the veil between the worlds is said to be at its thinnest, and the souls of the dead can slip effortlessly back and forth from the other side to Earth.

Scorpio is well acquainted with the dark mysteries of life. To most people, those mysteries seem melancholic; the young woman in the card, however, seems to have come to terms with them.

The young woman in the card is already familiar with Death, the Major Arcana card that corresponds to Scorpio. Because the woman in the card is young, part of the Minor Arcana, and positioned in the first decan of the sign, she might not have much firsthand experience with death. Even so, there's an understanding here that seems natural and innate.

Her familiarity is strengthened by the fact that the first decan of Scorpio is ruled by Mars, the warrior planet—and by the fact that Mars is also the natural ruler of the entire sign of Scorpio.

Every warrior—and every surgeon, who also fall under Mars' towering shadow—knows that death is a natural consequence of life. Sometimes it's even brought about by our insistence that the life we want to live is worth preserving and fighting for. Like the young woman's cloak, our bodies are easily shed, cast off, thrown aside. Compare the Five of Cups to the Death card, its counterpart in the Major Arcana, and you'll notice that both cards depict the process of loss, transformation, and change.

The Golden Dawn occultists called the Five of Cups "Loss of Pleasure" for a reason: in life, pleasure is fleeting and transitory. Spilled water, spilled blood … they're both the same. They are the river of life and time, and they flow inevitably to one inescapable conclusion.

Scorpio is ruled by Pluto, which corresponds to the Devil card in the Major Arcana. Many of our contemporary ideas about the devil are based in the mythology of Pluto, lord of the Underworld. Scorpio rules the eighth house of sex, death, and other people's money—often gained through inheritance.

Qabalistically, the Five of Cups depicts Geburah, the fifth sphere of strength, power, and severity. It corresponds to Mars, the planet of war. It's positioned in Briah, the watery world of fertility and creation. For the moment, the young woman pictured in the card is seeing her dreams washed away—but she'll become more cautious, focused, determined, and powerful as a result.

In a tarot reading, the Five of Cups often represents sadness, loss, and regret.

The first decan of Scorpio usually falls between October 23 and November 2, when the Sun is between 0 and 10 degrees Scorpio.

Six of Cups: Sun in Scorpio

Lord of Pleasure

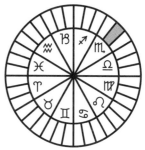

The Sun illuminates even the darkest corners of the zodiac. When the Sun becomes the subruler of Scorpio, it burns away the shadows of grief and loss, and brings a bright reminder of happier days.

Scorpio is the fixed water sign of the zodiac. That makes it intensely emotional and unwavering in its beliefs about life and love.

Scorpio does have a tendency to obsess silently over emotional relationships, as well as unquenched desires and unrequited love. Given enough time—and sunshine—someone in the throes of the second decan of Scorpio could even convince themselves that the past was always perfect.

And while Scorpio can be intensely sad, diving to the depths of despair when relationships fail, the sign can also rise to corresponding heights of happiness and joy. In fact, the Golden Dawn designers of this card called the Sun in Scorpio the "Lord of Pleasure," because it depicts the harmony of friendship and connection.

Qabalistically, the Six of Cups depicts Tipareth, the sixth sphere of beauty. It corresponds to the Sun, a symbol of light and recognition. It's positioned in Briah, the watery world of fertility and creation. That explains the beauty and sensitivity of the card: it depicts an overtly sentimental scene, filled with emotional attachments to both people and places.

In a tarot reading, the Six of Cups often represents nostalgia, happy childhood memories, lasting connections with siblings, and reunions with lifelong friends. It can symbolize a reconciliation after an insult, an argument, or a separation.

The second decan of Scorpio usually falls between November 3 and 12, when the Sun is between 10 and 20 degrees Scorpio.

Seven of Cups: Venus in Scorpio

Lord of Illusionary Success

When Venus, the benefactor, visits the third and last decan of Scorpio, she offers a tantalizing array of possibilities, including beauty, power, wealth, and happiness.

Unfortunately, if an offer sounds too good to be true, it probably is.

Venus, like the Empress, wants to make dreams come true. She wants to give her children every chance at success. She can present any number of options—but Venus is the planet of romantic illusion, and her promises can't be fulfilled without effort and time.

The Golden Dawn designers of this card called Venus in Scorpio the "Lord of Illusory Success," because it hints at a tantalizing array of possibilities, but it doesn't offer any guarantees of completion.

In fact, the card poses more questions than it answers: which path should the young man pursue? Which option is most likely to pay off in the end? For now, the card seems filled with empty promises. Talk is cheap—which is why actions always speak louder than words.

Qabalistically, the Seven of Cups depicts Netzach, the seventh sphere of victory. It corresponds to Venus, the planet of love and affection. It's positioned in Briah, the watery world of fertility and creation.

At the moment, the seven Cups are still in the process of manifestation. Their shape and structure hasn't yet materialized. For the time being, they offer nothing but promise and possibility—along with the tantalizing options of perfect happiness and joy. Think of them as unborn children: when women are pregnant, they dream of all the love and success they'll share. Before those infants actually emerge, squalling and demanding to be fed, those children are perfect and unblemished little people.

In a tarot reading, the Seven of Cups often represents fantasy, illusion, dreams, and a tendency to lose oneself in revelry and thought. It could symbolize dream lovers, fantasy romances, and imaginary relationship. The card could even depict an embarrassment of riches—but it could also suggest a tendency toward drunkenness, which could lead to promiscuity or violence.

If you're particularly mystical, the card's connection to Scorpio—the sign of sex, death, and other people's money—might even remind you of our connection to the spirit world. The seven Cups might symbolize the souls of the dead, lining up for their chance to connect with loved ones through a medium.

The third decan of Scorpio usually falls between November 13 and 22, when the Sun is between 20 and 30 degrees Scorpio.

Cosmic Connection: SEVENTH HEAVEN

Several intriguing layers of meaning are woven into the Seven of Cups. The seven vessels in the card correspond to the seven ancient planets, as well as their corresponding Major Arcana cards. Look closely and you'll recognize the symbols from those cards.

- **Mercury**—the Magician's lemniscate (In other decks, the lemniscate may be portrayed as a snake. Both are symbols of infinity; the Ouroborus is the serpent that bites its own tail in a symbolic depiction of eternity.)
- **Venus**—the head of the Empress
- **Mars**—the Tower
- **Jupiter**—the Wheel of Fortune (In other decks, the fortune is often depicted as a collection of gleaming jewels and treasure.)
- **Saturn**—the World's wreathlike crown
- **The Moon**—the High Priestess (In other decks, she appears as a veiled woman.)
- **The Sun**—Apollo's white horse (In other decks, it may be portrayed as a winged dragon, another symbol of solar movement and power.)

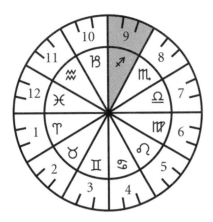

The Three Decans of Sagittarius
MUTABLE FIRE: THE EIGHT, NINE, AND TEN OF WANDS

◆ ◆ ◆

We'll continue our tour of the Minor Arcana with the three cards that correspond to the three decans of Sagittarius: the Eight, Nine, and Ten of Wands.

Because it's a fire sign, the cards come from the fiery suit of Wands. And since it's a mutable sign, illustrating conclusions and the corresponding transition to new beginnings, the cards come from the end of the suit.

As we study the cards, and the characters in the cards, remember that they'll all share the same attributes of the sign.

- **Sign:** Sagittarius, the ninth sign of the zodiac, is the sign of long-distance travel, higher education, and philosophy. All three cards in Sagittarius depict people who are expanding their world view and broadening their vision.
- **Mode:** Sagittarius is a mutable sign, transitioning the move from the last month of fall to the first month of winter. The corresponding cards from the end of the suit depict a versatile, flexible energy.
- **Element:** Sagittarius is a fire sign, so it corresponds to the suit of Wands. Both the element and the suit are impulsive, driven, courageous, direct, energetic, enthusiastic, and spontaneous.
- **Duality:** Fire signs are masculine. They are active, assertive, confident, direct, and energetic. They move in a linear fashion, from point A to point B.
- **Corresponding Majors:** Temperance is assigned to Sagittarius, and the Wheel of Fortune is assigned to Sagittarius's ruling planet, Jupiter.

Eight of Wands: Mercury in Sagittarius

Lord of Swiftness

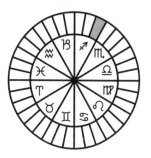

The Eight of Wands card combines the most familiar attributes of Mercury, the messenger, with Sagittarius, the sign of long-distance travel, philosophy, and higher education.

Mercury was the messenger of the gods. He moved at the speed of light—and thought—ferrying messages and communications across great distances in time and space. Like the Magician, his tarot-card counterpart, Mercury could transcend the limits and bonds of earthly existence, and transform the physical world into a sphere of mental activity.

Here in the Eight of Wands, he's traveling through the philosophical realm of high-minded Sagittarius—a sign that's happy to broadcast messages and communication to the world at large. In fact, the ninth house of Sagittarius is the natural home of publishing. The card that corresponds to Sagittarius, Temperance, symbolizes a bridge between two worlds—just as the written word bridges the divide between writers and readers.

While Wands cards usually convey a spiritual message, the eight missives in the card also conform to the laws of physics. They fly in formation, and gravity will eventually compel them to land.

At the moment, however, it's not clear whether the Wands are taking off or arriving at their destination, or whether they'll reach their target or miss their mark.

It's also not clear if anyone sees them overhead. Who sent them? Is anyone expecting their arrival? Since there are no people in the card, the Wands may simply be carrying a message from the universe at large.

Qabalistically, the Eight of Wands depicts Hod, the eighth sphere of splendor and glory. It corresponds to Mercury, the planet of thought and communication. It's positioned in Atziluth, the fiery world of inspiration. The soaring Wands in the card are bearing messages of creativity and drive; they're an undeniable call to action.

In a tarot reading, the Eight of Wands often symbolizes electronic communication—sailing across the airwaves, soaring through the stratosphere, bouncing off satellites, and crashing to a halt on your desktop or a device in the palm of your hand.

The Golden Dawn designers of this card called Mercury in Sagittarius the "Lord of Swiftness," because it depicted a hail of messages and communication flying through the air, soaring like the archer's arrows, connecting people and places to one another.

The first decan of Sagittarius usually falls between November 23 and December 2, when the Sun is between 0 and 10 degrees Sagittarius.

Nine of Wands: Moon in Sagittarius
Lord of Great Strength

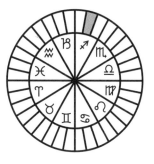

Sagittarius is an explorer and an adventurer—but here, under the meditative influence of the Moon, a soldier of fortune takes time to reflect on past missions and formulate plans for the next round of battle—as well as the next cycle of experience. In fact, you might want to think of her as a guarded version of the Moon's high priestess, tempered by time and experience in the darker realms of life. Sagittarius' journeys don't always confine themselves to bright and happy places, and the corresponding Temperance archetype often demands a balance between light and shadow.

In the card, the young warrior's posture is defensive: she's an experienced fighter, and she has allied herself with a spiritual force that's strong and organized enough to stand up to any onslaught.

Even so, she remains guarded and watchful. She knows that a surprise attack could come at any moment, and she doesn't dare let down her shield. While her back is against the wall, her body is angled, so that she can respond to a threat from any direction.

The Golden Dawn designers of this card called the Moon in Sagittarius the "Lord of Great Strength," because the calming power of the Moon gives Sagittarius the deep philosophical underpinnings he craves—especially when it comes to spiritual battles. That Sagittarian and lunar blend of emotion and reason can help us build a fortress of strength, resolve, and self-reliance.

Qabalistically, the Nine of Wands depicts Yesod, the ninth sphere of foundation. It corresponds to the Moon, the orb of reflection. It's positioned in Atziluth, the fiery world of inspiration. It's a reminder that no reward comes without patience. Just as a mother must wait months for the birth of a child, the wounded warrior must release the past in order to move forward.

In a tarot reading, the Nine of Wands often represents a wounded warrior—one who might have lost the battle, but plans to win the war.

The second decan of Sagittarius usually falls between December 3 and December 12, when the Sun is between 10 and 20 degrees Sagittarius.

Ten of Wands: Saturn in Sagittarius

Lord of Oppression

Saturn, the ringed planet of limitations and restrictions, reins in everything it touches. Here it burdens happy-go-lucky Sagittarius with baggage that's bound to weigh him down and slow his forward motion and progress.

Like Sisyphus, the young man in the card seems condemned to roll a boulder uphill for all eternity—or, in this case, to carry an armload of burning branches across an open field.

Sagittarius is normally footloose and fancy-free. The adventurous horseman likes nothing better than to ride off into the sunset in search of new lands, new people, and new philosophies to explore.

Saturn is also the planet of gravity. When Saturn assumes the rulership of Sagittarius' third decan, he brings the weight of the world along with him. It tempers his dreams and hopes, and limits his travels.

The young man might be carrying the burden of manifesting his dreams and ideas. Unfulfilled hopes weigh heavily on anyone's soul. He might also be struggling with guilt for past wrongdoings, like Marley's ghost, perpetually wrapped in a chain he forged link by link.

The Golden Dawn designers of this card called Jupiter in Saturn the "Lord of Oppression." For anyone who's unfamiliar with Saturn's limits and restrictions, the weight of responsibility can certainly seem oppressive.

Qabalistically, the Ten of Wands depicts Malkuth, our earthly realm. It's positioned in Atziluth, the fiery world of inspiration. It depicts the earthly realities of our dreams and ideas; sometimes, they take a lot of work to organize and manifest.

In a tarot reading, the Ten of Wands often represents overwork and disorganization.

The third decan of Sagittarius usually falls between December 13 and 21, when the Sun is between 20 and 30 degrees Sagittarius.

The Three Decans of Capricorn
CARDINAL EARTH: THE TWO, THREE, AND FOUR OF PENTACLES

◆　◆　◆

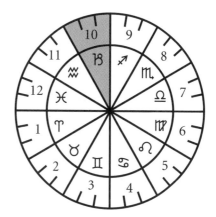

We'll continue our tour of the Minor Arcana with the three cards that correspond to the three decans of Capricorn: the Two, Three, and Four of Pentacles.

Because it's an earth sign, the cards come from the earthy suit of pentacles. And since it's a cardinal sign, illustrating initiation and new beginnings, the cards come from the beginning of the suit.

As we study the cards, and the characters in the cards, remember that they'll all share the same attributes of the sign.

- **Sign:** Capricorn, the tenth sign of the zodiac, is the sign of career and social status. All three cards in Capricorn depict issues of finance and worldly power.

- **Mode/Quality:** Capricorn is also a cardinal sign. Just as cardinal signs usher in a change of seasons, the characters in the cards that belong to Capricorn initiate change. They're decisive, quick, and energetic.

- **Element:** Capricorn is an earth sign, so it corresponds with the suit of pentacles. Both the element and the suit are solid, reliable, responsible, practical, physical, and enduring.

- **Duality:** Earth signs are feminine. They are receptive, reactive, magnetic, responsive, and patient, and their energy flows in a circular pattern.

- **Corresponding Majors:** Capricorn is associated with the Devil, while its ruling planet, Saturn, is associated with the World.

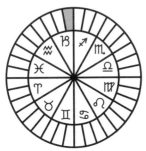

Two of Pentacles: Jupiter in Capricorn
Lord of Harmonious Change

All work and no play makes Jack a dull boy—but Jupiter's going to make sure that no one gets bored. When Jupiter visits the first decan of Capricorn, it shakes up the structure of the Saturnine World, and provides a welcome diversion from rules and regulations.

Jupiter, of course, is the happy-go-lucky Wheel of Fortune. Here in the Devil's tenth house of career and social service, the Greater Benefic seems a little out of place. In fact, Jupiter is in its fall in Capricorn—something of an unwelcome guest. He has a lot of work to do to get Capricorn to lighten up. Given the resistance he faces, the best he can do is to get Capricorn to jingle the coins in his pocket, try a little sleight of hand, and practice juggling his resources. Ultimately, Jupiter might even be able to bring out the devil-may-care aspect of Capricorn's otherwise serious personality.

The Golden Dawn designers of this card called Jupiter in Capricorn the "Lord of Harmonious Change," because the benefic Jupiter makes changes and material improvements happen smoothly and unobtrusively. The young man might need to spend money with one hand, but Jupiter will ensure that he can make money with the other.

Qabalistically, the Two of Pentacles depicts Chokmah, the second sphere of wisdom. It's positioned in Assiah, our earthly world. The young man in the card is learning to unite the forces of mind and body, and bring balance to his physical and spiritual existence.

In a tarot reading, the Two of Pentacles often represents a balancing act—the constant struggle to balance time and money, work and pleasure, and personal and professional obligations. His act may be time consuming, but sometimes, it's also performed for the benefit of an audience—who may or not be appreciative of his time, talent, or trouble.

The first decan of Capricorn usually falls between December 22 and 30, when the Sun is between 0 and 10 degrees Capricorn.

THREE OF PENTACLES

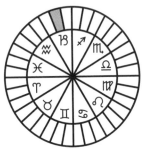

Three of Pentacles: Mars in Capricorn
Lord of Material Works

Mars, the warrior planet, puts on a suit and goes to work when he takes over as subruler of Capricorn's second decan.

Mars is exalted in Capricorn. He's an honored guest, and he's received with all the respect his station affords him.

Mars loves to get down to business, to establish goals and objectives, and execute a battle plan—or a business plan. He's more than willing to give the Devil his due, in exchange for a corner suite in an office tower. From that vantage point, high in the chart and high in the sky, Mars can see the world—and the world can see him at work, too. The tenth house describes career and social status. It's a prominent, visible position in a chart.

In fact, the earthy tenth house is the perfect home for Mars' Tower-like energy. Rather than wreaking havoc and destruction, however, Mars' lightning flashes of inspiration are grounded here—and that can lead to practical, profitable results. Simply picture the young man in the card as an aggressive captain of industry, with the full faith and credit of the investors and board of directors that are backing him.

The Golden Dawn designers of this card called Mars in Capricorn the "Lord of Material Works," because here Mars has the resources—and the savvy—to take action, make money, and create the change he wants in the world.

Qabalistically, the Three of Pentacles depicts Binah, the third sphere of understanding. It corresponds to Saturn, the planet of structure. It's positioned in Assiah, the earthly world of physical manifestation. The young man in the card is learning how to find his place in the hierarchy of business, as well as how to understand and structure the time he invests with others.

In a tarot reading, the Three of Pentacles often represents the creative work of building a business through partnership, investment, and commercial enterprise.

The second decan of Capricorn usually falls between December 31 and January 9, when the Sun is between 10 and 20 degrees Capricorn.

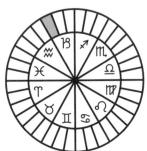

Four of Pentacles: Sun in Capricorn
Lord of Earthly Power

The Sun illuminates everything it touches. In this case, it emphasizes Capricorn's natural tendency to acquire money, power, and influence.

Most versions of the card feature a king on his throne, guarding four pentacles that symbolize his spiritual, intellectual, physical, and emotional realms.

He seems to have the Midas touch—but if you remember the classic myth, you'll realize that it's not necessarily a good thing. The ancient king turned everything he touched into gold—including his loved ones, who lost their lives when he embraced them. In this case, the figure in the Four of Pentacles is cut off from friends, family, and neighbors while he single-mindedly works to manage and control his investments of money, time, and energy. You could even think of him as a more humanized version of the Capricorn Devil, embracing the riches, rewards, and temptations of life in the physical world.

The Golden Dawn designers of this card called the Sun in Capricorn the "Lord of Earthly Power," because it highlights the sign's obsession with material resources—not only the acquiring of money for its own sake, but also for the power and protection it affords.

Qabalistically, the Four of Pentacles depicts Chesed, the fourth sphere of mercy. It corresponds to Jupiter, the planet of expansion. It's positioned in Assiah, the earthly world of physical existence. By isolating himself and guarding his resources, the young man in the card might actually be conserving and growing his wealth to share with future generations.

In a tarot reading, the Four of Pentacles often represents a keen business mind, control of material and spiritual resources, a tendency to hoard because of past injuries or insults, and the need to protect oneself against an uncertain future in an unfeeling world.

The third decan of Capricorn usually falls between January 10 and 19, when the Sun is between 20 and 30 degrees Capricorn.

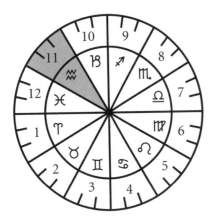

FIXED AIR: THE FIVE, SIX, AND SEVEN OF SWORDS

◆   ◆   ◆

We'll continue our tour of the Minor Arcana with the three cards that correspond to the three decans of Aquarius: the Five, Six, and Seven of Swords.

Because it's an air sign, the cards come from the airy suit of Swords. And since it's a fixed sign, illustrating established principles, the cards come from the middle of the suit.

As we study the cards, and the characters in the cards, remember that they'll all share the same attributes of the sign.

- **Sign:** Aquarius, the eleventh sign of the zodiac, is the sign of futuristic thinking, idealism, and social groups and causes. All three cards in Aquarius depict people dealing with utopian visions.

- **Mode/Quality:** Aquarius is a fixed sign, stationed securely in the middle month of winter. The corresponding cards from the middle of the suit embody a stable, persistent energy.

- **Element:** Aquarius is an air sign, so it corresponds with the suit of Swords. Both the element and the sign are intellectual, communicative, social, changeable, curious, and versatile.

- **Duality:** Air signs are masculine. They are active, assertive, confident, direct, and energetic. They move in a linear fashion, from point A to point B.

- **Corresponding Majors:** Aquarius is connected to the Star, and its ruling planet, Uranus, is connected to the Fool.

FIVE OF SWORDS

Five of Swords: Venus in Aquarius

Lord of Defeat

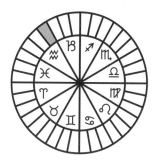

Like the Empress, Venus is a lover, not a fighter. Unfortunately, that's not necessarily a good fit for Aquarius, who loves social groups and causes just as much as people—and he's willing to fight for them.

That's the Aquarius we meet in the Five of Swords. He's a visionary crusader, and a firm believer in struggle and insurrection. Aquarius doesn't hesitate to pick up a sword of righteousness and fight for its own idea of justice. After all, Aquarius is ruled by Uranus, the planet of revolution and rebellion.

In the process of fighting for its favorite cause, Aquarius can sometimes forget—or conveniently ignore—the humanity of its opposition. Unlike Venus, this sign has a tendency to love humanity as a whole, but its easily annoyed by individual representatives of the group.

Like the Empress, Venus wants all of her children to get along. When she steps in to help manage starry-eyed Aquarius, her first order of business is to put an end to the squabbling and restore a sense of order and control.

The Golden Dawn designers of this card called Venus in Aquarius the "Lord of Defeat," because it depicts the aftermath of a skirmish, in which two of those on the losing side are walking away, dejected and humiliated by their defeat. Even the victor, collecting his spoils, realizes that his success wasn't necessarily a clean win. He's left to pick up the pieces and rebuild the utopia he wanted in the first place. Happily, the benefic Venus will be there to give him a hand.

Qabalistically, the Five of Swords depicts Geburah, the fifth sphere of strength, power, and severity. It corresponds to Mars, the planet of war. It's positioned in Yetzirah, the airy plane of thought. Perhaps the victor in the card is teaching his opponents a much-needed lesson about choosing one's battles.

In a tarot reading, the Five of Swords often symbolizes poor sportsmanship. It depicts the thrill of victory and the agony of defeat—and the disparity between winners and losers.

The first decan of Aquarius usually falls between January 20 and 29, when the Sun is between 0 and 10 degrees Aquarius.

Six of Swords: Mercury in Aquarius
Lord of Earned Success

We don't normally think of quick trips to be life-changing—but when they take us across the River Styx, guided by a specterlike Mercury, they can be the start of a whole new existence.

Mercury was the god of short journeys. He was also a psychopomp—an escort and a conductor of souls. The spirits of the dead would board his ferry, and he would shepherd them across the river into the Underworld.

Mercury himself could come and go as he pleased: he was one of the few gods who could enter and leave Hades at will.

Aquarius is the futuristic sign of social groups and causes. When Mercury steps in as ruler of the second decan of Aquarius, he maintains the broad perspective of the sign. Like the Star, the card that corresponds to the sign, Mercury understands long-term visions and goals. And like the Uranian Fool, Aquarius' ruling planet, Mercury is unafraid of death and rebirth.

The Golden Dawn designers of this card called Mercury in Aquarius the "Lord of Earned Success"—perhaps because it illustrates the final reward that awaits all of us at the end of our days.

Qabalistically, the Six of Swords depicts Tipareth, the sixth sphere of beauty. It corresponds to the Sun, the symbol of light and recognition. It's positioned in Yetzirah, the airy plane of thought. If the souls in Mercury's boat are those of the dead, their transition is a peaceful one.

In a tarot reading, the Six of Swords often represents travel, particularly on or over water. It symbolizes short, life-changing journeys, boundary crossing, and divine guidance from one phase of life to the next.

The second decan of Aquarius usually falls between January 30 and February 8, when the Sun is between 20 and 30 degrees Aquarius.

Seven of Swords: Moon in Aquarius
Lord of Unstable Effort

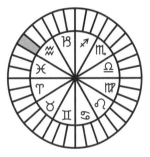

Shielded in shadows and obscurity, the Moon slips into Aquarius under the cover of night.

We normally see the Moon as a glowing High Priestess; here, in the third decan of Aquarius, she shows us her dark side, and her presence stirs primal fears of mystery and deception.

Aquarius, the sign of social groups and causes, isn't generally prone to reflection. The sign prefers starlight to moonlight—and its ruling planet, Uranus, often wants to mount rebellions and insurrections simply for the sake of revolution. The Seven of Swords depicts one of its agents of change: a spy, a thief in the night, an infiltrator in an enemy camp.

That thief could be an unwelcome opponent, collecting weapons to weaken, intimidate, or humiliate his opposition. He could be the rightful owner of the swords, reclaiming property that was unjustly taken from his own army of fighters. He might even be a commander, testing the readiness of his own troops.

In either case, the Seven of Swords illustrates the dark side of the Moon, and its corresponding landscape of loss and confusion.

The Golden Dawn designers of this card called the Moon in Aquarius the "Lord of Unstable Effort," because it illustrates the shifting world of shadows and gloom. The card could portray the death of a dream—or the difficult process of establishing a new reality.

Qabalistically, the Seven of Swords depicts Netzach, the seventh sphere of victory. It corresponds to Venus, the planet of love and affection. It's positioned in Yetzirah, the airy plane of thought. In that sense, the Seven of Swords might depict the brave warrior who dares to face his darkest fears for the sake of those whom he loves.

In a tarot reading, the Seven of Swords often represents an untrustworthy associate, a former friend bent on revenge, or the surreptitious recovery of stolen property.

The third decan of Aquarius usually falls between February 9 and 18, when the Sun is between 20 and 30 degrees Aquarius.

The Three Decans of Pisces
MUTABLE WATER: THE EIGHT, NINE, AND TEN OF CUPS

◆　◆　◆

We'll conclude our tour of the Minor Arcana with the three cards that correspond to the three decans of Pisces: the Eight, Nine, and Ten of Cups.

Because it's a water sign, the cards come from the watery suit of Cups. And since it's a mutable sign, illustrating conclusions and the corresponding transition to new beginnings, the cards come from the end of the suit.

As we study the cards, and the characters in the cards, remember that they'll all share the same attributes of the sign.

- **Sign:** Pisces, the twelfth sign of the zodiac, is the sign of secrets and hidden places. All three cards in Pisces depict people dealing with emotional issues.
- **Mode/Quality:** Pisces is a mutable sign, transitioning the move from the last month of winter to the first month of spring. The corresponding cards from the end of the suit depict a versatile, flexible energy.
- **Element:** Pisces is water sign, so it corresponds to the watery suit of Cups. Both the element and the suit are emotional, changeable, subtle, intuitive, and flowing.
- **Duality:** Water signs are feminine. They are receptive, reactive, magnetic, responsive, and patient, and their energy flows in a circular pattern.
- **Corresponding Majors:** Pisces is associated with the Moon, while its ruler, Neptune, is associated with the Hanged Man.

EIGHT OF CUPS

Eight of Cups: Saturn in Pisces
Lord of Abandoned Success

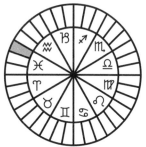

Like a cosmic disciplinarian, Saturn has certain expectations. He demands order and control wherever he travels—and when Saturn rules a decan, he puts a quick end to poorly planned ideas and flawed executions.

In this case, the loose organization of the Eight of Cups wasn't compelling enough to win Saturn's approval—but Saturn didn't have to work too hard to convince the young man in the card to walk away, either. Like a young Father Time—one of Saturn's secret identities—the man in the Eight of Cups has turned his back on a precarious arrangement of silver chalices.

That's because Pisces is a mutable sign, easily swayed, and readily persuaded to change course. It's reactive, not proactive. It's a watery sign, keyed to the fluid world of moods and emotions. While it can go with the flow, it's also easily diverted. It takes the shape of its container.

Pisces' ruling planet is Neptune, which corresponds to the Hanged Man. Other dreams and visions will rise to take the place of this one.

The Golden Dawn designers of this card called Saturn in Pisces the "Lord of Abandoned Success," because it illustrates the act of deserting a dream.

Qabalistically, the Eight of Cups depicts Hod, the eighth sphere of splendor and glory. It corresponds to Mercury, the planet of speed and communication. It's positioned in Briah, the watery world of fertility and creation. The young man in the card is off to find a message that will satisfy him emotionally.

In a tarot reading, the Eight of Cups often represents regret, abandonment, or a spiritual quest for completion and fulfillment.

The first decan of Pisces usually falls between February 19 and 28, when the Sun is between 0 and 10 degrees Pisces.

NINE OF CUPS

Nine of Cups: Jupiter in Pisces
Lord of Material Happiness

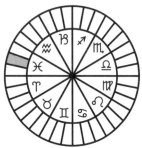

When Jupiter steps into the second decan of Pisces, he lives up to his reputation as the Greater Benefic and god of good fortune. He sets a bountiful table and invites everyone to have a seat.

The young High Priestess in the card is herself the picture of contentment as she prepares to welcome friends for an evening of socializing. Together, they'll raise their glasses to the blessings of health, wealth, and success—all the gifts they're sure to receive when Jupiter spins the wheel of fortune.

They'll share their joys and celebrations—and even if their reminiscences turn to less prosperous times, the Cups will serve as a barrier against sadness, and their contents will offer a buffer against the aches and pains of disappointment.

It's interesting to note that in classical astrology, Jupiter wasn't just the ruler of Sagittarius, as it is now. Jupiter also ruled Pisces, which means that Jupiter is in its dignity here. He's not just visiting: he's come home, to his own sign and its own house. That makes Jupiter's connection to the Nine of Cups even stronger. Study the illustration, and you'll see that Jupiter does lend a certain appeal to the Piscean principles of wine, women, and song.

Even so, Pisces people are usually cautioned about the risk of alcohol and drug abuse as an escape route from painful realities. That's augmented by the Nine of Cups' connection to the Moon, the Major Arcana card that corresponds to Pisces. The Moon rules the night, where dark shadows take on a life of their own and truth can be obscured. The Nine of Cups' relationship to Neptune is also cause for reflection. Neptune is the modern ruler of Pisces and corresponds to the Hanged Man, who lives in a state of altered consciousness.

The Golden Dawn designers of this card called Jupiter in Pisces the "Lord of Material Happiness," because Jupiter brings plenty and prosperity to everything it touches.

Qabalistically, the Nine of Cups depicts Yesod, the ninth sphere of foundation. It corresponds to the Moon, the orb of reflection. It's positioned in Briah, the watery world of fertility and creation. The young woman in the card recognizes that people need to bond together socially in order to create a happy life together.

In a tarot reading, the Nine of Cups typically represents happiness and celebration, large gatherings, and social functions hosted by a warm and welcoming organizer.

The second decan of Pisces usually falls between March 1 and 10, when the Sun is between 10 and 20 degrees Pisces.

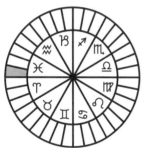

Ten of Cups: Mars in Pisces
Lord of Perfected Success

Mars, the planet of energy and aggression, goes after everything it wants. In the Ten of Cups, we see that Mars' passionate pursuits apply to family life, too.

Here, in a twilight tableau, a model family gathers under a crescent Moon of emotional satisfaction and contentment. They seem happy: the mother and father embrace each other and keep both their children close at hand.

The four family members don't simply represent a close-knit bond among kindred spirits, however. They also represent earth, air, fire, and water—symbols of physical, intellectual, spiritual, and emotional existence. Together, as a family unit, they symbolize individual and personal wholeness. In that sense, they resemble the four members of each royal family in the Court Cards.

Obviously, the family on the card is idealized. Pisces has a tendency to deny reality—and in the twelfth house of secrets and mystery, Pisces won't just deny his unhappy memories. He'll repress them, forget them, and lock them away like monsters in a closet.

The Minor Arcana cards of Pisces are connected to the Moon and the Hanged Man. Both contribute to the dreamlike nature of the card, as memories, dreams, and reflections lend an air of unreality to the image.

The card's placement on the horizon line of a horoscope, however, also seems to suggest that personal integration and family happiness is the birthright of every child. The card's position in the last decan of the horoscope wheel: a happy home life, surrounded by loved ones, is the ultimate proof of a life well lived.

Qabalistically, the Ten of Cups depicts Malkuth, the tenth sphere of our earthly reality. It's positioned in Briah, the watery world of fertility and creation. The card serves as a reminder that for most of us, there truly is no place like home.

In traditional tarot readings, the Ten of Cups often represents a happy marriage, beautiful children, and a comfortable home and family life.

The Golden Dawn designers of this card called Mars in Pisces the "Lord of Perfected Success," because Mars' determined energy has the power to turn dreams into reality.

The third and final decan of Pisces usually falls between March 11 and 20, when the Sun is between 20 and 30 degrees Pisces.

Astrology in Action: **The Past, Present, and Future Decan Spread**

A basic past, present, and future spread is familiar to most tarot readers. The cards take on a whole new layer of significance, however, when you associate them with astrological correspondences.

In this case, the astrological correspondences are based on both the client's birth date and the date he posed the question—much like a traditional horary reading, in which an astrologer bases his answer on the exact time that a question was asked.

Sample Reading: The Security Specialist

John specializes in security technology, and he's negotiating for a contract at a major university. How can he get the job?

Past: First, let's explore the experience that John brings to the question by looking at the cards that correspond to his birthday, December 20. (All of the correspondences are listed on page 220.)

John has a Sagittarius Sun, which corresponds to the Temperance card. Like most Sagittarians, he has a fiery interest in philosophical discussion and debate. He's honest, optimistic, and open-minded. He's good-natured and generous, and he likes to travel, because he has a burning desire to meet new people and see new places. Like the alchemist in the *Wizards Tarot* card, he's not afraid to mix things up.

Further, John was born during the last 10 days of Sagittarius, when the Sun was between 20 and 30 degrees of the sign. The Minor Arcana card assigned to that decan is the Ten of Wands, which symbolizes the oppression of Saturn in Sagittarius. While John might be a born adventurer, Saturn's influence also means that his dreams and visions have limits, as he's forced to reconcile them with the weight and responsibilities of the real world.

That theme comes up again with the Court Card assigned to his birth date, the Queen of Pentacles. As we learned previously, she's actually the guardian of the next sign, Capricorn. She is stationed here because it's her responsibility to reach back on the zodiac's Wheel of the Year and pull the tail end of Sagittarius forward into her sign. Capricorn is earthy and worldly, concerned with the practicalities of life and the importance of career and social status.

All told, John brings an interesting blend of skills and talents to any prospective client. He's a philosophical thinker, but he's grounded in the earthly realities of physical existence. It's no coincidence that he wants to use his gifts and talents to enhance the safety and security of an institute of higher education.

Present: Now let's look at the current state of John's contract negotiations by borrowing a technique from horary astrology. We'll interpret his question based on the date he asked it—January 11.

The Major, Minor, and Court cards that correspond to January 11

On that date, the Sun was in Capricorn, which corresponds to the Devil card. That fits perfectly. John isn't asking about a deeply spiritual or philosophical question. Instead, he's hoping to advance his career and social status. He's bedeviled by issues of money, power, and control.

January 11 falls in the third decan of Capricorn, corresponding to the Four of Pentacles. The Four of Pentacles, in turn, corresponds to the Sun in Capricorn. It tells us that those who are in positions of power are jealously guarding their domains; those with their hands on the purse strings are holding on to every penny they can.

The Court Card for this time period is the King of Swords. Like the Queen of Pentacles in the previous sample reading, he's also the guardian of the next sign—in this case, Aquarius—and he has reached back, too, to move the issue forward. That's actually a good sign. The answer John wants isn't in limbo; there's a steady push toward progress and decision-making.

The influence of future-oriented Aquarius further suggests that the decision makers are focusing on the long-term ramifications of their decision. The King of Swords also hints at the legalities involved. There may be a written contract in the works.

Future: Finally, let's address the specifics of John's question. How can he get the job? What actions should he take next? For the answer, we'll pull a single card at random from the deck.

A response comes in the form of the Magician—the powerful Major Arcana card that corresponds to Mercury, the god of orators and salesmen. The answer seems clear: John needs to keep talking! He needs to keep going with his sales pitch. He's already had several meetings and exchanges with the decision makers, but the deal is not yet closed. He should remember that he's performing a magic act before an audience that wants to be amazed. He needs to put on a show and astound them with the tools and tricks of his trade—his own credentials, experience, and initiative—and convince them to offer him the position.

◆　◆　◆

Eight

◆

The Court Cards

The Court Cards might be some of the most misunderstood cards in the tarot deck—but a basic understanding of the astrology that underlies their foundation can help you bring the characters to life.

The Court Cards all have elemental associations, just like the rest of the cards in the Minor Arcana. The four pages represent the four elements in their purest form, while the knights, queens, and kings represent a blend of the elements. Those blended elements, in turn, describe the astrological characteristics of the cards.

Pages, the students and messengers of the tarot, are the physical personifications of fire, earth, air, and water, untempered by other elemental influences.

Knights, the adventurers and rescuers of the deck, are fiery, spirited individuals. Each one combines the element of fire with the element of his own suit. The Knight of Cups, for example, is a blend of the energetic nature of fire with the emotional nature of water. Knights are also mutable: each one moves easily through the transitional signs of Gemini, Virgo, Sagittarius, and Pisces.

Queens, the nurturers and guardians of their realms, are emotional, receptive, and watery. They combine the element of water with the element of their respective suits. Queens are also cardinal: each one ushers in one of the four seasons and rules a corresponding cardinal sign: Aries, Cancer, Libra, or Capricorn.

Kings, the administrators and defenders of each kingdom, are intellectual, objective, and airy. They combine the element of air with the element of their suits. Kings are also fixed. They occupy the height of power, at the height of each season, during the months associated with Taurus, Leo, Scorpio, and Aquarius.

The elemental associations are especially easy to see in the *Wizards Tarot*, because the Court Cards all feature elemental creatures. Look closely, and you'll notice that the four royal families are humanized versions of fiery salamanders, earthy gnomes, airy sylphs, and watery undines.

Cosmic Connection: THE RULERS OF HEAVEN

The Golden Dawn's method of assigning the Court Cards is idiosyncratic. The Knights rule the mutable signs, the Queens rule the cardinal signs, and the Kings rule the fixed signs. What's left for the Pages?

According to the designers of the deck, the Pages might be the most privileged of all. Not only do they embody the elements of fire, earth, air, and water, but they also serve as the earthly "thrones"—the seat of power for the four Aces.

Cosmic Connection: COURT CARDS AND THE WHEEL OF THE YEAR

The Court Cards are stationed around the Wheel of the Year, spinning it forward and helping to ensure that one sign flows into the next.

This is a technical note, but if you follow strict Golden Dawn timing—which is the basis for this book—the dates for the Court Cards' control don't strictly adhere to the signs. The Queen of Wands, for example, doesn't rule all 30 degrees of Aries. Instead, she reigns over the first 20 degrees of Aries, along with the last 10 degrees of Pisces.

The knights, queens, and kings all follow the same pattern. Each one controls the first 20 degrees of his or her sign, along with the last 10 degrees of the sign that came before.

The process is a little like crochet: each member of the tarot court reaches back 10 degrees to draw one sign forward into the next.

PAGE OF WANDS

Page of Wands
The Personification of Fire

The Page of Wands is the personification of fire. She embodies the burning drives and desires of all three fire signs—Aries, Leo, and Sagittarius—along with their enthusiasm for spiritual development and understanding.

The Page of Wands is holy and pure, and she serves as a vessel of spiritual creation. Like Vesta, the goddess of hearth and home, generations of spiritual women can trace her lineage to her and through her. She connects the suit of Wands to the world of spirit and creativity, and she's the keeper of the flame we first saw in the Ace of Wands.

During the Renaissance, pages were the youngest members of the royal court. They would frequently serve as messengers; it was their job to carry news from one person to another. In addition, because they were young, pages were students, learning their future roles through apprenticeships.

Like her fellow pupils, the Page of Wands is youthful, with childlike enthusiasm and an unbounded capacity to learn. She burns with a passion for discovery. She's also impetuous: she can lie low, glowing like an ember for hours—but once you spark her imagination, she'll burst into flame. Add fuel to the fire, and she'll erupt into a conflagration that's hard to contain and almost impossible to extinguish.

Page of Pentacles
The Personification of Earth

The sturdy Page of Pentacles is the personification of earth. She embodies the steady, dependable energy of all three earth signs—Taurus, Virgo, and Capricorn—and her grounded energy connects the suit of Pentacles to the world of matter and physical existence.

Like all pages, the Page of Pentacles is young—but this page exemplifies the very nature of earth itself. She's heavy and low to the ground. She's solid, stable, and secure. She is steady and resolved, forthright and self-assured. She's patient and persevering, and she's determined to achieve a solid foundation for her understanding of the physical world. She moves slowly, but she moves with undeniable sureness and force.

Despite her high level of skill, however, she's usually extremely careful—even cautious—and she doesn't take many risks. She is consistent and conscientious, diligent and deliberative.

She is also a nurturing figure, like a young Mother Earth. At the moment, she's untouched, like the untilled soil, but eventually she'll serve as a vessel for physical creation. She holds the Ace of Pentacles for safekeeping; like Ceres, the goddess of earth's bounty, it's her destiny to safeguard and protect the physical world.

Page of Swords
The Personification of Air

The bright Page of Swords is the personification of air. She illustrates the highest qualities of the three air signs: Gemini, Libra, and Aquarius. Like a bird in flight, she embodies the fast-moving energy that connects the suit of Swords to the higher realms of intellect and communication.

The Page of Swords is intelligent and inquisitive, clear-headed and far-sighted. She's observant and alert: she has a bird's-eye view, and nothing can escape her eagle eye. She's versatile: she can flit readily from subject to subject. She moves at the speed of sound, and she can respond to even the slightest whisper.

She's also extremely communicative. Her voice—as well as her thoughts—carry on the wind. She can be a gentle breeze or a stormy gale. She might be nearly invisible, but her presence is unmistakable.

Like all pages, the Page of Swords is youthful, with childlike enthusiasm and an unbounded capacity to learn. She's a reader, a writer, and a talker. She's thoughtful and idealistic, and she's naturally drawn to scholars, scientists, and philosophers.

She contains multitudes of possibility, and it's her destiny to give birth to countless generations of students, teachers, and ideas. Like Pallas Athene, the goddess of wisdom, she carries a sword of logic and reason. It's the same sword that's pictured in the Ace of Swords, and she'll ensure that it always remains an instrument of truth and justice.

Page of Cups
The Personification of Water

The Page of Cups is the personification of water. She embodies the fluid undercurrents that connect the suit of Cups to the world of emotion, and she unites the three water signs of Cancer, Scorpio, and Pisces.

Like water itself, the Page of Cups is graceful—but she can also be unpredictable. She can be effervescent or still, choppy or smooth. She's adaptable: she readily takes the form of her container, and rises to the level of the emotions around her.

The Page of Cups She speaks the language of the sea: she communicates through the misty realm of dreams and watery psychic impressions. Her messages can be subtle, or they can roar like the pounding surf. You can find her in rivers and streams, lakes and ponds, or oceans and underground wells. She wades along the shoreline of emotions, and splashes in the liquid pool of the collective unconscious.

Like all pages, the Page of Cups is youthful, with childlike enthusiasm and boundless capacity to learn. She's extremely sensitive. She's gentle and kind, dreamy and imaginative. She's a poet, an artist, and a dreamer—and she's still innocent enough to be optimistic.

She holds the Ace of Cups, which is sacred to Juno, the goddess of marriage and childbirth. In time, the Page of Cups will drink from the cup herself, and taste the bittersweet nectar of wisdom and experience.

Aries and the Queen of Wands

The Leadership And Initiative of Cardinal Fire

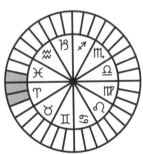

The four queens are all examples of ideal women. Each one combines the element of water with the corresponding element of her own suit. In that respect, the Queen of Wands personifies the steamy combination of water with the fire, energy, passion, and heat of the Wands cards. She's seductive, simmering, and surprisingly strong.

Queens, of course, are rulers—but traditionally, their rulership is based on the feminine principles of safeguarding and nurturing their realms. Like all of the tarot's queens, the Queen of Wands is a mature woman, gracious and wise in the ways of the world.

As an elemental creature, she embodies all the fire and passion of the Wands. She has energy to burn. She's mesmerizing, like a glowing campfire. She is sinewy and strong, willful and dynamic, confident and self-assured. Like fire itself, she's spontaneous and hard to contain.

The Queen of Wands also represents the cardinal fire sign of Aries. She's a natural leader who initiates change. She's impulsive, impatient, and impetuous. She's brave, bold, and downright brazen.

Like her Major-Arcana counterpart, the Emperor, she has a warrior's spirit. She's courageous and competitive, driven and direct. She moves quickly. In fact, she often embodies many of the attributes we think of as masculine. She takes direct, aggressive action, and she asserts herself in sudden energetic bursts.

The Queen of Wands rules the third decan of Pisces and the first and second decans of Aries. In the natural horoscope, her primary domain is the first house of self-identity and self-expression.

Taurus and the King of Pentacles
The Stability of Fixed Earth

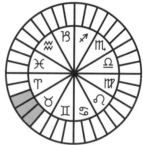

Like all of the kings in the tarot deck, the King of Pentacles is a seasoned, experienced man. He has successfully completed the mission he undertook as the former Knight of Pentacles. He was rewarded with the keys to the kingdom, and he now rules the entire realm—as well as its armies, which defend and conquer in the name of the throne.

Elementally, the four kings of the tarot are airy intellectuals. They simply combine the element of air with the corresponding element of their own suit. In that regard, the King of Pentacles embodies the heady combination of air with earth.

The Kings of Pentacles also represents the fixed earth sign of Taurus, which makes him a steady, reliable monarch. He's stable and grounded, determined and dependable, practical and realistic. He's honest and hard-working, He can be stubborn and slow-moving, but he's also patient and persevering. He's a man of substance, value, and worth. Like his Major-Arcana counterpart, the Hierophant, he values tradition, and his surroundings reflect his spiritual beliefs.

The King of Pentacles manages the affairs of his kingdom with mathematical, business-like precision. He has a flair for ingenious, practical solutions to complicated problems. It usually takes him a long time to get angry—but once he is roused, he can be fierce. He might be earthy and unrefined, but he's also loyal and honorable. His feet are firmly on the ground, and his body, mind, and soul are devoted to his cause.

The King of Pentacles rules the third decan of Aries and the first and second decans of Taurus. In the natural horoscope, his primary domain is the second house of values and personal belongings.

Gemini and the Knight of Swords
The Soaring Intellect of Mutable Air

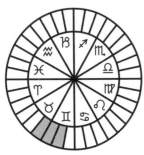

Knights—the adventurers and rescuers of the deck—are inherently fiery individuals. Each one combines the element of fire with the element of his own suit. In that regard, the Knight of Swords embodies the combustible combination of fire with air. He can literally ride like the wind.

The Knight of Swords is probably the one who best matches most people's conception of a knight. He is a skillful, brave warrior. His armor is always polished, and his horse is always ready to ride. Occasionally, he can be indecisive. Even more rarely, he can be deceitful. But the Knight of Swords didn't just memorize the code of chivalry—he helped write it.

He is truly a knight's knight. He's well suited for the battlefield of ideas. He's enthusiastic, energetic, and fearless. He's an explorer, and he soars through the stratosphere of ideas and imagination. He's fearless and adventurous: there's no sign of the ground beneath his feet.

The Knight of Wands also represents the mutable air sign of Gemini, which makes him versatile and quick thinking. He has lofty goals and aspirations, and he seeks them in the heady atmosphere of clouds and sky. He operates at a higher elevation than most other elementals. He's a migratory creature, never in one place for long, and always setting off on an expedition or an adventure. Like his Major-Arcana counterparts, the Lovers, he's interested in a wide range of people and experiences. He loves to exchange ideas, and he communicates with style and wit.

The Knight of Swords rules the third decan of Taurus and the first and second decans of Gemini. In a natural horoscope, his primary domain is the third house of neighborhood and communication.

Cancer and the Queen of Cups
The Maternal Devotion of Cardinal Water

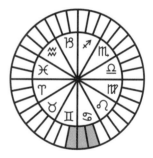

The Queen of Cups embodies the pure blend of water with the emotional depth of the Cups cards—giving her, in essence, a double dose of water qualities. She's usually pictured in the watery world of love and relationships, because she embodies the emotional energy of the suit of Cups.

The Queen of Cups also represents the cardinal water sign of Cancer, which makes her a natural homemaker and caretaker. She's nurturing, sensitive, loving, and caring.

Her maternal gifts also make her more powerful than many people realize: cardinal signs are decisive leaders. She knows, better than most, that the hand that rocks the cradle rules the world.

Like her Major Arcana counterpart, the Charioteer, she navigates through a realm of dangerous currents and tides, and she usually manages to steer clear of rocky reefs and shorelines. She effortlessly balances marriage and family life.

The Queen of Cups is creative and artistic—she can even be remarkably intuitive. At times, she's prone to psychic prophecies and mystical visions, inspired by her ruling planet, the Moon.

Like the Moon, she does have a dark side. Those who are caught in her wake can sometimes find themselves drowning in the eddies of her emotions. At times, she can be overprotective, and even smothering.

The Queen of Cups rules the third decan of Gemini and the first and second decans of Cancer. In a natural horoscope, her primary domain is the fourth house of home and family life.

Leo and the King of Wands
The Passion of Fixed Fire

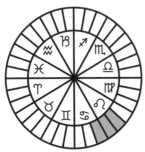

The King of Wands, the ruler of fire, embodies the spirit and passion of Leo—the sign of fixed fire. He's a combustible mix of the element of fire, combined with the airy intellectualism of the kings.

He's a confident, courageous monarch. Like his Major-Arcana counterpart, the lionesque card of Strength, he is forceful and brave—and like Leo's ruling planet, the Sun, he's a source of light and inspiration. He's not afraid to stand at attention, or to be the center of attention, either.

All the tarot's kings are leaders, but the King of Wands may be the most charismatic of the four. Admirers gravitate to him; his leadership style is inspiring, and he gives voice to his followers' deepest, most heartfelt desires. In the process, he imbues them with his own sense of pride and self-awareness.

As a result, the King of Wands can be egotistical and egocentric, dramatic, and occasionally dictatorial. He's forceful and aggressive, and he can even be explosive. In fact, the King of Wands won't hesitate to employ a scorched earth policy if he needs to make a point. He understands the cleansing, purifying power of fire, along with the renewal that will inevitably follow.

He can also be playful. The King of Wands rules the third decan of Cancer the first and second decans of Leo, and in a natural horoscope, his primary domain is the fifth house of recreation and procreation. Like the Sun, he can also be a source of life and creativity, and he can father countless generations of descendants.

Virgo and the Knight of Pentacles
The Slow But Steady Progress of Mutable Earth

The Knight of Pentacles doesn't fit most people's preconceptions of a knight. He doesn't move very fast, he's not especially flirtatious, and when the rest of the knights ride off on adventures, he usually stays behind to take care of the kingdom's routine border patrols.

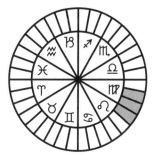

That's because the Knight of Pentacles embodies the rather disparate combination of fire with earth. Soil doesn't burn; in fact, dirt and sand will actually extinguish most small blazes. He's also an elemental creature of earth, and earth doesn't move on its own. It usually takes an earthquake or an avalanche for such a grounded being to overcome the forces of gravity and inertia that tie him to his favorite plot of land. While all knights are explorers, the Knight of Pentacles surveys the world at a slower pace than most.

At the same time, however, the Knight of Pentacles is far more attuned to physical needs and desires than the rest of his colleagues. He wants to master the material world. Once the Knight of Pentacles sets out on a mission, he'll finish it, no matter how long it takes.

In fact, the Knight of Pentacles is remarkably patient and calm, discerning and analytical. His mission in life seems to be taking care of the ordinary details and everyday responsibilities that the other knights overlook.

The Knight of Pentacles represents the mutable earth sign of Virgo. Like his Major-Arcana counterpart, the Hermit, he is conscientious and conservative, driven but cautious, and a bit of a perfectionist.

The Knight of Pentacles rules the third decan of Leo and the first and second decans of Virgo. In a natural horoscope, his primary domain is the sixth house of health, work, and service to others.

Libra and the Queen of Swords
The Decisiveness of Cardinal Air

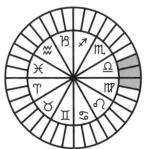

What do you get when you mix the emotional world of water with the intellectual realm of air? Meet the Queen of Swords, who uses both her head and her heart to make balanced decisions.

Each one of the tarot's queens combines the element of water with the corresponding element of her own suit. As a result, the Queen of Swords embodies a unique blend of logic and reason with understanding and feeling.

The Queen of Swords, as a ruler of the intellect, is a critical thinker. She's a clever conversationalist with a keen intelligence—and an occasionally sharp tongue. She knows that words have precise meanings, and she understands subtext, too. She can cut through extraneous information, and get right to the point of any discussion or debate.

She also knows that words are often a poor representative of deep-seated feelings and emotions, so she can read between the lines of any argument or dispute. She's clear headed and compassionate; the Queen of Swords is firm but fair.

In fact, according to tarot tradition, the Queen of Swords is well acquainted with sorrow and heartbreak. She is usually believed to be a widow or a divorcée, who has learned from her loss and developed an uncanny ability to empathize and draw accurate conclusions about other people and situations.

The Queen of Swords represents the cardinal air sign of Libra. She's a natural-born leader, willing and able to hear both sides of any story. She can play the role of peacemaker, mediator, or judge. Like her Major-Arcana counterpart, the goddess of Justice, she makes clear and fair decisions based on the facts—and like Libra's ruling planet, Venus, she's attuned and attracted to other people.

The Queen of Swords rules the third decan of Virgo and the first and second decans of Libra. In a natural horoscope, her primary domain is the seventh house of partners and relationships.

Scorpio and the King of Cups
The Emotional Depth of Fixed Water

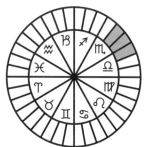

The King of Cups is the ruler of an underwater world, where he can submerge himself in the deepest mysteries of life.

Elementally, the four kings of the tarot are airy intellectuals. They simply combine the element of air with the corresponding element of their own suit. In that regard, the King of Cups embodies the vaporous combination of intellectual air with the deep, rolling waters of emotion.

The King of Cups is a husband and father—but the card also represents the fixed water sign of Scorpio, which makes him an intense and passionate ruler. He's perceptive and analytical. He's smart and sensual, and he craves a deep connection with an intellectual equal. He's comfortable in the darkest depths of emotion, and he can even be obsessive.

His corresponding Major-Arcana card is the Death card—and its ruling planet is Pluto, the god of the Underworld. All told, the King of Cups understands the ebb and flow of time, and the cycles of transformation and rebirth.

In the Wizards Tarot, the King of Cups looks like King Neptune. His trident and three-pronged crown are evidence of his reign, and his white beard and white hair signify his wisdom and experience.

Oceans rise and fall at his command, and all the animals of surf and sea respond to his call. He can raise storms and hurricanes. He can stir whirlpools of grave confusion. He can also raise his trident above the surface, and call on the forces of air and fire to bear down upon the waves.

The King of Cups rules the third decan of Libra and the first and second decans of Scorpio. In a natural horoscope, his primary domain is the eighth house of sex, death, inheritance, and joint resources.

Sagittarius and the Knight of Wands
The Unstoppable Explorer of Mutable Fire

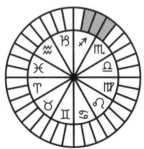

Like fire itself, the Knight of Wands can be spellbinding. Without a safe place to burn, however, he can also rage out of control, and he could become unstable, violent, and destructive.

Knights—the adventurers and rescuers of the deck—are inherently fiery individuals. Each one combines the element of fire with the element of his own suit. The Knight of Wands, however, is the only court card that embodies the passionate combination of fire with fire.

He's an explorer, with wide ranging interests and a craving for philosophical and spiritual conquest. He's fascinated by foreign people and ideas, and he'll go to great lengths to see the world, meet the multitudes, and experience all that life has to offer. Like his Major-Arcana counterpart, the alchemical angel of Temperance, he's willing to experiment, mix things up, and adapt along the way. He's impulsive, restless, and always on the move.

The Knight of Wands also represents the mutable fire sign of Sagittarius, which makes him outgoing and audacious. He's flexible and carefree. He'll try anything once—and maybe twice, for good measure.

His Sagittarian nature graces him with good fortune. As a result, he tends to think of himself as invincible, which leads to risky, dangerous behavior. Even so, he'd be the first to tell you that he's willing to go out in a blaze of glory.

The Knight of Wands rules the third decan of Scorpio and the first and second decans of Sagittarius. In the natural horoscope, his primary domain is the ninth house of long-distance travel, philosophy, and higher education.

Capricorn and the Queen of Pentacles
Leadership By Example: Cardinal Earth

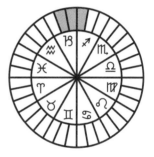

The Queen of Pentacles embodies the fertile combination of water with the earthy resources of the Pentacles cards. She's a patient and intractable woman. She has no hurried sense of time or pressure to conform. She has planted herself firmly in a granite garden, and that's where she'll bloom.

She represents the cardinal earth sign of Capricorn, which makes her a savvy businesswoman who can cultivate a wide range of resources for her people. She's a leader and a decision-maker. She's earthy and authoritative, disciplined and cautious. She believes in the values and structures of tradition.

Being patient and enduring also gives her time to think. Over the years, she's developed a dry sense of humor that catches many people by surprise. Like most Capricorns, she's an old soul who grows younger and more lighthearted with time.

The Queen of Pentacles is the guardian of earth, and she understands the importance of safeguarding and protecting the physical world for future generations. Even so, she's not a believer in unproven theories or rash environmentalism. She knows that Earth has resources most people can't imagine, and that the planet will outlive its population.

Like her Major Arcana counterpart, the devilish Dark Lord, she also understands the pleasures of the flesh—and the temptations of earthly existence. She's aware of her status and position. She leads by firm and resolute example, holding fast to her values and beliefs.

The Queen of Pentacles rules the third decan of Sagittarius and the first and second decans of Capricorn. In a natural horoscope, her primary domain is the tenth house of career and social status.

Aquarius and the King of Swords
The Intellectual Determination of Fixed Air

The King of Swords, the ruler of air, is a powerful, authoritative commander, who makes decisions based on solid logic and intellectual prowess.

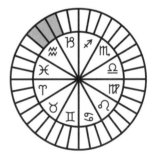

Elementally, the four kings of the tarot are airy intellectuals. They simply combine the element of air with the corresponding element of their own suit. In that regard, the King of Swords embodies the rarified combination of air with air.

Clearly, he's assertive and alert. He can even be aggressive. He guards his kingdom with passion and force, and he's not afraid to make arbitrary decisions. He's willing and able to defend his realm and dispense justice in accordance with his rule. He's forward thinking, determined, and idealistic. In other words, the King of Swords can be a firm friend—or a vengeful enemy.

The King of Swords also represents the fixed air sign of Aquarius, which makes him a forward-thinking, socially conscious monarch. Like his Major-Arcana counterpart, the Star, he's ethereal: from his position high in the sky, he can see the big picture. And like Aquarius' ruling planet, Uranus, he can overturn old ways of thinking and establish new institutions that better serve the needs of his kingdom.

The King of Swords rules the third decan of Capricorn and the first and second decans of Aquarius. In a natural horoscope, his primary domain is the eleventh house of social groups and causes.

KNIGHT OF CUPS

Pisces and the Knight of Cups

The Flowing Emotion of Mutable Water

The Knight of Cups, like all of the Court Cards in his suit, is watery and emotional. He is gallant, graceful, and generous. He is imaginative—even visionary. More than anything, he is a romantic idealist who believes that beauty is truth, and truth is beauty.

Knights—the adventurers and rescuers of the deck—are inherently fiery individuals. Each one combines the element of fire with the element of his own suit. In that regard, the Knight of Cups embodies the steamy combination of fire with water.

The Knight of Wands also represents the mutable water sign of Pisces, which makes him charming, sweet, beguiling, and sensitive. He's chivalrous, but he's also boyish, fickle, and forgetful.

Like his Major-Arcana counterpart, the Moon, the Knight of Cups sees the world through a misty glow, and he reflects the fondest wishes, hopes, and dreams of those around him.

The Knight of Cups is a romantic soul. He's a sensitive idealist, a dreamer, and an artist. He's intuitive, and he's not afraid to dive deep into the world of emotion. He'd be quite a catch for any woman—but undines, like fish, can be elusive.

The Knight of Cups rules the third decan of Aquarius and the first and second decans of Pisces. In a natural horoscope, his primary domain is the twelfth house of mysticism and hidden secrets.

Summary: The Court Cards

Court Cards and the Elements

The four elements blend together in the Court Cards. Look through this chart, and you'll see how the various combinations help define the characteristics of the four royal families.

	Wands Fire/Spirit	Cups Water/Emotion	Swords Air/Intellect	Pentacles Earth/Physical
Pages Earth/ Physical	Fire In Physical Form	Water In Physical Form	Air In Physical Form	Earth In Physical Form
Knights Fire/Spirit	Fire and Fire Spiritual	Fire and Water Spiritual and Emotional	Fire and Air Spiritual and Intellectual	Fire and Earth Spiritual and Physical
Queens Water/ Emotion	Water and Fire Emotional and Spiritual	Water and Water Emotional	Water and Air Emotional and Intellectual	Water and Earth Emotional and Physical
Kings Air/ Intellect	Air and Fire Intellectual and Spiritual	Air and Water Intellectual and Emotional	Air and Air Intellectual	Air and Earth Intellectual and Physical

Court Cards and the Seasons

The kings, queens, and knights are distributed around the wheel based on their astrological associations. In the process, two patterns emerge.

1. First, the cards fall into a seasonal lineup, with a queen, a king, and a knight for each season.

2. Second, each season also has a Court Card from a cardinal, fixed, and mutable sign.

	Cardinal Signs	Fixed Signs	Mutable Signs
Spring	♈ Aries Queen of Wands	♉ Taurus King of Pentacles	♊ Gemini Knight of Swords
Summer	♋ Cancer Queen of Cups	♌ Leo King of Wands	♍ Virgo Knight of Pentacles
Fall	♎ Libra Queen of Swords	♏ Scorpio King of Cups	♐ Sagittarius Knight of Wands
Winter	♑ Capricorn Queen of Pentacles	♒ Aquarius King of Swords	♓ Pisces Knight of Cups

Summary: Tarot and the Wheel of the Year

This chart shows how all of the major and Minor Arcana cards fit on the Wheel of the Year.

Signs and Planetary Rulers	Major Arcana Cards	Court Cards	Decans	Approx. Dates	Minor Arcana Cards	Planetary Sub-Rulers
Aries Cardinal Fire *Mars*	IV. The Emperor *XVI. The Tower*	Queen of Wands	1st 0°–10°	Mar 21–30	Two of Wands (fire)	Mars
		Queen of Wands	2nd 10°–20°	Mar 31–Apr 10	Three of Wands (fire)	Sun
		King of Pentacles	3rd 20°–30°	Apr 11–20	Four of Wands (fire)	Venus
Taurus Fixed Earth *Venus*	V. The Hierophant *III. The Empress*	King of Pentacles	1st 0°–10°	Apr 21–30	Five of Pentacles (earth)	Mercury
		King of Pentacles	2nd 10°–20°	May 1–10	Six of Pentacles (earth)	Moon
		Knight of Swords	3rd 20°–30°	May 11–20	Seven of Pentacles (earth)	Saturn
Gemini Mutable Air *Mercury*	VI. The Lovers *I. The Magician*	Knight of Swords	1st 0°–10°	May 21–31	Eight of Swords (air)	Jupiter
		Knight of Swords	2nd 10°–20°	Jun 1–10	Nine of Swords (air)	Mars
		Queen of Cups	3rd 20°–30°	Jun 11–20	Ten of Swords (air)	Sun

		Queen of Cups	1st 0°–10°	Jun 21–Jul 1	Two of Cups (water)	Venus
Cancer Cardinal Water *The Moon*	VII. The Chariot *II. The High Priestess*	Queen of Cups	2nd 10°–20°	Jul 2–11	Three of Cups (water)	Mercury
		King of Wands	3rd 20°–30°	Jul 12–21	Four of Cups (water)	Moon
Leo Fixed Fire *The Sun*	VIII. Strength *XIX. The Sun*	King of Wands	1st 0°–10°	Jul 22–Aug 1	Five of Wands (fire)	Saturn
		King of Wands	2nd 10°–20°	Aug 2–11	Six of Wands (fire)	Jupiter
		Knight of Pentacles	3rd 20°–30°	Aug12–22	Seven of Wands (fire)	Mars
Virgo Mutable Earth *Mercury*	IX. The Hermit *I. The Magician*	Knight of Pentacles	1st 0°–10°	Aug 23–Sep 1	Eight of Pentacles (earth)	Sun
		Knight of Pentacles	2nd 10°–20°	Sep 2–11	Nine of Pentacles (earth)	Venus
		Queen of Swords	3rd 20°–30°	Sep 12–22	Ten of Pentacles (earth)	Mercury
Libra Cardinal Air *Venus*	XI. Justice *III. The Empress*	Queen of Swords	1st 0°–10°	Sep 23–Oct 2	Two of Swords (air)	Moon
		Queen of Swords	2nd 10°–20°	Oct 3–12	Three of Swords (air)	Saturn
		King of Cups	3rd 20°–30°	Oct13–22	Four of Swords (air)	Jupiter
Scorpio Fixed Water *Pluto*	XIII. Death *XX. Judgment*	King of Cups	1st 0°–10°	Oct 23–Nov 2	Five of Cups (water)	Mars
		King of Cups	2nd 10°–20°	Nov 3–12	Six of Cups (water)	Sun
		Knight of Wands	3rd 20°–30°	Nov 13–22	Seven of Cups (water)	Venus

		Knight of Wands	1st 0°–10°	Nov 23– Dec 2	Eight of Wands (fire)	Mercury
Sagit-tarius Mutable Fire *Jupiter*	XIV. Temperance *X. The Wheel of Fortune*	Knight of Wands	2nd 10°–20°	Dec 3–12	Nine of Wands (fire)	Moon
		Queen of Pentacles	3rd 20°–30°	Dec 13–21	Ten of Wands (fire)	Saturn
		Queen of Pentacles	1st 0°–10°	Dec 22–30	Two of Pentacles (earth)	Jupiter
Capricorn Cardinal Earth *Saturn*	XV. The Devil *XXI. The World*	Queen of Pentacles	2nd 10°–20°	Dec 31– Jan 9	Three of Pentacles (earth)	Mars
		King of Swords	3rd 20°–30°	Jan 10–19	Four of Pentacles (earth)	Sun
		King of Swords	1st 0°–10°	Jan 20–29	Five of Swords (air)	Venus
Aquarius Fixed Air *Uranus*	XVII. The Star *0. The Fool*	King of Swords	2nd 10°–20°	Jan 30– Feb 8	Six of Swords (air)	Mercury
		Knight of Cups	3rd 20°–30°	Feb 9–18	Seven of Swords (air)	Moon
		Knight of Cups	1st 0°–10°	Feb 19–28	Eight of Cups (water)	Saturn
Pisces Mutable Water *Neptune*	XVIII. The Moon *XII. The Hanged Man*	Knight of Cups	2nd 10°-20°	Mar 1–10	Nine of Cups (water)	Jupiter
		Queen of Wands	3rd 20°–30°	Mar 11–20	Ten of Cups (water)	Mars

The dates in this chart are approximate. Check an astrological calendar or an ephemeris of planetary movements if you're researching specific dates and times.

The Aces are not included in this chart, because they represent the elements. The Ace of Wands is fire, the Ace of Cups is water, the Ace of Swords is air, and the Ace of Pentacles is earth.

Part Three

◆

ASTROLOGY IN DEPTH

Now that we've covered the basics of tarot, the signs, and the planets, it's time to bring them all together in the houses of the horoscope.

Nine

◆

The Houses of the Horoscope

Horoscope Charts

The planets, signs, and houses all come together in a horoscope chart—a visual snapshot of the sky at a given point in time. Like a map of the cosmos, it's a convenient way to plot the positions of the planets in the signs, and the houses are a convenient way to divide the chart into manageable sections.

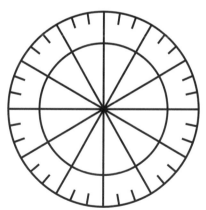

The word horoscope actually comes from the Greek word *hora*, or hour, plus *skopos*, watching. An astronomer could read a horoscope chart like an atlas of the solar system. Astrologers and tarot readers, however, can read a horoscope chart like a treasure map, filled with symbols that describe our journey through life.

Divisions of Space and Time

You've already seen horoscope charts in this book—but only in the context of tarot cards. Horoscope charts, in fact, were the basis for distributing the cards around the Wheel of the Year.

You probably noticed that every horoscope chart is a circle, designed to represent our view of the solar system from our position on earth. Every horoscope chart is also divided into twelve pie-shaped houses—one for each sign of the zodiac. The word zodiac, in fact, is Greek for "circle of animals."

Like any map, astrologers use the houses of a horoscope chart to pinpoint the positions of the planets as they move through the signs. One look will reveal the sign each planet is passing through, as well as the planets' relationship to one another.

While the houses might add a layer of complexity to astrological analysis, they also offer valuable context and background information of their own.

The sun is in a different sign of the zodiac every month—but it moves through the twelve houses of a horoscope chart every day. The rest of the planets do, too. That's because we're not just revolving around the sun, facing a new sign of the zodiac every month. The earth is also spinning on its axis, making a full rotation every twenty-four hours. In the process, every location on earth faces a different sign of the zodiac for about two hours at a stretch.

Don't be too confused by this concept: just picture the Sun moving across the sky over the course of the day, rising in one location and setting in another. If you were to plot the sun's movement on a map of the sky, you would simply mark its travel by charting its path along the way.

That's what happens on a horoscope chart, too: the sun, the moon, and the planets all move through the houses of the horoscope as the earth gently cycles through space. The houses of the horoscope simply illustrate our rotating view of the solar system as we spin in place.

The houses are a useful astrology tool because they offer a measure of context, perspective, and background information about the planets as they move through the signs.

True to their roots, the houses derive much of their significance from the zodiac signs.

The Natural Horoscope

In a natural horoscope—an idealized map of the sky—each house of a horoscope is ruled by one sign of the zodiac. And because every sign is ruled by a planet, every house of the horoscope has a planetary ruler, too. Aries, for example, rules the first house. The planet Mars rules Aries. Together, that means Aries and Mars are always associated with the first house of a horoscope.

In real life, however, there's no such thing as a perfect natural horoscope chart, with every planet in its own sign, and every house occupied by its rightful owner. That's because the planets are constantly on the move, perpetually orbiting the sun. Along the way, they pass through every sign of the zodiac—not just their own. Given that there are twelve signs to visit, it's not hard to see why most planets don't spend much time in their own sign.

Throw in the fact that our view of the houses is constantly changing, too, and you'll soon realize that we're not likely to find a planet in its own house, either. That's because we calculate the houses based on our own perspective, as the Earth rotates on its axis. From our standpoint, the planets are constantly cycling through all twelve houses of the horoscope. Ultimately, when a planet actually does land in both its own sign and its own house on a horoscope chart, it's almost a happy accident.

Even so, astrologers keep the natural horoscope in mind when they assess a chart, because the planets and signs that naturally rule a house always have a certain measure of power in them. The planets and signs might be absentee landlords, but they're still the owners of each house, and their presence can be felt even when they're not at home.

Zodiac Houses

In the next few pages, we'll study the houses, one by one. Here's a brief overview of the significance of all twelve houses, along with their ruling signs and planets.

House	Rulership	Ruling Sign	Ruling Planet
First House	Physical appearance, first impressions	Aries, the Ram; associated with leadership	Mars, planet of energy and aggression
Second House	Money, possessions, values	Taurus, the Bull; associated with property	Venus, planet of love and attraction
Third House	Communication, siblings, neighborhoods	Gemini, the Twins; associated with communication	Mercury, planet of speed and communication
Fourth House	Motherhood, home, and family	Cancer, the Crab; associated with protection and nurturing	The Moon, orb of reflection and feminine cycles
Fifth House	Creation, procreation, and recreation	Leo, the Lion; associated with courage and showmanship	The Sun, source of energy and enlightenment
Sixth House	Work, duty, responsibility, service to others	Virgo, the Virgin; associated with health and cleanliness	Mercury, planet of speed and communication
Seventh House	Marriage, partnerships, intimate relationships	Libra, the Scales; associated with justice, equality, and balance	Venus, planet of love and attraction
Eighth House	Sex, death, other people's money	Scorpio, the Scorpion; associated with the dark mysteries of life	Pluto, planet of death, resurrection, and unavoidable change
Ninth House	Philosophy, long-distance travel, higher education	Sagittarius, the Archer; associated with honesty and exploration	Jupiter, planet of luck and expansion
Tenth House	Ambition, status, career, and public image; fathers and authority figures	Capricorn, the Goat; associated with work and rewards	Saturn, planet of structure, boundaries, and limitations
Eleventh House	Social groups, causes, long-term thinking	Aquarius, the Water Bearer; associated with visions of a better world	Uranus, planet of independence, revolution, and rebellion
Twelfth House	Psychic ability, the occult, hidden places	Pisces, the Fish; associated with intuition	Neptune, planet of mysticism and illusion

Astrology in Action: **The Houses** ◆
of the Horoscope Spread

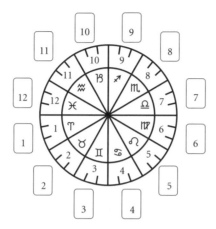

The houses of the horoscope lend themselves naturally to use as a tarot spread—even without an actual horoscope chart in hand. The twelve cards in the spread derive their significance from the houses of the horoscope and the signs and planets that naturally rule each house.

Notice that the cards are laid out in the same order the houses appear, starting with the first card in the nine o' clock position, and moving counter-clockwise around the wheel.

1. **Aries:** Self-awareness, leadership, drive, and initiative; physical appearance, first impressions

2. **Taurus:** Money, possessions, values, security, creature comforts, material resources

3. **Gemini:** Communication, thought process, siblings, neighborhoods

4. **Cancer:** Motherhood, home, and family; the ability to nurture and be nurtured, intuition

5. **Leo:** Creation, recreation, procreation, and children

6. **Virgo:** Work, duty, service, health, attention to detail, and inheritance

7. **Libra:** Marriage, partnerships, intimate relationships, balance, and social skills

8. **Scorpio:** Sex, death, joint resources

9. **Sagittarius:** Philosophy, long-distance travel, higher education

10. **Capricorn:** Ambition, status, career, and public image

11. **Aquarius:** Social groups, causes, inventiveness, futuristic and long-term thinking

12. **Pisces:** Psychic ability, the occult, hidden places, the subconscious mind, psychological health

Sample Reading: Rose's Romance

Rose, a twenty-one-year-old education major, hasn't had a boyfriend—or even a date—for the last year. "I just want to know what I should be looking for in a man," she said. "What are my prospects for romance?"

A houses of the horoscope spread, with cards pulled randomly from a well-shuffled tarot deck, offers a starting point for analysis.

Surprisingly, it seems that Rose's search for love and romance is closely tied to her career goals—and that romance won't be in the cards until she can align her love life with the rest of her life's dreams and plans.

1. **Two of Wands**: The young and handsome Mars in Aries—a younger version of the Emperor—suggests that leadership and drive is important to Rose—both in herself and in a partner.

2. **Queen of Wands:** The fiery Queen of Wands, who rules most of Aries, points out that Rose's priorities extend into the realm of money and possessions, too. Rose wants a boyfriend with a job and a future—just as she expects to establish herself in a secure profession, too.

3. **Page of Cups:** The Page of Cups personifies the element of water, and symbolizes lessons and messages about relationships. The third house describes sibling connections and communication styles. Rose has always shared a close bond with her sister, and the card's placement here suggests that Rose learned much of what she knows about relationships from her sister.

4. **Queen of Pentacles:** The earthy Queen of Pentacles, who rules most of Capricorn, addresses Rose's need for physical comfort and stability. The fourth house describes motherhood and nurturing. Rose identifies closely with her mother, and she hopes

to provide for a family of her own someday. Her choice of a partner and a mate plays a crucial role in that plan.

5. **Three of Wands:** The fifth house is the house of creativity, procreation, and recreation. The fiery Three of Wands—a depiction of the Sun in Aries—suggests that Rose wants a man who can inspire her and fuel her creative drives. In tarot, Threes often symbolize creativity, because they represent the children—literal or symbolic—that are born of partnerships.

6. **The Star**: which embodies the vision and ideals of futuristic Aquarius, has fallen in Rose's sixth house of work, duty, responsibility, service to others. As a future teacher, Rose has chosen an idealistic profession, and she'll need a partner who can support her in that cause.

7. **The World:** Rose certainly has high hopes—and high expectations—when it comes to sixth-house issues of partnership and marriage. Just as Saturn's rings define its outer boundaries, Rose might have a tendency to define herself by the people she attracts, which could be why she's being so particular about the men she dates.

8. **Four of Swords:** The eighth house describes joint resources that stem from partnerships and intimate relationships. The unconscious knight on the Four of Swords suggests that Rose could ultimately benefit from a certain amount of luck in this department. It corresponds to Jupiter in Libra, which blesses everything it touches with good fortune. Of course, the fact that Rose hasn't fallen for any of her suitors so far could indicate that Rose is making a calculated decision to wait for her lucky break, until she finds a partner with assets to share.

9. **Six of Cups:** Here we see Rose's career goals merging once again with her relationship ideals. The ninth house is home to her philosophy and higher education—which, in this case, focuses on teaching children like those in the Six of Cups. Astrologically, the card corresponds to the Sun in Scorpio—the Lord of Pleasure. Scorpio can be intensely nostalgic. On some level, it's possible that Rose is hoping for a reunion with a former boyfriend.

10. **Ten of Cups.** The happy family in the Ten of Cups makes another child-focused appearance in the tenth house of ambition, status, career, and public image. Astrologically, the Ten of Cups corresponds to Mars in Pisces—the Lord of Perfected Success. Rose won't accept anything short of a "perfect" mate, job, or family life.

11. **King of Wands.** The fiery King of Wands, who rules most of Leo, brings a sense of passion and commitment to Rose's eleventh house of social groups and causes, as well as her long-term vision and plans.

12. **The High Priestess.** Despite the overwhelming focus on career in the rest of this reading, the mystical High Priestess makes an appearance where she's comfortable: in the twelfth house of psychic ability, the occult, and hidden places.

◆　　◆　　◆

Houses of Cards

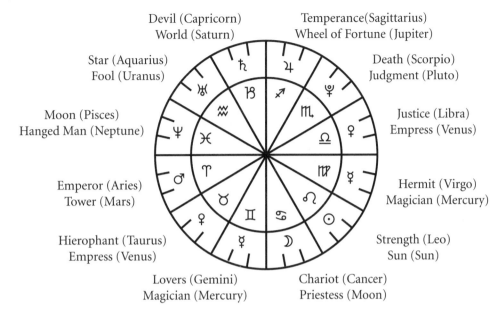

Devil (Capricorn)
World (Saturn)

Temperance(Sagittarius)
Wheel of Fortune (Jupiter)

Star (Aquarius)
Fool (Uranus)

Death (Scorpio)
Judgment (Pluto)

Moon (Pisces)
Hanged Man (Neptune)

Justice (Libra)
Empress (Venus)

Emperor (Aries)
Tower (Mars)

Hermit (Virgo)
Magician (Mercury)

Hierophant (Taurus)
Empress (Venus)

Strength (Leo)
Sun (Sun)

Lovers (Gemini)
Magician (Mercury)

Chariot (Cancer)
Priestess (Moon)

All of the planets and signs—and by association, tarot cards—occupy their own houses in a natural horoscope.

The Houses of the Horoscope

Each house of a zodiac chart represents a separate area or zone of activity. As you explore the twelve houses, visualize them as rooms in a house, with each room dedicated to a specific function. To get a feel for the signs and planets in the houses, picture them in the guise of their tarot-card counterparts. Simply think of the planets and signs as the people who live in each room.

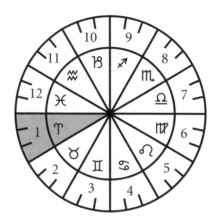

First House

If a zodiac chart were a real home, the first house would be the front entry. It describes first impressions, physical appearance, and the public face we show the world.

In fact, for many astrologers, the first house really is the entrance into a chart, because it represents the first thing we notice about anyone we meet. It's a natural starting point for analyzing a horoscope.

The first house is ruled by Aries, which means it's the natural outpost of Aries' signature card, the Emperor. He's the king of the castle—and he's perfectly at home in the first house, guarding the front door and deciding who will gain admission to the inner chambers.

Aries is ruled, in turn, by Mars, the red planet of energy and action. That adds some Tower energy to the first house of the horoscope. A tower, after all, is designed to impress friends, intimidate foes, shelter valuables, and protect the inhabitants from would-be assailants.

In a real-life horoscope chart, you'll probably find that other signs and planets in the first house, where they'll stand guard in the Emperor's stead. Whether it's their job to welcome visitors or protect the Tower against potential attacks, they'll try to fill the Emperor's commanding presence as best they can. In fact, any planets in Aries or the first house will assume some Aries and Emperor-like characteristics, such as forthrightness and martial assertiveness.

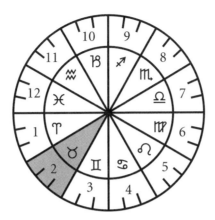

Second House

If a zodiac chart represented a real residence, the second house would be the living room. That's because the second house describes the material possessions that surround us and make us comfortable and happy—not only physically, but also spiritually. Wealth comes in many forms—money, property, and values—and the second house relates to anything we treasure.

The second house is ruled by Taurus, which means that Taurus' signature card, the Hierophant, is naturally in charge of the decor. Not surprisingly, the Hierophant favors traditional styles, with richly varnished wood, velvet upholstery, scented candles, classical music, and fine art masterpieces on the walls—like the stained-glass windows of a church.

The Hierophant inherits his taste from his ruling planet, Venus—the Empress' planet of love, affection, and attraction. Venus rules the throat, which means that both the Hierophant and the Empress will do more than fill their living rooms with furnishings. They'll also equip their living space with the sound of great music. If they're not playing orchestral songs on their state-of-the-art sound systems, they're probably singing hymns, opera, or classics themselves.

In most horoscope charts, you'll probably find that other signs and planets are sitting in the living room, and that they surround themselves with furnishings and property that appeal to their own tastes and sensibilities. Because they're still on Taurus' home turf, however, they'll naturally assume some of the Hierophant's craving for comfort, stability, and tradition.

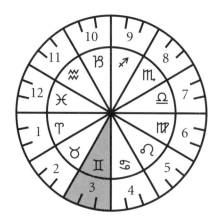

Third House

The third house of the horoscope is the communications center of the home. It's the room with a computer, a phone, a stack of household mail, and a file drawer filled with birth certificates and important papers. Whether the third house takes the form of a dedicated home office, a desk in the living room, or a corner of the kitchen table, it's the place where bills are paid, appointments are scheduled, and the details of daily life are managed.

Typically, the third house focuses on routine communications, sibling relationships, and neighborhood affairs. That's because the third house is ruled by Mercury, the messenger of the gods. His work took him all over Mount Olympus, ferrying communiqués to and from the pantheon of gods—most of whom were related to one another. In fact, the third house also covers interactions with extended family members, such as uncles, aunts, and cousins.

The Gemini Lovers also rule the third house, and their emphasis on communication echoes Mercury's focus. They're versatile, engaged, and enmeshed in a busy day-to-day routine. They're not tidy—but there's a method to their madness. And like their more organized counterpart, the Virgo Hermit that's also ruled by Mercury, they can find what they need in a jumbled pile of papers, books, and files.

During the course of your astrology pursuits, you'll probably find other signs and planets in the third house, which puts them in charge of the communications department. But because they're still in Mercury's realm, they'll try to fill his winged shoes to the best of their own ability.

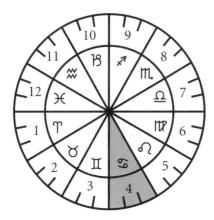

Fourth House

The fourth house, like the kitchen, is the heart of the home, where both body and soul can find nurturing and sustenance. Because the kitchen is usually a mother's domain, the fourth house usually describes mothers and caregiving parents. Positioned at the bottom of the chart, the fourth house is also the symbolic foundation of a horoscope: it's the place where we look for information about the foundations of home and family life.

In the natural zodiac, the fourth house is ruled by Cancer. Cancer rules the breasts and stomach, which symbolize the nurturing power of food. Of course, most modern mothers don't spend a lot of time in the kitchen. Many of them are modern-day Charioteers, commuting to work, and shuttling their children to school and extracurricular events.

Cancer is ruled, in turn, by the Moon, the celestial sphere of reflection and cyclical change. With time and experience, most young mothers will eventually become wise women, like the High Priestess in the Moon card. When you sit down at the High Priestess' kitchen table, you might feel like you're having tea with an old, familiar soul—or even a loving, patient grandmother. The Moon's influence also explains why astrologers look to the fourth house for information about the lunar landscape of childhood memories, dreams, and reflections.

As you build your astrological practice, you'll probably find that other signs and planets in the fourth house. Just remember that when they're around, they're cooking in another woman's kitchen. They may have their own secret recipes—but their placement means they'll naturally assume some Cancer characteristics, as well as some of the Moon's glow.

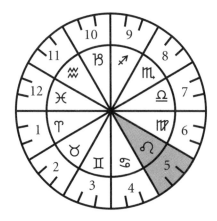

Fifth House

If a zodiac chart represented a real home, the fifth house would be the rec room—because the fifth house is the house of recreation, procreation, and creativity. It's the house of children and childlike pleasures and pursuits. It's also a party room; it's a place for fun and frolic, amusement and play, as well as arts, crafts, and entertainment.

In the natural zodiac, the fifth house is ruled by Leo, which makes it home to the sign's signature card, Strength. Left to her own devices, the wild child transforms playroom into a lionesque den of amusement and enjoyment. You might find games in the fifth house, or sporting events and athletic competitions. The fifth house sometimes describes gambling; it might even look like a poker room or a casino.

Leo is ruled, in turn, by the Sun, the showman of the zodiac. He uses the fifth house as a stage, where he can perform for the pleasure of his company. Like Apollo, the godlike figure in the Sun card, he's a golden child—confident, self-assured, and in command. And as the marker of annual events, the Sun is always ready to celebrate birthdays, anniversaries, and special occasions.

During the course of most astrology readings, you'll probably find that other signs and planets also take the stage in the fifth house—but while they're in residence, they'll naturally assume some of the Sun's zest for life, and the lion's flair for dramatic play.

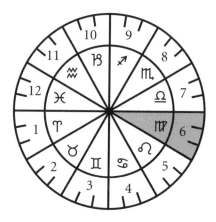

Sixth House

If a zodiac chart represented a real house, the sixth house would be the workspace. It typically takes the form of a home office, but it might also take shape as a workshop or a library, filled with tools and resources to share with others. That's because the sixth house is the house of service. It describes the work we do in service to others, out of a sense of duty and responsibility.

It's the natural home of Virgo—who, in the form of the tarot's Hermit, lives a life of dedication and resolve. In the process, he strives for clean and simple living.

If you see any similarity between Virgo's sixth-house home office and Gemini's third-house communication center, it's for a reason: both Gemini and Virgo are ruled by Mercury, the planet of communication. Here, however, Mercury places special emphasis on the Hermit's critical thinking and communication skills. Virgo is deeply analytical, and he can drive others to distraction with his attention to detail.

Occasionally, the sixth house might also describe a home's medicine cabinet, fully stocked with first-aid remedies, healing herbs, and nutritional supplements. That's because the sixth house traditionally corresponds to sickness and health.

When you work with horoscope charts, you'll probably find that other signs and planets also operate in the sixth house. Because they're still in Virgo's space, they'll naturally assume some of the Hermit's focus on conscientious service and well-being.

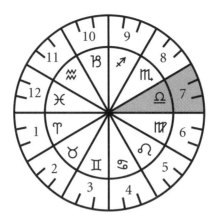

Seventh House

If a zodiac chart represented a real home, the seventh house would be the back door—the "friends and family" entrance to the chart. The seventh house describes marriages, partnerships, and personal relationships—and it symbolizes allies and open enemies alike. It's the place where astrologers look for information about commitments and lifelong attachments, as well as people who know the intimate details of our private lives, such as doctors, lawyers, and accountants.

The seventh house is ruled by Libra, the sign of relationships. That means it's the natural outpost of Libra's signature card, Justice. Like the goddess in the card, Libra carefully weighs both sides of any story, and finds the truth about existence by comparing and contrasting her experience to those of the other people in her life.

Libra is ruled, in turn, by Venus, the Empress-like planet of love and attraction. She's the archetypal wife and partner of the tarot.

When they're in charge of welcoming friends and family members at the back door, both Justice and the Empress usher in loved ones with affection and respect. Justice delights in listening to everyone's stories. The Empress meets her children at the door with cookies, and greets her husband with a kiss.

During the course of your astrological studies, you'll probably find other signs and planets in the seventh house. Because they're still in Libra's domain and the Empress's home, they'll naturally welcome guests with their hostesses' balance, grace, and charm.

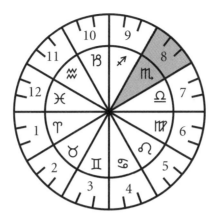

Eighth House

If a zodiac chart represented a real home, the eighth house would be the bedroom—the place where we're transformed by darkness. That's because the eighth house is ruled by Scorpio, the master of transformation. After all, we retreat to the darkness for rest and recuperation. We climb into bed at night so we can be reborn in the morning. And when we fall sick at the end of our days, we lie in our deathbed and wait for Pluto's sweet release.

Pluto, of course, is Scorpio's ruler. It's the planet of death, destruction, and deliverance. It's a chilling fact that planets in the eighth house will often describe how we'll die—either literally or metaphorically.

Scorpio corresponds to the Death or Transfiguration card. Death never sleeps—but he doesn't mind lying in state every now and then. His bedroom is a dark refuge, as quiet as the grave, and it's his favorite place to watch escapist television shows.

In most horoscope charts, you'll probably find that other signs and planets are sleeping over. When the master bedroom is transformed into a guest bedroom, the visitors will naturally assume some of Scorpio and Pluto's intensity, drives, desires, and focus. They only pray that they won't be carried out of the room feet first.

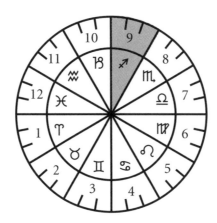

Ninth House

If a zodiac chart represented a real home, the ninth house would be the library. That's because the ninth house is the domain of philosophy, religion, and higher education—all of which feed the publishing world, too.

The ninth house is ruled by Sagittarius, so it's the natural outpost of Sagittarius' signature card, Temperance. Both are explorers, literally and symbolically. They bridge wide distances of time and space to experience the wonders of a far-flung world. They're restless, and easily bored by routine. It's their nature to be adventurous and outgoing, meet new people, and test the boundaries of human imagination.

Sagittarius, in turn, is ruled by Jupiter, the planet of luck and expansion. It's said that travel broadens a person, and like the spinning Wheel of Fortune, the Jupiterian spirit wants to keep growing. Under Jupiter's divine guidance, we all want to experience the gifts life has to offer, test our luck, and prove our faith in a benefic universe.

What will you find on the shelves of a true Sagittarian library? Philosophy books, of course, along with textbooks on comparative religions and alternative spirituality. You'll also discover foreign-language dictionaries, maps, and travel guides designed for real-life voyagers and armchair tourists alike.

In a real-life horoscope chart, you'll probably find that other signs and planets in the ninth house, and that they fill the library with materials that reflect their own spiritual journeys and special interests.

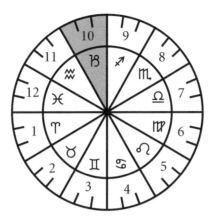

Tenth House

The tenth house is the house of career and social status—both of which often come at great expense. No one understands that cost better than a Capricorn, who will pay almost any price for the privilege that power can bring.

If a zodiac chart represented a real home, the tenth house would be the exterior—the front of the house, visible to everyone, even from across the street or down the block. The size and style of most houses is a clear indication of the occupants' social status, income, and career success.

The tenth house is ruled by Capricorn, which means it's the natural outpost of Capricorn's signature card, the Devil. He lives in the finest house money can buy: an executive mansion.

Capricorn is ruled, in turn, by Saturn, the ringed planet of limitations, restrictions, boundaries, and structure. Like any dark lord, Saturn lives in a world of his own making and design—a gated community, strictly off-limits to those who have no business being there.

As you survey the neighborhood of astrological charts and horoscopes, you'll probably find that other signs and planets also affect curb appeal. Because they're still in the Dark Lord's domain, they'll naturally assume some of his concern for material possessions, as well as public image and appearance.

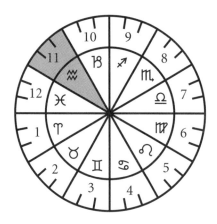

Eleventh House

If a zodiac chart represented a real home, the eleventh house would be the dining room, where fellow travelers and kindred spirits gather around the table to share their hopes, dreams, and visions of a better future.

Astrologers turn to the eleventh house for information about social groups and causes. You might even say it's a club house, where groups and organizations meet to focus on special interests and long-term goals. If you've ever hosted a book club meeting, a PTA planning event, or a reception on behalf of your favorite candidate for city council, you've shared your eleventh house with others.

The dining room isn't the only place where social groups meet, however. It's not always practical for larger groups to get together in private homes, so some planets move their assemblies to more public places, like coffee houses, community centers, and corporate board rooms.

The eleventh house is ruled by Aquarius. In tarot, Aquarius is represented by the Star— the blithe spirit of space and sky, with a long-range view of the cosmos. She draws kindred spirits into her futuristic realm. Together, they fill the space with utopian dreams and visions.

The Star is ruled, in turn, by Uranus, the planet of revolution and reform. Uranus is a Fool for almost any errand, and will often climb on board any cause the Star supports.

When other signs and planets step into the eleventh house, they bring their own friends and causes with them. Because they're still in the Star's heavenly corner of the sky, however, they'll naturally assume some of her starry-eyed dreams and visionary goals.

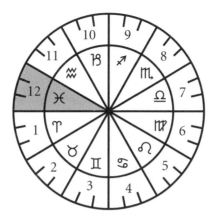

Twelfth House

If a zodiac chart represented a real home, the twelfth house would be a locked room, a secret chamber, or a closet you're forbidden to open. It might also be a dark and scary basement, or an inaccessible attic. In short, he twelfth house is a place of mysteries and secrets, hidden from view and banished from our thoughts.

Obviously, the twelfth house isn't always a pleasant place. The things we keep here are those we'd like to hide, both from other people and from ourselves. At their core, those issues represent our most secret fears. They're the concerns we have to work through, which could include deceptions, hidden enemies, and the issues and torments that we hide away from public view. In some cases, those confinements are literal: the twelfth house occasionally describes the isolation of prisons, asylums, and hospitals.

On a less frightening note, the twelfth house also describes spirituality, psychic ability, mysticism, meditation, past-life issues, and the subconscious. A twelfth house that's opened and allowed to air out will often lead to stunning—and healing—revelations and discoveries.

The twelfth house is ruled by Pisces. It's the natural outpost of the Moon's card, with its deep reflecting pools and an entire underwater world submerged beneath its depths. The goddess of the Moon, like her sister, the High Priestess, can keep any secret until it needs to be revealed.

Pisces, in turn, is ruled by Neptune, the Hanged Man, the mystic visionary who suspends himself in an alternate reality.

As you immerse yourself further, you'll probably find that other signs and planets in the twelfth house. They have secrets and fears of their own, which they'll hide away as best they can, and bring to light when the time is right.

Astrology in Action: **The Planet, Sign, and House Spread**

Astrologers sometimes describe a horoscope chart as the outline of a drama. The planets are the actors, the signs are the costumes they wear, and the houses are the sets.

A simple three-card spread based on planets, signs, and houses can illustrate almost any personal story, and provides another example of how easily tarot and astrology work seamlessly together.

Sample Reading: Alice's Adventures in Australia

After thirty-seven years of marriage, Alice and her husband Richard are planning a week-long vacation at an Australian resort. She has high hopes for the experience.

"This holiday is supposed to be relaxing," she says. "It's meant to give us some time out, and some time for each other. There's a pool there, so I hope to swim, but I also hope to get some writing done. At the same time, I want to be able to get out and about a little, too. What should I expect?"

For the answer, we shuffled a tarot deck and pulled three cards at random to represent the energies of a planet, a sign, and a house.

Planet: The Empress card corresponds to Venus

Sign: The Sun card corresponds to the Sun, Leo's ruling planet

House: The Knight of Wands corresponds to Sagittarius, the sign that rules the Ninth House

1. **Planet:** *Venus.* The Empress corresponds to Venus—the goddess of love and attraction. When Alice is on vacation, she'll be playing that role herself. Not only will she be surrounded by the beauty of a lush tropical setting, but she'll be perceived

as an ideal mate for her husband—who apparently is an Emperor in his own right. In tarot, the Empress is the embodiment of creative energy, which bodes well for Alice's creative writing pursuits, too—although, in this case, she may find herself surrounded by a garden of ideas that she'd like to plant and nurture over time, rather than commit to paper all at once.

2. **Sign:** *Leo.* Thanks to a random quirk of fate, the card we pulled to represent a sign actually depicted a planet. That's not a problem: we simply looked for the corresponding sign associated with that planet. In this case, we turned to Leo, the sign that's ruled by the Sun. Leo is the sign of ego and self-esteem. Leos love to clothe themselves in the adoration of their partners and bask in the spotlight. All told, the week will be a huge boost to Alice's self-image. Not only will she be the focus of her husband's attention, but Leo—the ruler of creative drives—suggests that she'll find time to unleash her imagination on the printed page, too.

3. **House:** *Ninth.* The Knight of Wands corresponds to Sagittarius, which rules the ninth house of philosophy, higher education, and long-distance travel. It's the perfect symbol of Alice's adventures in a vacation wonderland. This card suggests that her experiences will probably be more intellectual than physical; she might not find much time for relaxing or floating in a pool. Instead, she'll be exploring her own spirited brand of thought and self-expression—and like the fiery Knight of Wands, she'll probably make time to explore a few nearby tourist attractions as well.

◆　◆　◆

Polar Opposites

One of the best ways to get a feel for the houses—and the signs they rule—is to study them in pairs. Every sign has an equal and opposite counterpart on the other side of the chart wheel.

Aries and Libra

The Self and the Partner

The first house of Aries represents the self, while the seventh house of Libra represents partnerships.

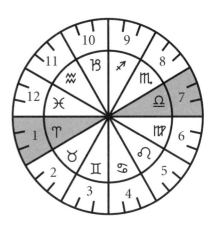

In tarot, Aries is the Emperor, and Libra is Justice. The Aries Emperor asserts his independence, but the woman in the Libra Justice card tries to balance her needs against the needs of other important people in her life.

Aries is ruled by Mars, the lightning-struck Tower. Libra is ruled by Venus, the Empress. Both are channels for cosmic energy. In the Tower, the energy is destructive. In the Empress card, the energy is constructive. Both have their rightful place in the cycle of life.

Taurus and Scorpio

Personal Property and Shared Resources

The second house of Taurus describes personal possessions, while the eighth house of Scorpio describes shared resources.

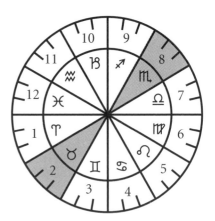

In tarot, Taurus is the Hierophant, and Scorpio is Death. The Taurus Hierophant wants to maintain his traditions and the status quo, but the angel of Death demands transfiguration and change. The Hierophant wants to hold on to all the spiritual and material treasure he's accumulated; Death will eventually take them all away.

Taurus is ruled by Venus, the Empress' planet of love and beauty. Scorpio is ruled by Pluto, Judgment's planet of endings and new beginnings. They all find common ground in the graveyard: Death may have its way, but the Hierophant will enrich his church in the process, as a result of planned giving and bequests.

Gemini and Sagittarius

Self-Expression and the Higher Self

Gemini, the sign of communication and self-expression, finds its counterpart in Sagittarius, the sign of philosophy, higher education, and long-distance travel.

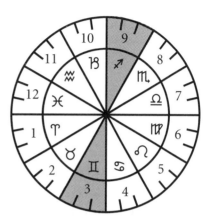

Curious Gemini wants to know and understand his neighbors, but far-sighted Sagittarius wants to meet foreigners. While Gemini busies himself with elementary education, Sagittarius wants to pursue an advanced degree. And when Gemini takes short trips and runs neighborhood errands, Sagittarius heads off on distant journeys.

In tarot, Gemini is represented by the Lovers, and Sagittarius is represented by Temperance. The Lovers want to plunge head-first into a relationship, but Temperance cautions them to take a more balanced approach, and to see the world before they commit to settling down.

Gemini is ruled by Mercury, the Magician's planet of speed, skill, and communication. Sagittarius is ruled by Jupiter, the planet of luck and the Wheel of Fortune.

Cancer and Capricorn

Private versus Public

The fourth house of Cancer represents the privacy and comfort of home, while the tenth house of Capricorn describes the public face of career, social status, and reputation.

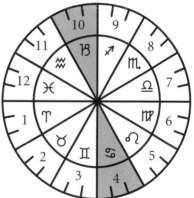

Cancer is safe and nurturing, and it praises personal achievements. Capricorn, however, makes those achievements visible, where they're exposed to challenge and criticism. The two signs demonstrate the difference between unconditional love and public responsibility.

Cancer is the Charioteer, safely ensconced in a crablike shell. Capricorn is the Devil, facing the cold, cruel material world in exchange for recognition and reward.

Cancer is ruled by the Moon, the mystical planet of the High Priestess, while Capricorn is ruled by Saturn, the tarot's World at large.

Leo and Aquarius

Instant Gratification versus Long-Range Planning
Leo, the sign of creativity and play, pairs off against Aquarius, the sign of long-range vision and planning.

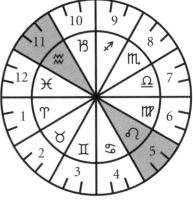

In tarot, Leo is Strength, and Aquarius is the Star. Leo is the star of his own show, but Aquarius wants to be part of a constellation. Leo wants to play with his kids, but Aquarius is thinking about tomorrow's children—so her work needs to start today. Leo wouldn't mind a quick romp through the park, but Aquarius wants to organize a fundraiser.

Together, they should be able to find a happy medium. Leo is ruled by the Sun, the planet of creative self-expression. Aquarius is ruled by Uranus, the Fool's planet of revolution and reform.

Virgo and Pisces

The Everyday World and the World of Dreams
Virgo, the sign of health, work, and service, finds its counterpart in Pisces, the sign of dreams and secrets.

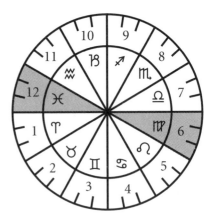

Virgo is practical; Pisces is mystical. Virgo is intelligent; Pisces is intuitive. Virgo wants to control every detail of his existence, but Pisces would rather go with the flow. In short, Virgo focuses on the responsibilities of physical existence, while Pisces focuses on the rewards of spirituality.

In tarot, Virgo is the Hermit, and Pisces is the Moon. Left to their own devices, both could easily lose touch with reality.

Virgo is ruled by Mercury, the Magician's planet of thought and communication. Pisces is ruled by Neptune, the Hanged Man's planet of mysticism and illusion.

Ten

◆

How to Read a Horoscope Chart

A horoscope chart is a snapshot of a moment in time, plotted on a map of the sky. You can read it as you would read any other map—but there are a few things to keep in mind.

First of all, it's important to note that a horoscope chart is designed to give you a view of the entire solar system, as seen from one spot on Earth. It's not a map of Earth, or any place on Earth. Instead, it's a geocentric map of the solar system.

Most horoscope charts are circular, like a celestial globe. When you look at a horoscope chart, imagine the planet Earth as a small focal point in the center of the chart, surrounded by the sphere of heaven.

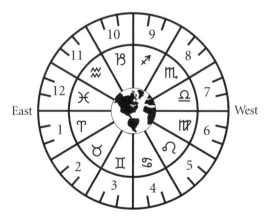

The exact center of the chart represents a specific latitude and longitude on Earth. In theory, if you were to stand on that spot, you could look east and west along the horizontal line that separates the top half of the chart from the bottom. That's because the horizontal line actually does represent the visual horizon.

The compass points, however, aren't what you'd expect: the eastern horizon is on the left, and the western horizon is on the right. North is at the bottom, and south is at the top. That's because charts are constructed from the perspective of the northern hemisphere, where the ancients first stood to survey the heavens. When you read a chart, picture yourself standing on the top half of the globe, looking south. East will be on your left, and west will be on your right.

From that position, if you were to look straight up, you'd be looking at open sky above your head. If you were to look straight down, you'd see the Earth beneath your feet.

In real life, you could only see the top half of the chart from where you were standing. The sky above the horizon would be visible, but the rest of the cosmos would be hidden from view, rolling along on the other side of the world. That's an important thing to remember when you start to analyze the symbolic meaning of a chart.

We all know that the Sun rises in the east. Astrologers also chart all the planets and signs that rise and set in their own due course. They move around the chart in a counter-clockwise direction, which means that any planets and signs that are rising on the eastern horizon are indicated near a chart's first house. Any planets or signs that are setting on the western horizon are plotted near the seventh house.

Here's another tip to keep in mind as you survey a chart wheel: it's also like a clock. Conceptually, the eastern horizon marks the dawn. If a chart is cast for sunrise, you'll see the Sun there, ascending on the cusp of the first house. The western horizon denotes the sunset; that's the descendant. High noon is straight up, on the Midheaven between the ninth and tenth houses of the horoscope, and the midnight hour is positioned at the bottom of the chart, between the third and fourth houses. It's called the *Imum Coeli* (I.C.), which is Latin for "bottom of the sky."

Those four angles of the chart are important, because they each symbolize a separate form of awareness and interaction with the outside world.

Cosmic Connection: PLANETARY MOTION

The signs and planets are in constant motion. A few minutes can make a big difference in the rising sign, the signs of the subsequent houses, and the position of the Moon—which means it's important to start any horoscope with an accurate time.

- The Moon moves approximately one degree every two hours, or twelve degrees a day.

- The Sun, Venus, and Mercury move about one degree a day.

- There are twelve zodiac signs, and the Earth revolves to face them all during the course of a twenty-four-hour day. That means the rising sign changes every two hours.

- The twelve houses of the horoscope are simply divisions of space. As the world turns throughout the day, the planets also move through the various houses.

While exact times are optimal, astrologers can develop a horoscope chart based on any information you can find. Some astrologers will cast a chart for sunrise on the day in question, to symbolize the potential that dawned that day. Others will cast a chart for noon. Advanced astrologers can also rectify a chart, which means they'll make an educated guess at an unknown birth time based on important life events such as marriages, births, and deaths in the family.

House Cusps

The cusps—the dividing lines between the houses—mark the transition from one astrological sign to another. Even though planets often land close to the cusps, the divisions are firm: a planet can only be in one house at a time. Even so, their energy might be felt in the adjoining house, just like a noisy neighbor can be heard through a wall.

Empty Houses

All ten planets and twelve signs appear in every horoscope chart. Because they're constantly cycling through space at different speeds, however, most charts usually have at least one or two empty houses.

That doesn't mean that empty houses are bereft of energy or activity. They're still ruled by a sign, which means they offer one avenue of expression for the planet that rules the sign. They'll also be visited, over time, by transiting planets.

The Moon, for example, visits every sign during the course of a month. The Sun travels through all twelve signs every year.

An empty house could even be a good thing: it could indicate that the energy of the sign and house is peaceful and easy, and mastery of its realm comes naturally to the subject.

Intercepted Houses

Occasionally, an entire sign will fall completely inside a house, with other signs bracketing the cusps on either side. In those cases, the qualities of the intercepted sign won't be readily apparent. They'll be hidden, almost like a secret identity, but their qualities will manifest at critical junctures.

Cosmic Connection: TYPES OF HOROSCOPE CHARTS

Horoscope charts can be drawn up for any moment in time—past, present, or future—for any reason.

- **Natal** charts are calculated for the exact moment of birth. Natal charts are popular, because they can be used as tools for personality profiles or prediction.

- **Electional** charts can be drawn for choosing an auspicious time for an important event, like a wedding, business deal, major purchase, or elective surgery.

- **Horary** charts answer a question based on the moment the question was asked. They can be useful for finding lost or missing objects.

- **Synastry** charts compare the natal charts of two people. They're usually drawn up to describe the compatibility of romantic partners, family members, or friends.

- **Composite** charts combine two individual charts into one, to illustrate the relationship between two people.

- **Transit** and **Progressed** charts compare the current positions of the planets to their positions at an earlier time.

- **Solar Return** charts are based on the Sun's return to the same degree it occupied at the moment of birth. These "birthday" charts are interpreted as a snapshot of the year ahead.

- **Mundane** charts are cast for geopolitical entities, like countries, cities, provinces, and states. This is one of the oldest forms of astrology, because kings and potentates once used them as a decision-making tool. One branch of mundane astrology, astro-meteorology, focuses on forecasting the weather.

- **Relocation** charts can help some people choose the best place to live, by repositioning a birth chart in a new location.

Eleven

◆

A Simplified Guide to Chart Interpretation

You could spend years studying a chart and never exhaust every level of detail you'd find there.

Most astrologers, however, don't have that luxury. They stick to a few basic principles and techniques. Over time, every astrologer develops his or her own system of assessing a horoscope.

If you're just starting to read charts, here's a step-by-step checklist of the key points you should consider.

1. The Sun
2. The Moon
3. The Ascendant
4. The Ruler of the Chart
5. The Angles of the Chart
6. The Planets, Signs, and Elements in the Houses
7. Patterns
8. Aspects

Keep reading for details and step-by-step instructions.

Cosmic Connection: YOUR NATAL CHART

Here are some starting points for a discussion and analysis of your chart, starting with your Sun, Moon, and Ascendant. Once you get a feel for the kinds of questions you could be asking, you can carry on with the other planets in your chart, too.

Your Sun

Sign: Which Major Arcana card corresponds to your Sun sign? How does that card describe your personality, individuality, and sense of self?

Element: Is your Sun in a fire, earth, air, or water sign? Are you fundamentally fiery, earthy, airy, or watery? Are you spiritually passionate, physically grounded, reasoned and intellectual, or tapped into the waters of intuition?

Mode: Were you born during the first, second, or third month of a season? Is your Sun in a cardinal, fixed, or mutable sign? Do you tend to initiate projects, work steadily until they're finished, or remain flexible and take life as it comes?

House: If you know what time you were born, which house does your Sun fall into? In other words, where does your Sun shine, and what area of your life does it enlighten? *(If you don't know your birth time, don't evaluate the house position.)*

Your Moon

Sign: Which Major Arcana card corresponds to your Moon sign? How does that card describe your overall temperament and mood? How does it reflect your emotional makeup?

Element: What does your Moon sign—and its corresponding elemental nature—say about how you behave in relationships? Are you fiery and passionate, earthy and steadfast, airy and intellectual, or watery and sentimental? Do you see any corresponding symbolism in the card that represents your Moon sign?

House: Where does your Moon glow? Which area of life is reflected by your Moon sign? *(If you don't know your birth time, don't evaluate the house position.)*

Complexity: How well do your Sun and Moon relate to each other? Are they in compatible signs, elements, and houses? Do they share a similar outlook? Or do they have different perspectives on life, love, and objects of fascination?

Your Rising Sign/Ascendant

If you don't know your birth time, your ascendant is difficult to determine. Skip this step.

Sign: Which sign was rising at the moment of your birth? Which Major Arcana card corresponds to that sign?

Description: How does that card describe the face you show the world? What does it say about the first impression you make when you meet new people? The answer may surprise you.

Step 1. The Sun

The Sun is the central focus of any horoscope chart. In a natal chart, it describes the essence of the self: the ego, the sense of personal identity, one's life force, and the defining drives and desires of an individual's basic nature. The Sun can also describe powerful relationships with husbands, fathers, and other strong masculine presences.

Start your chart assessment by noting the Sun's sign and house placement, as well as its element and mode—whether it's cardinal, fixed, or mutable. For additional insight, take a look at the Major Arcana card that corresponds to the Sun's sign.

Step 2. The Moon

The Moon's position describes one's emotional makeup, memory, and mood. The Moon can also describe a person's basic female nature, intuitive sense, nurturing ability, and relationships with nurturing women, such as mothers and wives.

Just as you did with the Sun, consider the Moon's sign, house, element, and mode, and pull the Major Arcana card that corresponds to its sign, too.

Step 3. The Ascendant

In a natal chart, the ascendant, or rising sign, is the face you show the world. It's based on the sign that was rising on the eastern horizon at the moment of your birth, and it symbolizes the first impressions you make when you first appear on the horizon of other people's awareness. It describes your attitude, physical appearance, and overall disposition.

The ascendant is also the cusp of the first house. You can find it at the 9 o'clock position on the chart wheel.

Step 4. The Ruler of the Chart

The sign on the ascendant determines the planetary ruler of the chart. That planet will have a strong influence on the subject—and that influence will be further colored by the ruling planet's position in the chart. Consider its sign, house, element, and mode. For added detail, pull the cards associated with the ruling planet and its sign.

On a related note, you can also check the rulers of each house, based on the signs you'll find on the cusp of each house.

Astrology in Action: **The Sun, Moon, and Ascendant Spread**

The Sun, Moon, and Ascendant are arguably the three most important indicators in a chart. The three corresponding tarot cards can give you remarkable insight into someone's makeup, and serve as the foundation for a personality profile. Let's see how the three play out in Gene Roddenberry's chart.

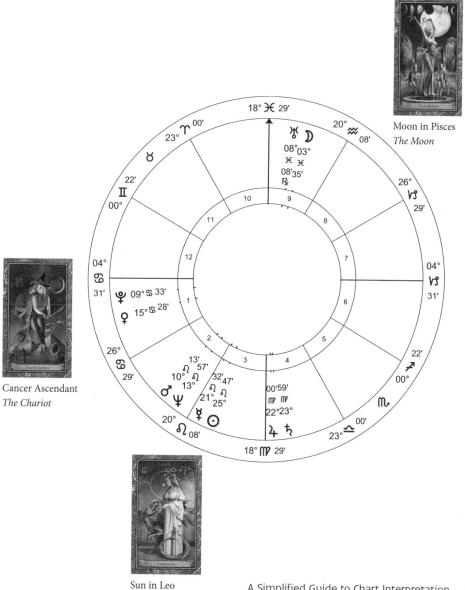

Moon in Pisces
The Moon

Cancer Ascendant
The Chariot

Sun in Leo
Strength

Gene Roddenberry
August 19, 1921
1:35 a.m.
El Paso, Texas
Time Zone: 07:00 (MST)
Longitude: 106° W 29' 11"
Latitude 31° N 45' 31"
Placidus Houses
Tropical Zodiac

Sample Reading: Gene Roddenberry's Futuristic Vision

The power of the Sun, Moon, and rising sign are dramatically illustrated in Gene Roddenberry's chart.

Cancer Ascendant. Roddenberry, of course, was the visionary creator of the *Star Trek* universe. And how did he present himself to the world? As an interstellar voyager who had the courage to travel through time and space where no man had gone before—just like the Charioteer on his Cancer ascendant.

Sun in Leo. Like the characters he created, Roddenberry's Sun and Moon are highly archetypal, which suggests that he was clearly in tune with the rhythms of the universe.

Both fall in their own signs. His Sun was in fiery Leo, the sign of willpower and drive. His attraction to broadcasting isn't surprising: it Sun was positioned in the third house of communication. The Magician's powers of communication (and sales, and sleight of hand) worked hand-in-hand with Strength's creativity, willpower, and drive.

Moon in Pisces. His Moon was also dignified, this time in Pisces, the sign of mysticism, the unknown, the subconscious, and hidden mysteries. And with that Moon in the ninth house of philosophy, higher education, and long-distance travel, it seems that Roddenberry was destined to explore the outer limits of human experience and understanding.

◆　◆　◆

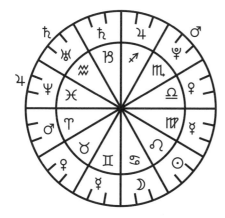

Aries: Mars
Taurus: Venus
Gemini: Mercury
Cancer: Moon
Leo: Sun
Virgo: Mercury
Libra: Venus
Scorpio: Pluto (Mars)
Sagittarius: Jupiter
Capricorn: Saturn
Aquarius: Uranus (Saturn)
Pisces: Neptune (Jupiter)

A Note on Rulerships

Most contemporary astrologers use modern rulerships, which are pictured in their correct houses, above. In traditional astrology, Jupiter, Saturn, and Mars had dual rulerships: those are pictured outside the wheel.

Step 5. The Four Angles of the Chart

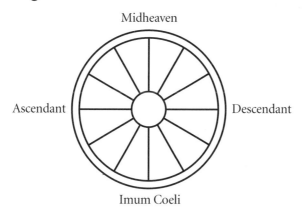

Four of the house cusps are called *angles*, and they have special significance.

1. **The ascendant** is the most important angle of the chart, but there are three others to consider: the *Imum Coeli* (I.C.), the descendant, and the Midheaven. Look for any planets near the four angles, and give them extra emphasis in your interpretation of the chart.

2. **The *Imum Coeli*—**a Latin phrase that means "bottom of the sky"—is the cusp of the fourth house. It's the nadir, or lowest point of the chart, so it symbolizes foundations.

   It's interesting to note that both houses adjacent to the I.C. relate to childhood experiences. The third house rules sibling relationships and elementary education, while the fourth house rules home and family life.

3. **The Descendant**, directly opposite the ascendant, describes the impression we make on the people who know us best. The ascendant is the face we show to the world; the descendant is the face we show to intimate partners and friends.

   On that note, the adjacent sixth house describes how we fulfill our duties of work and service; in classical astrology, it related to servants and employees. The seventh house symbolizes close personal relationships with spouses, doctors, lawyers, accountants, and anyone who knows the private details of our lives.

4. **The Midheaven**, at the top of the wheel, is the most public point in the chart. Located directly opposite the *Imum Coeli,* it's sometimes called the *Medium Coeli* (M.C.), Latin for "middle of the heavens."

   The planets and signs at the Midheaven are in full view for all to see; they correspond to accomplishments, profession, and prestige. In fact, the adjacent ninth house describes higher education, while the tenth house describes career. Anything on the Midheaven is a solid indicator of social standing and reputation.

The four angles of the chart are significant, and a reading based on the angles gives us quick insight into a birth chart. You can see their importance in Salvador Dali's chart.

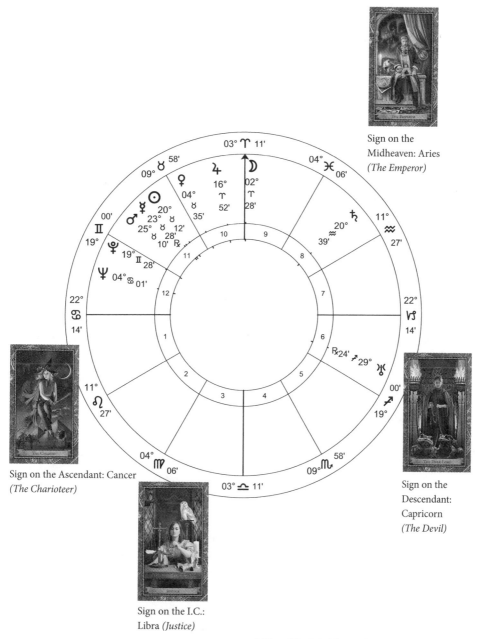

Sign on the
Midheaven: Aries
(The Emperor)

Sign on the Ascendant: Cancer
(The Charioteer)

Sign on the I.C.:
Libra *(Justice)*

Sign on the
Descendant:
Capricorn
(The Devil)

Salvador Dali

May 11, 1904

8:45 a.m.

Figueras, Spain

Time Zone: 00:00 (UT/GMT)

Longitude: 002° E 58'

Latitude 42° N 16'

Placidus Houses

Tropical Zodiac

Sample Reading: The Surreal Salvador Dali

Salvador Dali was one of the twentieth century's most original artists. He was also one of its most eccentric. The signs on the four angles of his natal chart, along with the planets in close proximity, offer clues to his off-the-chart personality.

Cancer Ascendant: Dali's Cancer ascendant made him a child of the Moon. He was intuitive, insightful, and closely connected to feminine energy. His mother adored him and women inspired him; in fact, he even created a custom tarot deck, reportedly at the behest of his wife Gala.

Midheaven (and Chart Ruler): The planet that rules the ascendant is also the ruler of the chart, which makes Dali's lunar connection even more pronounced. In this case, the Moon that rules Cancer is at the top of the chart, almost exactly conjunct the Midheaven—which itself is represented by the Emperor. Because his Moon was in Aries, Dali was able to channel much of his lunacy into his creative work. It's interesting to note that Jupiter isn't far away, either, and it's in Aries, too. As the planet of luck and expansion, Jupiter also seems to suggest that Dali was able to parlay his hard work into good fortune.

Capricorn Descendant: Dali had a Capricorn descendant. The seventh-house cusp is associated with relationships and partnerships, and Capricorn is represented by the Devil. In Dali's case, ritual, taboo, and physical fetishes were a major part of his relationship with his wife.

Imum Coeli: At the foundation of his chart, however, you'll find Libra, the sign of balance. Libra is an artist's sign: it's ruled by Venus, the planet of beauty and attraction. That Venusian influence kept Dali's work grounded, despite the far-ranging influences of the other angles in his chart.

◆　◆　◆

Cosmic Connection: HOUSE SYSTEMS

Every chart wheel, like every circle, contains 360 degrees—and every chart wheel is divided into twelve houses.

There are many systems of house division. Placidus is the most popular one, but other systems include Koch, equal house, and whole sign houses. Choosing a system is strictly a matter of personal preference and convenience.

Most systems start with the ascendant as the cusp of the first house, and the descendant as the cusp of the seventh house. Many also use the Midheaven as the cusp of the tenth and the Imum Coeli as the cusp of the fourth house. Those four angles will be the same in almost every system.

The intermediate house cusps, however, can shift dramatically based on the system you choose. The planets' relationship to each other doesn't change, but they can land in different houses, which affects their interpretation.

Step 6. The Planets in the Houses

You've examined the Sun, the Moon, and any planets on the angles of the chart. Now consider the rest of the planets in turn. Check their house placement, sign, and element.

House Placement

Find each planet's place in one of the twelve houses, and remember that the planets will focus their energy on the activities of that house.

1. First house: Physical appearance, first impressions

2. Second house: Money, possessions, values

3. Third house: Communication, siblings, neighborhoods

4. Fourth house: Motherhood, home, and family

5. Fifth house: Creation, procreation, recreation, and children

6. Sixth house: Work, duty, responsibility, service to others; attention to detail and health

7. Seventh house: Marriage, partnerships, intimate relationships

8. Eighth house: Sex, death, joint resources, and inheritances

9. Ninth house: Philosophy, long-distance travel, higher education

10. Tenth house: Father figures, discipline, ambition, status, career, and public image

11. Eleventh house: Social groups, causes, utopian vision, and long-term thinking

12. Twelfth house: Psychic ability, the subconscious, the occult, confined and hidden places

Signs and Elements

Consider the sign each planet occupies, and use that information to determine whether it will express itself through the fiery domain of spirit, the earthy plane of matter and property, the airy realm of thought and communication, or the watery world of emotion.

1. Aries: Cardinal Fire

2. Taurus: Fixed Earth

3. Gemini: Mutable Air

4. Cancer: Cardinal Water

5. Leo: Fixed Fire

6. Virgo: Mutable Earth

7. Libra: Cardinal Air

8. Scorpio: Fixed Water

9. Sagittarius: Mutable Fire

10. Capricorn: Cardinal Earth

11. Aquarius: Fixed Air

12. Pisces: Mutable Water

If you notice a preponderance of any one element or mode, pay attention. If you notice a lot of planets in fixed signs, for example, or in the element of earth, you could be dealing with an overall theme that echoes the fixed earth qualities of Taurus—even if there are no planets actually *in* Taurus.

Step 7. Patterns

Planets also fall into a number of configurations that you can spot at a glance. Most are easy to recognize, and each one has symbolic significance.

Step back and look at how the planets are distributed around the chart. Scattered planets scatter their energy. Clustered planets focus their energy.

- Planets in the eastern hemisphere are either rising above the horizon, or they've just risen. They're in the process of coming out into the world. A predominance of planets on the left half of the chart suggests an emphasis on independence.

Cosmic Connection: ESSENTIAL DIGNITIES

You can assess the comfort level of the planets in each sign, based on their essential dignities and debilities. A planet in its own dignity is at home. A planet in exaltation is an honored guest. A planet in detriment is working with energies that are completely different from its own, putting it at a disadvantage, while a planet in fall is an unwelcome visitor.

Planet	Dignity (Domicile)	Exaltation	Detriment	Fall
Sun	Leo	Aries	Aquarius	Libra
Moon	Cancer	Taurus	Capricorn	Scorpio
Mercury	Gemini/Virgo	Virgo	Sagittarius	Pisces
Venus	Taurus/Libra	Pisces	Aries	Virgo
Mars	Aries/Scorpio	Capricorn	Libra	Cancer
Jupiter	Sagittarius/Pisces	Cancer	Gemini	Capricorn
Saturn	Capricorn/Aquarius	Libra	Cancer	Aries

Mutual Reception

Take the dignities one step further, and you can determine which planets might be in *mutual reception*. In that case, two planets are in each other's signs of dignity, so they're in a position to help each other.

- Planets in the western hemisphere are either setting, or they've already set. They're in the process of retreating to the privacy of their homes at night. The right side of the chart describes a focus on relationships.
- Planets above the horizon are all visible in the bright light of day. They're public.
- Planets below the horizon are shielded by the darkness of night. They're private.

Step 8. Aspects

The ten planets on an astrological chart can work well together, or at cross purposes—depending on their positions.

Astrologers look for aspects—the geometric angles where planets intersect with each other and the angles of the chart. It's simple geometry, but the implications can be profound. Those interactions affect the planets' energy and determine how well they'll relate to each other.

Major Aspects

Some of the most commonly studied aspects are oppositions, conjunctions, squares, trines, sextiles, and quincunxes. In a tarot reading, those aspects can even be converted into meaningful spreads and layouts.

Conjunctions: Planets in conjunction share the exact same position in a chart. As a result, they share a common viewpoint because they usually have the same sign, element, mode, and polarity in common. They operate, in effect, as a powerful combined force.

How do planetary conjunctions play out in a horoscope chart? Again, picture the planets as their tarot-card counterparts.

- **Sun:** While a conjunction with the golden child can overshadow some planets, the Sun god can also energize and enlighten their strengths.
- **Moon:** A conjunction with the High Priestess causes other planets to express their energy in the emotional realm, and makes their qualities seem more intuitive and innate.
- **Mercury:** The Magician helps communicate the message of any other planet in his sphere of influence. He adds intellectual energy to its usual characteristics.
- **Venus:** The graceful Empress enhances the beauty, charm, and creativity of every planet she touches.

- **Mars:** Like a cosmic lightning rod, the Tower card illustrates how Mars can energize any planets in its electrical field.
- **Jupiter:** Planets that brush up against the Wheel of Fortune are expanded. Their energy is magnified. Their effect become more philosophical and more influential.
- **Saturn:** The World likes clearly defined boundaries. When Saturn bumps into another planet, it starts building fences and imposing orderly limitations, restrictions, structure, and discipline.
- **Uranus:** The Initiate—the Fool—invites innovation, revolution, and rebellion. It can overturn the other planet's usual way of operating.
- **Neptune:** The Hanged Man, used to seeing the universe from alternate vantage points, combines a planet's usual energy with his own hazy view of reality.
- **Pluto:** The god of transformation breaks down the influence of other planets and reveals the dark side of their energy. It deconstructs them so that they can be remade and reborn, better than they were before.

Oppositions: Two planets in opposition to each other are 180 degrees apart. That might seem confrontational, but there's also plenty of room for communication and agreement, because each has a clear view of the other's position. Planets in opposition also share the same masculine or feminine polarity, which makes them both either active or receptive.

Trines: The trine is an easy combination, in which two planets are 120 degrees apart. They share the same element—fire, earth, air, or water—so their energy flows freely back and forth.

Squares: Planets that square off in a chart are 90 degrees apart. The aspect can be troublesome because they work at cross-purposes. While they share the same modality—cardinal, fixed, or mutable—each has a different polarity. One will be masculine and active, while the other will be feminine and receptive.

Sextiles: Planets in sextile are separated by 60 degrees. As a result, they share the same polarity—masculine or feminine—and compatible elements. A sextile is usually considered an easy aspect that represents a window of good fortune or a doorway of opportunity.

Quincunxes (inconjuncts): Quincunx planets are 150 degrees apart. They don't have anything in common: their elements, qualities, and modes are all different. The aspect stresses them both and often has an impact on physical health.

Aspect Patterns

Some planetary aspects form patterns and designs on a chart.

Stelliums: When three planets share the same sign and house, they form a stellium. They'll act in conjunction with each other, and they'll add a tremendous amount of emphasis to a chart.

Grand trine: Three planets, each 120 degrees from the others, form an equilateral triangle. They usually share an elemental association of fire, air, earth, or water. Their shared energy flows easily and naturally, and leads to a comfortable harmony of their abilities and power.

Grand cross: When two pairs of opposing planets square off against each other, the result is a stressful, make-or-break configuration. The respective planets can block each other, or they can join forces and find a way to strengthen each other.

T-square: Three planets align in a T-square. Two of them will oppose each other, and the third will serve as a focal point for the release of that pent-up energy.

Grand sextile: Six planets, in six different signs, meet at 60-degree angles to each other. Together, they emphasize the combination of fire and air or earth and water. It can be a marker of high achievement.

Yod (Finger of God): Two planets, sextile to each other, both find themselves in quincunx to a third, focal planet. In a natal chart, the Finger of God often points to a radical point of view that could lead to periodic crises in relationships and self-development.

Cosmic Connection: CLOSENESS COUNTS

While an exact conjunction means two planets are positioned in the same degree, minute, and second of a sign, astrologers normally allow a few degrees of wiggle room in either direction. Most astrologers allow an orb—a sphere of influence—of five or six degrees. Aspects that involve the powerful Sun and Moon have larger orbs—typically around ten degrees. Tight aspects, obviously, are more powerful than loose aspects.

◆ Astrology in Action: **The Solar System Spread** ◆

A 10-card spread, based on every planet's sign and house position, is an intriguing way to gain insight into anyone's life story. Simply use the corresponding Major Arcana cards to help you visualize the characteristics of each planet and sign. In this case, we'll look at Marilyn Monroe's birth chart.

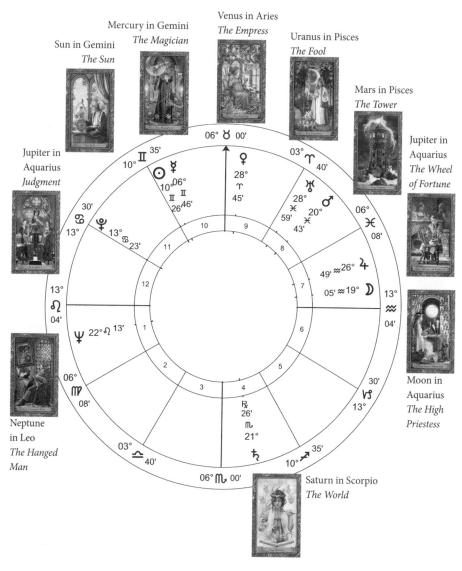

Mercury in Gemini
The Magician

Venus in Aries
The Empress

Sun in Gemini
The Sun

Uranus in Pisces
The Fool

Mars in Pisces
The Tower

Jupiter in
Aquarius
Judgment

Jupiter in
Aquarius
*The Wheel
of Fortune*

Moon in
Aquarius
*The High
Priestess*

Neptune
in Leo
*The Hanged
Man*

Saturn in Scorpio
The World

Marilyn Monroe
June 1, 1926, 9:30 a.m.
Los Angeles, California
Time Zone: 08:00 (PST)
Longitude: 118° W 14' 34"
Latitude 34° N 03' 08"
Placidus Houses
Tropical Zodiac

Sample Reading: Marilyn Monroe's Star Power

Marilyn Monroe, the legendary sex symbol and goddess of the silver screen, was far more than an image on film. Her birth chart, and the corresponding tarot cards, clarifies the distinction between her public image and her true self.

She understood that difference better than any of her fans or devoted admirers. "I've never fooled anyone," she once said. "I've let people fool themselves. They didn't bother to find out who and what I was. Instead they would invent a character for me. I wouldn't argue with them. They were obviously loving somebody I wasn't."

Leo Ascendant. The ascendant provides a starting point for assessing the planets, because it determines the ruler of the chart as well as the physical appearance of the subject. Marilyn Monroe had a Leo ascendant, and the sign of the lion is perfectly fitting for a sex kitten with a curly platinum mane. What's more, the Leo ascendant makes the Sun the ruler of Monroe's chart—and that gave her a fiery boost of star power.

The Sun in Gemini in the Tenth House. Monroe's Sun was in Gemini, the sign of communications, placed in the tenth house of career and achievement. Is it any surprise that Gemini's corresponding tarot card is the Lovers? For decades, Monroe has been one of the world's best-loved sex symbols. Even after death, she remains the object of adoration and unrequited devotion from countless lovesick admirers.

The Moon in Aquarius in the Seventh House. After you find the Sun in any chart, look for the Moon. Here it's placed in Monroe's seventh house of marriage and partnerships, in futuristic, forward-thinking Aquarius—which you can visualize as the Star card. Her Aquarius Moon illuminated her imagination and creativity, and it may have heightened her ability to shock some with her overt sexuality.

Mercury in Gemini in the Tenth House. Monroe's Sun is conjunct Mercury, the planet of speed and communication, in Gemini, Mercury's own sign. The conjunction bonded the Sun and Mercury together and supercharged Monroe's Gemini wit, versatility, and quick thinking. She was a master communicator, not only with the dialogue she delivered on screen and the surprising pronouncements she made in public, but also in the way she expressed herself non-verbally, through cues of body language.

Venus in Aries in the Ninth House. Venus, the planet of love, pleasure, and attraction, is the highest planet in Monroe's chart, near her Midheaven. Her beauty was on display for the whole world to see. Its Aries placement, however, added a fiery, no-nonsense quality to her physical appearance. Like the Empress, Monroe knew that her beauty was both a tool for success and a weapon in her arsenal. It also made her impulsive in affairs of the heart.

Mars in Pisces in the Eighth House. Monroe's beauty would ultimately prove to be her undoing. Her Mars, the fiery planet of energy, aggression, and self-defense, is submerged in watery Pisces, the sign of secrets, mysticism, and escape. Its placement enhanced her emotional sensitivity and vulnerability—two of her most endearing qualities. Sadly, it also explains her physical frailty and susceptibility to drugs and alcohol—like the Tower at the mercy of the elements on an eroding shore.

Jupiter in Aquarius in the Seventh House. Monroe's Jupiter, the planet of luck and expansion, is placed in Aquarius, in the seventh house of marriage and partnerships. When it came

to relationships, Monroe was an idealist. She was married three times—and at the time of her death, she was engaged to remarry her second husband Joe DiMaggio.

Saturn in Scorpio in the Fourth House. The ringed planet, which symbolizes boundaries and limitations, is linked to Scorpio, the enigmatic sign of sex, death, and other people's money. As the Death card implies, she transformed herself from an ordinary girl named Norma Jean into one of the world's most recognizable figures. She created her image, just as the figure in the World card manifests a reality from the pages of an open book. Indeed, decades after her mysterious and troubling death, Monroe's legend lives on.

Uranus in Pisces in the Eighth House. Like Mars, Monroe's Uranus—the Fool's planet of rebellion—is also immersed in watery Pisces. On the one hand, the planet symbolizes her idealism and unwavering sense of hopefulness. On the other, it could have contributed to her desire to escape the harsher realities of life through the Piscean, lunar landscape of drugs, alcohol, or sex.

Neptune in Leo in the First House. Neptune, the ethereal planet of glamour and illusion, is perfectly poised in Monroe's first house, where it lent her the movie-star quality that set the standard for generations of subsequent starlets. In tarot, Neptune corresponds to the Hanged Man; at times, Monroe seemed disconnected from the real world, but Neptune's placement in Leo ensured that her sex appeal would be highlighted in every public appearance, regardless of her state of mind.

Pluto in Cancer in the Eleventh House. Pluto, the planet of transformation, endings, and new beginnings, ushered in the sexual revolution of mid-century America—and Marilyn Monroe was one of its most iconic representatives. Despite Monroe's obvious sex appeal, she also embodied a the wholesome, All-American qualities of the girl next door—much like the home-loving woman in the Chariot card.

◆   ◆   ◆

Astrology in Action: **The Natal Chart Spread**

You can combine as many elements of tarot and astrology as you like. Here's a sample reading featuring young Prince William, who is slated to assume the throne of England.

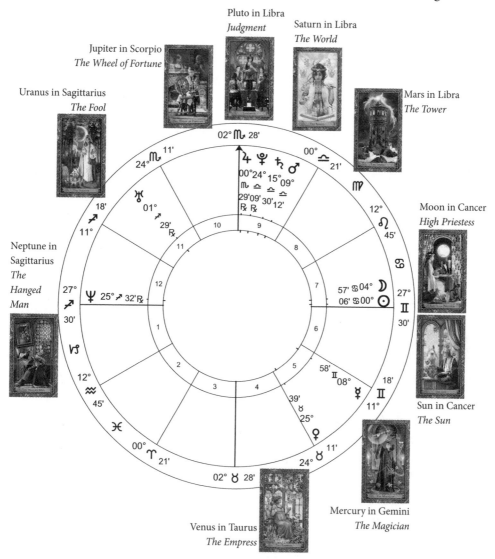

Pluto in Libra
Judgment

Saturn in Libra
The World

Jupiter in Scorpio
The Wheel of Fortune

Mars in Libra
The Tower

Uranus in Sagittarius
The Fool

Moon in Cancer
High Priestess

Neptune in
Sagittarius
*The
Hanged
Man*

Sun in Cancer
The Sun

Mercury in Gemini
The Magician

Venus in Taurus
The Empress

Prince William
June 21, 1982
9:03 p.m.
Paddington, United Kingdom
Time Zone: -01:00 (BST)
Longitude: 000° W 12'
Latitude: 51° N 32'
Placidus Houses
Tropical Zodiac

Sample Reading: Prince William, the Man Who Would Be King

Prince William, the charismatic young heir to England's throne, has a fascinating chart, and tarot cards add a surprising level of detail and description.

Sagittarius Ascendant. People who meet him for the first time are struck by his friendly demeanor and outgoing personality. His Sagittarius ascendant also makes William high-spirited, adventurous, honest, forthright, and open—much like the explorer in the Temperance card. The Sagittarius ascendant might even be taken literally: William is often seen on horseback.

Jupiter in Scorpio in the Ninth House. Sagittarius is ruled by Jupiter, which makes Jupiter the ruler of his chart. As it happens, Jupiter is William's highest planet, conjunct his Midheaven—and that's one of the traditional markers of a king.

Jupiter rules the ninth house of a natural horoscope, which means it's completely at home in William's ninth house of philosophy, long-distance travel, and foreign relations. Jupiter, in the guise of the Wheel of Fortune, also seems to promise a life filled with a wide range of adventures and experiences.

Jupiter happens to share the ninth house with three other planets. It's part of a stellium, which means that they'll all work together in unison. And there at the top of the chart, for the whole world to see, they take on a dramatic, larger-than-life significance.

Jupiter is the Great Benefic—the bringer of gifts. Pluto and Saturn, however, are the traditional "malefics"—and their gifts often come at a painful cost.

Mars, Saturn, and Pluto in Libra in the Ninth House. Part of the price has already been paid. Pluto, the planet of dramatic transformation, is sometimes associated with death. When William was just 15, his mother Diana was killed in tragic car crash—and William's childhood came to a shocking and sudden end, too. But as he solemnly accompanied her body in the procession to her funeral at Westminster Abby, he seemed to come of age. With the whole world watching, William was transformed from a child to a man.

Saturn is the planet of boundaries, limitations, and restrictions. It corresponds to the World card. At birth, William was given a gift that most people could never imagine—the gift of an empire, the throne of England. That destiny, however, is tied to countless limitations and restrictions. He will never have a quiet, normal life. He is bound to centuries of traditions, and a lifetime of obligations and expectations. William can't easily refuse his destiny.

Jupiter also shares the ninth house with Mars, the planet of energy, self-assertion, and aggression. Mars, like the Tower card, can be associated with sudden shocks, surprise attacks, and accidents like the car crash that claimed his mother.

It's interesting to note that even Jupiter, the planet of luck and good fortune, hints at a certain dark intensity in its gifts. That's because it's in Scorpio—the sign of sex, death, and other people's money.

Clearly, transformation is a major theme in William's life. That theme is softened, however, by the fact that Pluto, Jupiter, and Mars are all in Libra, the sign of balance and relationships. In tarot, it's depicted as Justice. Together, the stellium suggests that William could very well transform and rebalance the monarchy during his reign.

Uranus in Sagittarius in the Eleventh House. The idea that William is destined to reform the monarchy also is reinforced by Uranus, the planet of futuristic thinking and social change. It corresponds to the Fool card, the Initiate and the rebel. It's in its own domicile, the eleventh house of social groups and causes, and it's in philosophical, far-seeing Sagittarius. Along the way, Jupiter will bestow him with the gifts of popularity, public approval, and friends, family, and advisors.

Sun and Moon in Cancer in the Seventh House. In his private life, close personal relationships are of prime importance. William's Moon is in its own sign, Cancer, which rules home and family life—and his Moon is conjunct the Sun, which means that his head and his heart are united in their need for children and partnership. The marriage, in this chart, of the goddess of the Moon and the god of the Sun, suggests that William couldn't imagine a life by himself, and that he'll rely on his wife to help him reach his full potential, both in public and private.

It's interesting to note that William's mother had a Cancer Sun and a Sagittarius ascendant, suggesting a closeness and similarity between the two. After her death, the teenage William took on the responsibility of the causes and charities his mother supported.

Mercury in Gemini in the Fifth House. The Moon isn't the only planet in its own sign. Lucky William is also gifted with Mercury, the planet of communication, in Gemini. Don't let his good looks fool you: William is smart, well-spoken, quick-witted, and able to think on his feet. He's playful, too: that Gemini Mercury is in the fifth house of creativity.

Venus in Taurus in the Fifth House. Venus, the planet of love, beauty, and attraction, is also comfortable in Taurus—the sign of material and physical comfort. In the fifth house, his appreciation and pleasures also express themselves through play and recreation—a gift he inherited from his mother, the playful Empress that corresponds to Venus.

Neptune in Sagittarius in the Twelfth House. While his public persona, career highlights, and private relationship planets seem perfectly placed for a man who would be king, William's chart also offers one surprise that will please any astrologer or tarot reader. Neptune, the planet of mysticism, is also in its own domicile, the twelfth house of the unknown, the subconscious, and mysteries and secrets. The planet's connection to the Hanged Man, the card of suspension, also suggests that William's ascension to the throne won't happen quickly; he will have to wait his turn.

◆　◆　◆

Conclusion

The art of tarot and the study of astrology are lifelong pursuits. Both have the power to capture your imagination, enrapture your spirit, and carry you to distant lands.

Like a travel guide, this book has given you a preview of the new worlds that await you. You've seen some of the scenery in the cards and charts, and you've learned some of the words and phrases you'll need to talk with the strange and fascinating people you'll meet along the way.

Now it's time for you to plan the next leg of your journey. Like the Fool and the Initiate, the innocent wanderer in the first card of the tarot deck, it's time to pack your bags, take a deep breath, and begin the next phase of your adventure.

Start with your own chart, and apply the principles of tarot and astrology to your own life. Explore the questions and concerns that mean the most to you—and then test your methods on people you know. Recruit willing volunteers from your family and friends, or practice doing readings for celebrities and people in the news.

Take your time along the way. Don't rush, and don't worry about seeing everything at once. You don't need to master tarot and astrology to practice them, just as you don't need to eat dinner at every restaurant in Paris to experience the City of Light, or see every artifact at the British Museum to comprehend its wealth of history.

Instead, start small. Pick a few favorite techniques that appeal to your sense of adventure and exploration. Proceed step by step, and build your repertoire as you grow in comfort and experience.

You might also want to find a few real-world traveling companions. Join a tarot or astrology group, and register for any classes, workshops, or conferences that are offered in your area. If you happen to live in an isolated part of the world, look for fellow travelers online.

A few of my favorite books and authors are listed in the recommended Reading section—and with the plethora of tarot books and astrology books on the market, you'll soon find other teachers that you like, too.

Be warned, however, that no guide can help you discover a direct route to the mastery of tarot and astrology. That requires practice, and the development of your own talents. But the minute you start venturing into the field, you'll spot intriguing roadside attractions, compelling byways, and irresistible sightseeing opportunities.

Explore them all. Follow any avenue into tarot and astrology that catches your eye. After all, you're not bound by anyone's itinerary but your own—and as every traveler knows, getting there is half the fun.

When you do hit the road, keep this book and a tarot deck in your travel bag. That way, you can come back as often as you like—and you won't be charged extra for a return ticket.

Glossary of Astrological Terms

Air One of the four elements. Considered active, masculine, mental, intellectual, and communicative.

Air Signs The "thinkers" of the zodiac: Gemini, Libra, and Aquarius.

Angles The cusps of the angular houses of a horoscope chart: Ascendant (ASC), Descendant (DSC), Midheaven (MC), and *Imum Coeli* (IC).

Angular Houses The powerful first, fourth, seventh, and tenth houses of a horoscope chart.

Aquarius, the water bearer. Fixed air. Humanitarian, progressive, futuristic, visionary, utopian, nonconforming, independent, unconventional, impersonal, detached, aloof. Original and scientific. Ruled by Uranus. Rules the eleventh house of social groups and causes. Corresponds to the Star card.

Arabic Parts are sensitive points in a chart, and are calculated using specific formulas whereby two planets or points are added together, and a third planet or point is subtracted from that result.

Aries, the ram. Cardinal fire. Energetic, assertive, impulsive, commanding, courageous. Ruled by Mars. Rules the first house of the self.

Ascendant Also known as the rising sign. The sign on the cusp of the first house, the point at which planets and signs rise like the Sun on the eastern horizon. It reflects the face you show the world; the persona, personality, and self-perception.

Aspect An angular, geometric relationship with another planet. Commonly used aspects include the conjunction (0°), opposition (180°), trine (120°), square (90°), sextile (60°), and quincunx (150°).

Benefic In classical astrology, Jupiter and Venus are benefic; they are fortunate planets that grace everything they touch. Saturn and Mars are malefic. Other planets are neutral.

Cadent Houses The third, sixth, ninth, and twelfth houses of a chart; the last house in each quadrant of a horoscope. Classical astrologers believed planets in cadent houses were weakened.

Cancer, the crab. Cardinal water. Emotional, nurturing, protective, sensitive, sentimental, sympathetic, intuitive, instinctual. Ruled by the Moon. Rules the fourth house of home and family.

Capricorn, the goat. Cardinal earth. Pragmatic, responsible, disciplined, dutiful, methodical, organized, patient, persistent, cautious, ambitious, reserved, somber. Ruled by Saturn. Rules the tenth house of career and social status.

Cardinal Signs Aries, Cancer, Libra, and Capricorn mark the start of each new season, and symbolize leadership and initiative.

Celestial Equator An extension of the Earth's equator out into space.

Chart Ruler The planet that rules the sign on the ascendant also rules the chart.

Chiron An asteroid between Saturn and Uranus, named for the wounded healer of Greek mythology.

Classical Planets The seven that can be seen with the naked eye: Sun, Moon, Mercury, Venus, Mars, Jupiter, and Saturn.

Conjunction An aspect that conjoins, unifies, and intensifies the energy of two planets that share the same sign and degree in a chart.

Cusp The dividing line between signs or houses in a chart, and the degree where one sign ends and the next begins.

Decan A 10-degree division of a sign. Also known as a decanate.

Declination The distance of a celestial body north or south of the celestial equator.

Degree One of the 360 degrees of a circle.

Descendant The cusp of the seventh house; the point at which planets and signs descend like the setting Sun on the western horizon.

Detriment A planet's weakness, found in the sign opposite its own rulership.

Dignities Classifications of a planet's power: rulership, exaltation, detriment, and fall.

Direct A planet that seems to be moving forward through the zodiac, as seen from our perspective on Earth.

Dispositor The planet that rules a sign also holds some power over any planet that happens to be in that sign; technically speaking, a dispositor may dispose of, or rule over, the visiting planet as it sees fit.

Diurnal Chart A chart cast for the daytime hours when the Sun is above the horizon.

Diurnal Planets The Sun, Jupiter, and Saturn are day planets, which are strongest in diurnal charts. Mercury is diurnal if it rises before the Sun. See *Nocturnal Planets*.

Domicile A planet's natural home; its place in the sign or house that it rules.

Earth One of four ancient elements. Symbolizes the physical world, materialism, practicality, and earthly reality.

Earth Signs The "maintainers" of the zodiac: Taurus, Virgo, and Capricorn.

Eclipse A solar eclipse occurs when the Moon passes between the Earth and the Sun; lunar eclipses occur at the full Moon, when the Earth is between the Sun and the Moon. In astrology, eclipses represent sudden and dramatic change.

Ecliptic The great circle of the Sun's apparent path through the sky, as seen from Earth.

Electional Astrology Used to choose favorable dates and times for an event.

Elements The four ancient elements are fire, water, air, and earth. The zodiac is divided into elements, and signs of the same element share the qualities of that element.

Ephemeris A list of planetary positions by date and degree.

Equinox A time when days and nights are of equal length; the vernal equinox occurs when the Sun enters Aries, and the autumnal equinox occurs when the Sun enters Libra.

Exaltation A planet is exalted in the sign of its greatest power and influence, like a visiting dignitary in a foreign court. Exaltation is a planet's second-strongest placement; rulership is its first.

Fall A planet's weakest placement, found in the sign opposite its exaltation.

Feminine Signs Earth and water signs: Taurus, Cancer, Virgo, Scorpio, Capricorn, and Pisces. Feminine signs are also called receptive, reactive, negative, magnetic, and passive.

Fire One of four ancient elements. Represents spirit, will, inspiration, enthusiasm, desire, zeal, warmth, idealism, and creativity.

Fire Signs The initiators of the zodiac: Aries, Leo, and Sagittarius.

Fixed Signs Taurus, Leo, Scorpio, and Aquarius mark the middle month of each season. They are stable, consistent, constant, patient, and reliable.

Gemini, the twins. Mutable air. Versatile, intellectual, quick, restless, communicative, curious, scattered. Ruled by Mercury. Rules the third house of communication, sibling relationships, and neighborhoods.

Geocentric A model of the universe that puts the Earth at the center of the solar system.

Glyphs Symbols for the signs, planets, elements, and aspects.

Grand Cross A stressful configuration that involves four or more planets, in two sets of oppositions that combine to form four squares. The planets are usually related by mode: cardinal, fixed, or mutable.

Grand Sextile A rare configuration that involves six planets in sextile to each other in six different signs.

Grand Trine A beneficial configuration that involves three planets 120 degrees apart; they form an equilateral triangle. The planets in a grand trine are usually in the same element.

Horary Astrology The art of answering a question by analyzing a horoscope chart drawn for the precise moment the question was asked.

Horoscope An astrological chart. The word comes from the Greek word *hora*, or hour, and *skopos*, watching.

House Ruler The planet that rules a house in a horoscope.

Houses The 12 divisions of a horoscope chart that correspond to the 12 zodiac signs.

Imum Coeli (I.C.) The cusp of the fourth house; the lowest point in a horoscope chart; it relates to foundations, home, and family life. It's Latin for "bottom of the sky," and is directly opposite the *Medium Coeli* (M.C.) or Midheaven.

Inner Planets The Sun, Moon, Mercury, Venus, and Mars. See *Personal Planets*.

Interception A sign that is completely contained within a house.

Jupiter The expansive planet of luck and generosity. Symbolizes good fortune, prosperity, extravagance, higher thought, religion, law, and long journeys. Rules Sagittarius and the ninth house of philosophy, long-distance travel, and higher education.

Leo, the lion. Fixed fire. Regal, warm-hearted, loyal, generous, dramatic, proud, creative, domineering. Ruled by the Sun. Rules the fifth house of creativity, procreation, and recreation.

Libra, the scales. Mutable air. Gracious, charming, social, cooperative, fair, balanced, refined, harmonious, indecisive, indolent. Ruled by Venus. Rules the seventh house of marriage and partnership.

Luminaries The Sun and the Moon.

Lunation In astrology, the exact moment the new moon is conjunct with the Sun.

Malefic In classical astrology, Saturn and Mars are malefic; they bring misfortune. Jupiter and Venus are benefic. Other planets are neutral.

Mars The fiery red planet of energy, action, assertiveness, aggression, courage, desire, passion, drive, will, and initiative. Rules Aries and the first house of self.

Masculine Signs Fire and air signs: Aries, Gemini, Leo, Libra, Sagittarius, and Aquarius. Masculine signs are also referred to as active or positive.

Medium Coeli (M.C.) See *Midheaven*.

Mercury the fast-moving planet of speed and communication. Represents logic, reason, wit, writing, and speech. Rules Gemini and Virgo, and the third and sixth houses.

Midheaven The cusp of the tenth house; the highest, most elevated point in a horoscope chart; it signifies career, public image, status, and recognition. It's also known as the *Medium Coeli* (M.C.), which is Latin for "middle of the heavens."

Midpoint An equidistant point between two planets, angles, or cusps, used for additional chart interpretation.

Moon Phases New, waxing, full, waning.

Moon The luminous orb of reflection, inner life, and the cycles of life. Symbolizes emotion, memory, mood, and motherhood. Rules Cancer and the fourth house of home and family.

Mundane Astrology The study of countries, cities, provinces, and states. Weather forecasting is also a form of mundane astrology.

Mutable Signs Gemini, Virgo, Sagittarius, and Pisces mark the third and final month of each season. They are transitional, adaptable, and flexible.

Mutual Reception Planets placed in each other's signs of dignity enhance each other's strength.

Natal Chart A horoscope chart based upon the date, time, and place of birth.

Native The person for whom a natal chart is erected.

Neptune The planet of imagination, dreams, illusion, spirituality, idealism, escapism, sacrifice, confusion, and deception. Rules Pisces and the twelfth house of mysteries and secrets.

New Moon A new or dark Moon is the beginning phase of a lunar month, when the Moon and Sun are conjunct. See *Lunation*.

Nocturnal Chart A chart cast for the nighttime hours when the Sun is below the horizon.

Nocturnal Planets The Moon, Venus, and Mars are night planets, which are strongest in nocturnal charts. Mercury is nocturnal if it sets after the Sun. See *Diurnal Planets*.

Nodes The mathematical points where the Moon's orbit around the Earth crosses the ecliptic, the apparent path of the Sun around the Earth. The south node symbolizes gifts and talents that are inborn; the north node represents lessons that must be learned.

Opposition An aspect between two planets that are 180 degrees apart. While teir opposites attract, their energy can also be confrontational.

Orb The degree within which an aspect is considered to have an effect. The luminaries generally have a greater orb than the planets.

Outer Planets Uranus, Neptune, and Pluto. See *Transpersonal Planets*.

Part of Fortune A mathematical point in the chart that shows natural talent and suggests where joy and fortune can be found. One of the Arabic Parts.

Personal (Inner) Planets The Sun, Moon, Mercury, Venus, and Mars have a personal and direct effect on personality. See also *Transpersonal Planets*.

Pisces, the fish. Mutable water. Imaginative, compassionate, self-sacrificing, impressionable, empathetic, illusionary, secretive, victimizing or victimized. Ruled by Neptune. Rules the twelfth house of the unknown, mysteries, and secrets.

Planetary Rulers Each sign is ruled by a planet that shares its qualities.

Planetary Sect The division of day planets from night planets. See *Diurnal Planets* and *Nocturnal Planets*.

Planets Sun, Moon, Mercury, Venus, Mars, Jupiter, Saturn, Uranus, Neptune, and Pluto.

Pluto The planet of transformation, regeneration, unavoidable change, endings, death, destruction, elimination, power, compulsion, and analysis. Rules Scorpio and the eighth house of sex, death, and other people's money.

Polarities Active signs are masculine; receptive signs are feminine. Polarities may also refer to signs that are 180 degrees apart.

Prime Meridian The line of longitude that runs through Greenwich, England, and divides the eastern and western hemispheres.

Predictive Astrology Used to forecast trends and events in an individual's life, typically through the analysis of transits and progressions.

Progression An astrological technique that advances the planets' positions in a chart forward through time. The usual formula is a day for a year.

Quadrants Four divisions of a chart. The quadrants start at the cusps of the first, fourth, seventh, and tenth houses.

Quadruplicities The four elements: fire, earth, air, and water.

Qualities Polarities, modes (quadruplicities), and elements.

Quincunx The angular relationship between planets that are 150 degrees (or five signs) apart. A stressful aspect.

Rectification The process of determining an unknown birth time based on life experiences and events.

Retrograde From our viewpoint on Earth, the planets (with the exception of the Sun and Moon) periodically seem to move backward through the zodiac. The phenomenon is an optical illusion with symbolic significance. The qualities of retrograde planets in a natal chart are internalized, reversed, or slower to develop.

Rising Sign See *Ascendant.*

Sagittarius, the archer. Mutable fire. Adventurous, philosophical, optimistic, enthusiastic, candid, tactless. Ruled by Jupiter. Rules the ninth house of philosophy, higher education, and long-distance travel.

Saturn The ringed planet of boundaries and limitations. Symbolizes responsibility, restriction, structure, discipline, caution, control, ambition, inhibition, delay, father figures, authority, and old age. Rules Capricorn and the tenth house of career and social status.

Scorpio, the scorpion. Fixed water. Intense, penetrating, secretive, jealous, introspective, passionate, strong-willed, possessive, intimate, psychic, fascinated with the dark mysteries of life. Ruled by Pluto. Rules the eighth house of sex, death, and other people's money.

Sextile The angular relationship between planets that are 60 degrees apart; the aspect can be cooperative and offer opportunity.

Sign Ruler The planet that rules a sign. Planets are strongest in the signs they rule.

Signs Aries, Taurus, Gemini, Cancer, Leo, Virgo, Libra, Scorpio, Sagittarius, Capricorn, Aquarius, and Pisces.

Solar Return A birthday horoscope, calculated for the moment when the Sun returns to the exact degree, minute, and second of celestial longitude it occupied at birth.

Solstice The longest and shortest days of the year, when the Sun reaches its maximum distance north or south of the equator.

Square The angular relationship between two planets that are 90 degrees apart; it can be a challenging and stressful aspect.

Stellium Three or more planets in the same sign or house; a stellium adds emphasis.

Succedent Houses The second, fifth, eighth, and eleventh houses of a chart, which follow the cadent houses in succession. According to classical astrology, they derive their power from the cadent houses.

Sun The center of our solar system, it symbolizes self, ego, will, purpose, vitality, individuality, pride, authority, and fatherhood. Rules Leo and the fifth house of creativity, recreation, and procreation.

Synastry The practice of comparing the natal charts of two or more people to assess their compatibility.

Taurus, the bull. Fixed earth. Determined, stubborn, materialistic, possessive, security oriented, sensual, patient, stable, practical. Ruled by Venus. Rules the second house of values and possessions.

Transit A planet's movement through signs and houses.

Transpersonal (Outer) Planets Uranus, Neptune, and Pluto are slow moving, so their effect is as much generational as it is personal. See also *Personal Planets.*

Trine The angular relationship between two planets that are 120 degrees (or four signs) apart; the aspect is usually friendly and flowing, because the planets share an element.

Triplicities Zodiac signs that share an element. The fire triplicity is Aries, Leo, Sagittarius. Earth: Taurus, Virgo, Capricorn. Air: Gemini, Libra, Aquarius. Water: Cancer, Scorpio, Pisces.

Tropical zodiac A system that defines the signs in relation to the position of the vernal or spring equinox, commonly used in Western astrology.

T-square A stressful combination in which two planets square each other, and a third focal planet squares both of them.

Uranus The planet of sudden change, disruption, and revolution. Symbolizes technology, originality, and futuristic thinking. Rules Aquarius and the eleventh house of social groups and causes.

Venus The planet of love, beauty, and attraction. Represents affection, artistry, harmony, and values. Rules the second house of Taurus values and possessions, and the seventh house of Libra relationships and partnerships.

Virgo, the virgin. Mutable earth. Analytical, practical, detail-minded, organized, discriminating, productive, health conscious, critical. Ruled by Mercury. Rules the sixth house of sign of work, health, and service to others.

Void-of-Course Moon A designation that describes the Moon at the end of one sign, about to enter the next. When the Moon is void of course, it has completed all its major aspects to other planets, and symbolically, it's disconnected from the rest of the universe until it enters the next sign.

Waning Moon The gradually diminishing Moon, following the full Moon and before the new Moon. Symbolizes endings and completion.

Water Signs The feelers of the zodiac: Cancer, Scorpio, and Pisces.

Water One of four ancient elements. Symbolizes emotions, intuition, compassion, relationships, and femininity.

Waxing Moon. The gradually increasing Moon, following the new Moon and before the full Moon. Symbolizes beginnings and growth.

Western Astrology Founded by Ptolemy in the second century CE; a continuation of Hellenistic and Babylonian astrology.

Yod (Finger of God) A configuration that suggests a radical point of view; it consists of two planets in sextile to each other, and quincunx a third.

Zodiac The elliptical belt of space surrounding the Earth, divided into twelve signs; the planets travel from west to east, transiting through one sign after another in their order from Aries to Pisces. In Greek, zodiac means "circle of animals."

Quick Reference Guide
Horoscope Keywords

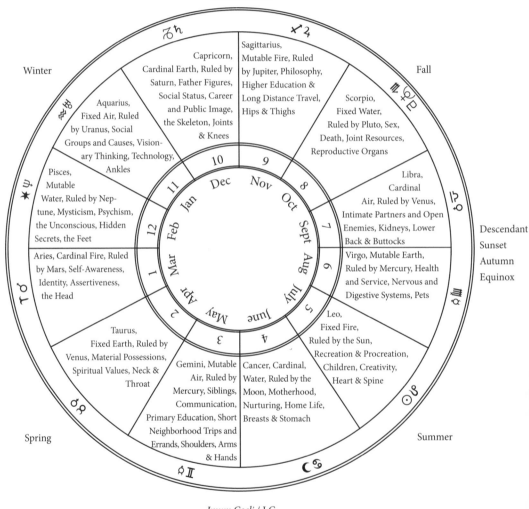

Midheaven
Medium Coeli / M.C.
"Middle of the Heavens"
Noon
Winter Solstice

Winter

Fall

Capricorn, Cardinal Earth, Ruled by Saturn, Father Figures, Social Status, Career and Public Image, the Skeleton, Joints & Knees

Sagittarius, Mutable Fire, Ruled by Jupiter, Philosophy, Higher Education & Long Distance Travel, Hips & Thighs

Aquarius, Fixed Air, Ruled by Uranus, Social Groups and Causes, Visionary Thinking, Technology, Ankles

Scorpio, Fixed Water, Ruled by Pluto, Sex, Death, Joint Resources, Reproductive Organs

Pisces, Mutable Water, Ruled by Neptune, Mysticism, Psychism, the Unconscious, Hidden Secrets, the Feet

Libra, Cardinal Air, Ruled by Venus, Intimate Partners and Open Enemies, Kidneys, Lower Back & Buttocks

Aries, Cardinal Fire, Ruled by Mars, Self-Awareness, Identity, Assertiveness, the Head

Virgo, Mutable Earth, Ruled by Mercury, Health and Service, Nervous and Digestive Systems, Pets

Taurus, Fixed Earth, Ruled by Venus, Material Possessions, Spiritual Values, Neck & Throat

Leo, Fixed Fire, Ruled by the Sun, Recreation & Procreation, Children, Creativity, Heart & Spine

Gemini, Mutable Air, Ruled by Mercury, Siblings, Communication, Primary Education, Short Neighborhood Trips and Errands, Shoulders, Arms & Hands

Cancer, Cardinal Water, Ruled by the Moon, Motherhood, Nurturing, Home Life, Breasts & Stomach

Ascendant
Rising Sign
Sunrise
Spring
Equinox

Descendant
Sunset
Autumn
Equinox

Spring

Summer

Imum Coeli / I.C.
"Bottom of the Sky"
Midnight
Summer Solstice

Recommended Reading and Resources

Astrology Books for Beginners

Antepara, Robin. *Aspects* (Woodbury, MN: Llewellyn Worldwide, 2006).

Burk, Kevin. *Understanding the Birth Chart* (Woodbury, MN: Llewellyn Worldwide, 2001).

Frawley, John. *The Real Astrology* (London: Apprentice Books, 2001).

Gerwick-Brodeur, Madeline and Lisa Lenard. *The Complete Idiot's Guide to Astrology* (New York: Alpha Books, 1997).

Guttman, Ariel and Kenneth Johnson. *Mythic Astrology: Archetypal Powers in the Horoscope* (Woodbury, MN: Llewellyn Worldwide, 1996).

Hampar, Joann. *Astrology for Beginners: A Simple Way to Read Your Chart* (Woodbury, MN: Llewellyn Worldwide, 2007).

MacGregor, Trish. *The Everything Astrology Book* (Holbrook, Massachusetts: Adams Media Corporation, 1999).

Scofield, Bruce. *The NCGR-Professional Astrologers' Alliance (NCGR-PAA) Education Curriculum and Study Guide for Certification Testing* (www.astrologersalliance.org)

Astrological Charts and Software

Software for Windows: AstrolDeluxe ReportWriter www.halloran.com

Free horoscope charts: www.astro.com

Online celebrity chart data: www.astro.com/astro-databank

Tarot Books for Beginners

Bunning, Joan. *Learning the Tarot* (Boston: Red Wheel/Weiser, 1998).

Kenner, Corrine. *Simple Fortunetelling with Tarot Cards*. (Woodbury, MN: Llewellyn Worldwide, 2007).

Louis, Anthony. *Tarot Plain and Simple* (Woodbury, MN: Llewellyn Worldwide, 2002).

Masino, Marcia. *Easy Tarot Guide* (San Diego: ACS Publications, 1987).

Michelson, Teresa C. *The Complete Tarot Reader: Everything You Need to Know from Start to Finish* (Woodbury, MN: Llewellyn Worldwide, 2005).

Moore, Barbara. *Tarot for Beginners* (Woodbury, MN: Llewellyn Worldwide, 2010).

Pollack, Rachel. *Tarot Wisdom* (Woodbury, MN: Llewellyn Worldwide, 2009).

Further Reading on Tarot and Astrology

Decker, Ronald and Michael Dummet. *A History of the Occult Tarot: 1870-1970* (London: Gerald Duckworth & Co. Ltd., 2002).

DuQuette, Lon Milo. *Understanding Aleister Crowley's Thoth Tarot* (San Francisco: Red Wheel/Weiser, 2003).

Gurney, Joseph. "The Tarot of the Golden Dawn." *Journal of the Western Mystery Tradition* (No. 17, Vol. 2, Autumnal Equinox 2009).

Hulse, David Allen. *The Key of It All, Book Two: The Western Mysteries* (Woodbury, MN: Llewellyn Worldwide, 1996).

Huson, Paul. *Mystical Origins of the Tarot* (Rochester, VT: Destiny Books, 2004).